The So-Called "Hebrew Israelites"

Formerly Known As
The Black Hebrew Israelites
(BHI)

Elder Robert L. Anderson
Minister Andrew E. Hooper

Detroit MI USA

The So-Called "Hebrew Israelites"

Copyright © 2019 Robert L. Anderson & Andrew E. Hooper.

All scripture quotations, unless otherwise indicated, are taken from the HOLY BIBLE, KING JAMES VERSION and are marked (KJV).

Scripture quotations marked (ESV) are from the ESV® Bible (The Holy Bible, English Standard Version®), copyright © 2001 by Crossway, a publishing ministry of Good News Publishers. Used by permission. All rights reserved.

All rights reserved. No part of this publication may be reproduced, stored in a retrieval system, or transmitted in any form or by any means – electronic, mechanical, photocopy, recording, or any other – except for brief quotations in printed reviews, without the prior permission of the publisher.

NOTE:

Bullet points and bold text are added by the author to provide emphasis on the borrowed references.

Truth Seekers Read Publications
P. O. Box 23345 • Detroit, MI 48233
E-mail: truthseekersread@att.net
URL: http://www.truthseekersread.com

KDP: ISBN 13: 978-1-9987221-1-5

ISBN 10: 1-9987221-1-5

Editing by Jerome Smith & Joann Anderson

Cover, and Interior design by Robert L. Anderson

Printed in the United States of America

TABLE OF CONTENTS

Endorsements 1
Acknowledgments 3
Introduction 5
PROBLEM ONE 9
  Why On Earth Would You Want To Be A Christian? 9
  How To Read And Teach The Bible 14
    Definition of Precept: 16
    Commentaries On Precept: 16
PROBLEM TWO 21
  The Identity Crisis: 21
    Has The Church Lost Its Biblical Mind? 21
    I Used To Be A Christian 26
  The People Who Follow The Pied Piper 30
    Noble Drew Ali: 30
    ELIJAH MUHAMMAD: 31
    Louis Farrakhan 34
    Clarence 13X: 34
    Spiritual Israel Church and It's Army 35
    The Israelite Nation World Wide Ministries 36
    The Black Hebrew Israelites - Abba Bivens – BHI: 37
    Beliefs Not Shared Among Hebrew Israelism: 43
    Shared Common BHI Beliefs concerning the Europeans (white-man) and other nations 44
    Basic Beliefs That Most BHI Inconsistently Profess to Subscribe: . 45
    The dilemma of A people: 46
  Hijacking The Word Black In The Bible: 46
    BHI Do Not Believe All BLACK People Are Of The Tribe Of Judah: 47
    So-Called Hebrew Israelites Belief About Jesus Christ 48

Jews/Israel Were Black People: 51
   King Solomon was a black Israelite: 51
   The Jews (Judah) Were Black: 52
   Hebrew Israelites Are Bursting Through The Doors Of Churches ... 53
Deuteronomy Chapter 28 53
   Related Questions That Must Be Addressed By BHI: 53
ISRAEL UNITED IN CHRIST: What's In The Name? 61
Israelite School of Practical Knowledge: ISUPK 63
The Gathering of Christ Church (GOCC) Provides Some BHI History Background. 66
Is The So-Called Hebrew Israelites (BHI) a racist group? ... 68
So-Called Hebrew Israelites Belief About Grace 68

PROBLEM THREE 71
   The Birth of Christ – The Seed 71
   The Virgin Birth 71
      Mary: 71
      Holy Ghost: 72
      Joseph: 73
      Problem with Hebrew Israelism Birth Assumption 73
      The Lineage of Christ 77
      The Seed 79
   The Comforter (Holy Spirit) Is A Black Man 82

PROBLEM FOUR 85
   The Immaculate Conception Is Not The Virgin Birth 85
   Religion Is Biblical 87
   Hebrew Israelites Create Their Own Hebrew Language 90
   The False So-Called Hebrew Israelite Prophet Ahrayah ... 94

PROBLEM FIVE 97
   Christians 97
      Before Joining a Church: 97

Regeneration is not Reincarnation: 98
Ten Refutations of Reincarnation 99
Hebrew Israelites and Reincarnation: 101
Will The Real Church Please Come Forth? 102
    Israel Is Not The Church That Jesus Built: 104
    What Defines A Christian: 108
    Christians Are Not The Israel of God 109
    BHI Camps are Void of Biblical Love 110
    Suffering As A Christian: 111

PROBLEM SIX 115
    The Law: 115
        Shared Common BHI Beliefs About The LAW: 115
        The Law vs. Commandment 115
        The Law vs. Faith: 121
    Did The Apostles Keep The Law? 131
    Did Jesus Keep The Mosiac Law? 136

PROBLEM SEVEN 145
    Hebrew Israelites Blame The Women For The Woes of The Family 145
    Hebrew Israelites Distorted View of Women 147
    The Nation Of Israel Is Not The True (Root or Vine)! 148
        ISRAEL IS NOT THE ROOT! 148
        Christ Is The True Root and Vine: 149
    So-Called Hebrew Israelites Ignorance of The Trinity Concept 150
        The Chart For Trinity Thought: 153
        Scripture Evidence For Trinity Doctrine: 154
        TRINITY ACTING IN UNITY 155
        Plurality Scriptures: 157

PROBLEM EIGHT 159

The Sabbath And Sunday 159
Did Constantine Change the Sabbath to Sunday? 159
    Scripture Determined The Lord's Day Not Constantine 159
    Before Constantine – The Church - Sabbath or Sunday 161
    After The Cross, Christians – Followers Of Jesus Christ 162

PROBLEM NINE 163
Who Are The GENTILES? 163
    So-Called Hebrew Israelites Belief about the Gentiles 163
    DEFINING YOUR TERMS 165
    Certain Gentiles are prominent characters in the Bible: 172
    Hellenists Does Not Refer to Greeks 173
    Does The Bible Teach or Endorse Racism? 174
    Proselytes Gentiles 175
Can Gentiles Be Saved? 177
    Gentiles (non-Jews) Into The Body of Christ 177
In The Beginning There Were Gentiles 180
    The Gentile Who Was called Out: 182
    The Gentile Who Was Anointed And The Servant Of God 182
Heaven and Hell 183
    So-Called Hebrew Israelites Belief about Heaven and Hell 183
    Esau Shall be Lead Into Captivity In The Kingdom 189

PROBLEM TEN 191
So, KING JAME WAS BLACK? 191
    Why Is The Apocrypha NOT In You Christians Bible? 192
Cussing and Foul Language 203
BHI Camp Believes Rape Is Ok 207
What are Hebrew Israelites sources of AUTHORITY? 208

PROBLEM ELEVEN 211
Would you Like To Accept Christ, today? 211

Questions To Address Before Dialoguing with So-Called Hebrew Israelites:...213

APPENDIX..215

   Glossary..215

   Hebrew Israelite - Subject Links 223

   About The Authors.. 225

   Other Books by Elder Robert Anderson..228

   Book Order Form.. 229

ENDORSEMENTS

In recent years, the "so-called" Hebrew Israelite have bombarded the religious world with aggressiveness; persuasive speech. Some of these sects even dress in special attire to draw attention to their false doctrines. Once again, Robert Anderson along with co-author Andrew Hooper unveil the false teachings propagated by these groups. There are many sects within this movement who do not believe or teach consistently; they have many different nuisances. These differences in teaching cause confusion for those who are investigating the "Hebrew Israelite's" historical origin, evolution, and doctrines.

Robert Anderson and Andrew Hooper analyzed the various splinters of the Black Hebrew Israelites for us. Their book is full of information showing the biblical contrast to the false teachings of these groups: Their dangerous tactics of twisting Scripture, the aggressive nature by which they intimidate people, and the way they lure some into believing what they say. Anderson and Hooper share historical data regarding the birth or this group, their leaders, and even internal friction among this group's sects.

Unfortunately, even some "Christians" are led away from the Truth of the Scriptures, and convert to the Hebrew Israelite movement.

I recommend their book, The So-Called Hebrew Israelites Formerly known as The Black Hebrew Israelites. The book has a "straight- forward" approach; with scripture references that defend their position on why the "Hebrew Israelite" movement is false and not inspired by God. Upon reading this body of work you will be blessed with solid information to prepare you to defend the true faith, The Gospel of Jesus Christ, which was once and for all delivered to the saints.

Blessings.

Pastor Quinton W. Wingate
Power Hope & Grace Bible Church
6495 West Warren Ave.
Detroit Michigan 4810

Endorsements

You have written a wonderfully clear, well-organized, carefully documented, and most instructive book about the so-called "Hebrew Israelites."

You have furnished information on what they teach and believe in their own words. You have presented excellent Bible-based refutations of their mistaken doctrinal positions.

I thoroughly enjoyed reading it, and trust your book will help others to be inoculated against the false doctrines of these groups or to help deliver some in these groups out of their bondage to error.

Yours in Christ

Jerome H. Smith

www.realbiblestudy.com
Author of *The New Treasury of Scripture Knowledge, Nelson's Cross Reference Guide to the Bible,* and *The Ultimate Cross Reference Treasury* (Premium Module available for the free e-Sword Bible software program)

ACKNOWLEDGMENTS

I, Pastor Robert Anderson, gratefully acknowledge:

My Lord and Savior Jesus Christ for renewed strength, energy, and courage. Without Him, this book would not be possible.

Sister Jo Ann Anderson, my wife, whose love and patience were often tried during my many long nights of research and writing for this book, and for her continual support with whatever I endeavor to do, especially when it comes to God and the church. *Honey, I Love You!*

Bishop Quinton W. Wingate under whose Pastor-ship and sound Biblical teaching keeps me grounded in the Word. Thanks, Pastor Wingate, for the ear that you have always provided to me even before becoming a member of PHGBC; and your valuable theologian input provided in this book.

Pastor Emery Moss, whose Biblical and Apologetic teachings unlocked the door for me to understand Biblically what I believe and why I should believe and defend it! *Thanks, Pastor Moss, you keep me studying and my head in the Bible and books.*

Special thanks to Elder Michael Holloway, for his valuable contribution to this book.

My Apologetic Ride or Die brother, Minister Andrew Hooper. We have witnessed and defended the faith together; you're always ready when I call for the Biblically throw-down. And now God has allowed and directed us in collaborating on this Book project together. All I can say is Brother in Christ!

Vivian Barnes, my late mother. She cried and prayed many nights over and for me.

Family and friends (too many to mention; brothers and sisters in Christ): for your embraced and continued support, I say thank you, and I love you in Christ!

I Dedicate this Book To Those Who Are Yet to Let The Elephant Out of The Closet!

Acknowledgments

I, Minister Andrew Hooper, graciously acknowledge:

The Father, The Son, & Holy Spirit for the work and sacrifice that was put in to save my life and produce this work.

I thank Pastor Emery Moss of Strictly Biblical Bible Teaching Ministry; thank you for all your classes and hard work.

Also, a huge thank you to Pastor Robert Anderson for all the encouragement and support during this journey keep up the great work

My Mother Saundra Robinson for all the support and unconditional love these many years. Thanks, mom, it has been a journey.

To my five children and grandchildren never leave the path that has been set before you, TO GOD BE THE GLORY.

INTRODUCTION

The title for this book "**So-Called Hebrew Israelites**" formerly known as **The Black Hebrew Israelites** has in mind the verse:

> "Can the **Ethiopian change his skin** or the **leopard its spots**? Then may you also do good who are accustomed to do evil." Jeremiah 13:23 (NKJV)

While adherents of **The Black Hebrew Israelites**[1] no longer wish to be identified by this title (for various reasons that we will explore later in the book), they still vehemently use Scriptures out of context with an attempt to prove that Jesus and the Jews (Judah) were black, and that the American negroes who experienced the Transatlantic Slave Trade were black Jews.

As many other minorities began to gravitate to their message, the word **BLACK** was dropped. Now they desire only to be known as **Hebrew Israelites**; hence, the development of their Twelve Tribes Chart.[2][3]

The term **Hebrew Israelism** was borrowed from Dr. James White and Vocab Malone to differentiate "**So-called Hebrew Israelites**" from the Messianic Jews who do believe in Jesus Christ and are members of the Body of Christ (Jews and Gentiles).

- Malone, Vocab. Barack Obama vs. The Black Hebrew Israelites: Introduction to the History & Beliefs of 1West Hebrew Israelism (p. 4). Thureos Publishing / Lionhouse Publishing. Kindle Edition.
- Vocab Malone and Hebrew Israelism: Mesa Edition with Calls![4]

We, *TruthSeekersRead*, use the term, **Hebrew Israelism** in a broad sense to go beyond **the religious practices and errors** of **1-West**, and for the purpose of including,

---

[1] https://www.youtube.com/watch?v=RL9QyhkjF4k (May 11, 2019)
[2] https://www.youtube.com/watch?v=iNz1fDQhzeA (May 7, 2019)
[3] https://www.youtube.com/watch?v=NBq0SluYxXs&feature=youtu.be&fbclid=IwAR0TL_6m_CDD0OEt3mucKdEOsLTprZYj5byNc1DKA0HJyGFt6o8dXiQIHrU (May 11, 2019)
[4] https://www.youtube.com/watch?v=FhsfuTjFBHs (May 7, 2019)

Introduction

lumping, and summarizing any group's erroneous practices under the guise of **Hebrew Israelites**.

- First, it is a False Premise to equate the belief of biblical Hebrew Israelites (of origin) to **Hebrew Israelism**.
- Second, All So-called Hebrew Israelites don't believe or practice the **SAME** thing and errors.

However, many of the groups (persons) we've researched are in error (biblically and historically), hence Error is Error, regardless of the Error. As related to the term **Hebrew Israelism**, we avoid getting into "this error is different than that error" scenarios. If it is contrary to Scripture, as far as we are concerned, it is **ERROR**, period.

Many may question what do the so-called Hebrew Israelites under the guise of Hebrew Israelism have to do with them? I know what I believe, so why should I care? It is my prayer that we answer these questions for you before you reach the end of this book.

Far too often, people are seeking our help after the fact. After their loved ones are dialoguing with the Hebrew Israelites or have joined a camp. They are not only recruiting on the corners but on campuses, online through Facebook and YouTube, etc. There aren't any quick tips to give you for pulling anyone out. But what we do encourage is dig deep into your Bible through study and prayer.

And it is not just the Hebrew Israelite camps, but many pastors that were under the Christian umbrella have begun to embrace Hebrew Israelism. You may have heard the terms **Christian Israelite** and **Spiritual Israel**.

If you studied and thought you knew your Bible before, you will really get an exercise in knowledge and context of the simple passages that they manipulate, twist, distort, and sadly our loved ones and friends believe.

Finally, we come against all cults and false doctrines. However, this one, the so-called **Hebrew Israelites**

Introduction

(formerly known as the Black Hebrew Israelites), cuts close to home in its entrapping's:

1. It targets people of color and other minority groups preaching nationalism under the guise of Skin color and the Bible.
2. It promotes hatred of others and Caucasians with the Bible in hand.
3. While many of the other cults and false doctrines do not target Christians (the Church) with a vengeance, the so-called Hebrew Israelites are on a mission. They are in the streets, and some have been bold enough to walk through the church doors spewing their perverted doctrine. One pastor even allowed them to pass out flyers in the church sanctuary.

Even so, nothing catches God by surprise. Jesus said,

> "And I say also unto thee, that thou art Peter, and upon this rock I will build my church; and the gates of hell shall not prevail against it." **Matthew 16:18 (KJV)**

BHI is a three-letter acronym used for "Black Hebrew Israelites." It will be used (at times) throughout this book in place of "**Black Hebrew Israelites**" and "**Hebrew Israelites**."

Introduction

PROBLEM ONE

WHY ON EARTH WOULD YOU WANT TO BE A CHRISTIAN?

Based on the so-called **Hebrew Israelites** skewed view of Christianity being The White man's religion; I believe this is a view that should be addressed first in a book such as this.

I asked Bishop Quinton Wingate, of Power Hope & Grace Bible Church, what does Christianity offer the believer that no other so-called religious group could ever offer?

He replied, one of the things that Christianity offers the believer is a real live risen savior. When you study the life of Christ, reportedly there have been atheists who have done research only to find out that there was a real historical Jesus. A real person, and not just a myth or figment of someone's imagination. A real person, Jesus, who lived in history.

The real interesting thing about this is that as they pursued their studies, it had been claimed that there was a real Jesus at one point in time who died and a few days later his disciples were boasting of His resurrection; in addition, those who went to visit the tomb where He was buried, found the tomb empty. The Apostle Paul talks about, **1 Corinthians chapter 15**, the number of people that saw Jesus after His resurrection:

> "and that **He was seen** by Cephas, then by the twelve. 6 After that **He was seen** by over five hundred brethren at once, of whom the greater part remain to the present, but some have fallen asleep. 7 After that **He was seen** by James, then by all the apostles. 8 Then last of all **He was seen** by me also, as by one born out of due time." **1 Corinthians 15:5-8 (NKJV)**

This becomes undeniable evidence that really cannot be refuted or proven to be refuted. Acknowledging these facts, Christians serve a risen Savior. There is no other religion, cult, or whatever group that can claim a Savior who lived, who died, and who was resurrected. So as Christians, when we preach Jesus, we are preaching the Christ ~ The risen Savior. The very foundation of Christianity hinges on the fact that we serve the risen Savior.

And not only that but through the working of the Holy Spirit in us that is confirmed in our life. I believe there are many Christians who can testify that when they truly accepted the Lord Jesus Christ, according to the Scriptures and believed in Him, that they could testify of the real transformation that took place in their lives. And the beauty of this is not only can they testify, but the power of this is that other people that they know (family, former friends, former associates) also know when a believer truly embraces Jesus Christ; And that a transformation has taken place in the believer's life, and there is a change. The Apostle Paul said it this way:

> "Therefore, if anyone is in Christ, he is a new creation; old things have passed away; behold, all things have become new." **2 Corinthians 5:17 (NKJV)**

It is a real historical fact that there was someone called Jesus, and they claimed that he died and there was proof from those who lived in that day. And historians have studied that He died, a few days later His tomb was empty, and that His disciples went around preaching Him. When you accept Him, and when I accept Him, and when anyone accepts Him, a transformation takes place.

I asked Bishop Wingate about those people who say," I used to be a Christian."

He replied, one of the things that become so very important when accepting Jesus Christ, is understanding that it is not just an intellectual assent of saying I believe in Jesus Christ. But it is intellectual as well as what comes from the heart. When the gospel message is preached, as the Apostle Paul says it this way it is the power of God unto Salvation:

> "For I am not ashamed of the gospel of Christ, **for it is the power of God to salvation for everyone who believes**, for the Jew first and also for the Greek." **Romans 1:16 (NKJV)**

So when the gospel message is preached, and a person embraces it and receives it from the heart; What is in their heart, they will confess it with their mouth. And when that true transformation takes place, it comes from that genuine confession.

There was a statistical study that said approximately 80 to 86% of Americans who claimed that they were Christians. But if we were to look at how they are living, 80 to 86% of Americans don't live like they are Christians. But there is that percentage that lives their lives like Christians because when they came to know Him, it was real. It was not just saying but something from the heart. And when it came from the heart, the Holy Spirit began to work in them and through them, so that the transformation is real.

Along with transformation comes conviction. If there is no conviction, then that is going to hinder any process of transformation. This is why I use the term "It Is From The Heart." What happens in the heart ultimately makes itself known on the outside. So when true conviction takes place in the heart, the believer's life is going to be transformed.

Of course, since I am a Christian, I know what God has done for me. A quick testimony: When I was a young fellow and came to the Lord and accepted Jesus Christ as my Lord and Savior: Just prior to that there was a fellow that I felt that I literally hated with a passion because of who he was and the things he used to do. He was the type of person that I was ready to egg on just so we could go at it. I got saved and gave my life to the Lord. That same day I felt the Holy Spirit working in me and just as clear as I'm talking to you now; it came to my mind what about (and I said the person's name) how do you feel about him? And I just felt an overwhelming love for this person. I was like, *my Lord,* something must have happened to me for me to love this person. I thought I hated him with a passion.

I learned that is the working of the Holy Spirit, the working of the Word of God that when you are convicted and want God; Jesus says this in the Scripture:

> "All that the Father gives Me **will come to Me, and the one who comes to Me I will by no means cast out.**" **John 6:37 (NKJV)**

So, when that conviction takes place, there is transformation. If there is **NO** transformation, the conviction has to be questioned.

So, we understand that a person can be a member of a church and simply be going through the motion, but there is no transformation and no conviction because these go hand in hand. And this transformation and conviction can happen long before a person has all the head knowledge.

And for me, it demonstrated how real God is, and the Holy Spirit is. It wasn't me, and I couldn't of my own do that. I had wanted to bring harm to that individual, but when I accepted Christ and got the understanding of what it means to accept Jesus, I didn't know a lot about the Scriptures and all about quote-unquote holy living and being fully-totally committed to the Christian lifestyle. The Apostle Paul had a similar type of experience:

> "Then Saul, **still breathing threats and murder against** the disciples of the Lord, went to the high priest 2 and asked letters from him to the synagogues of Damascus, so that if he found any who were of the Way, whether men or women, he might bring them bound to Jerusalem." **Acts 9:1-2 (NKJV)**

> "As he journeyed he came near Damascus, **and suddenly a light shone around him from heaven**. 4 Then he fell to the ground, and heard a voice saying to him, "Saul, Saul, why are you persecuting Me?" 5 And he said, "Who are You, Lord?" Then the Lord said, "**I am Jesus, whom you are persecuting. It is hard for you to kick against the goads.**" 6 So he, trembling and astonished, said, "Lord, what do You want me to do?" Then the Lord said to him, "**Arise and go into the city, and you will be told what you must do.**" **Acts 9:3-6 (NKJV)**

Paul, from that moment on, was convicted and transformed. His life was changed. He who was once persecuting Christianity, which was known as "the way" became a preacher of "the way" and now became a Christian himself. Even people who knew him, prior to his conversion, those who had seen and/or heard about him, could not believe it themselves but became witnesses of Paul's (Saul) transformation.

I asked Bishop Wingate what about those people who say if Christianity was right; why don't we see the conditions of people, neighborhoods, communities, cities, etc. in the world changing?

He replied, Jesus Himself said:

> "Jesus said to him, "'Thomas, because you have seen Me, you have believed. **Blessed are those who have not seen and yet have believed.**'" **John 20:29 (NKJV)**

When Jesus said those, who have not seen and yet have believed, he is not just talking about an arbitrary faith or belief or just some crazy off the wall belief. Our belief is based on historical facts that are based on Spiritual interaction. That is the Spirit of God working in us and through us. Our faith is not just built upon what Jesus or God can do for us here and now, but rather; it is built on a real genuine relationship of faith. This is another thing which makes Christianity so unique: We serve a Savior who came, died, was resurrected, left, and promised us that He is coming again. No matter what this life offers us, we don't just live our lives about what we can get and see now. We live our life by faith in a coming King; The return of Jesus Christ.

> "For what will it profit a man if he gains the whole world, **and loses his own soul**? 37 Or what will a man give in exchange for his soul?" **Mark 8:36-37 (NKJV)**

He who came over 2000 years ago, walked the face of this earth, and ascended on High and gave us a promise. That is why the Lord said Thomas, blessed are those who have not seen what you have seen. Because our hope is in the glorious appearing of our great God and Lord and Savior Jesus Christ.

We believe Him now for the benefits and blessings that He has in store for us believing now; His blessings far outweigh anything that the world could offer to us. And things of this world are only temporal. Every Religion that comes up with some type of their so-called faith, or so-called Messiah, the truth be told when you look at it closely, there is nothing in these religions where they can say or with proof demonstrate it has done anything for them. We can conclude that being a Christian doesn't change my neighborhood, but it changes what I do in the neighborhood. Being a Christian changes me and what I do. Now, as a result of that God can use us to help bring changes to whatever level that He deems necessary. But the key is for Christianity: those that are followers of Jesus Christ are one life changed at a time. How God uses us to affect others, so be it.

It is a myth that the so-called white-man gave "*the black-man*" Christianity. Christianity was born and birthed out of the experiences of early Christians who followed Jesus. At the end of the day, the simple meaning of Christianity **is to live like Christ**. That is what the word Christian means. It is not a white man's thing or a black man's thing. It is for whosoever comes to believe in the Jesus of the Bible.

Only the foolish would think it necessary to even utter the oxymoronic words "**Jesus was not a Christian**." Biblical integrity says **Jesus is the Christ** who lived a spotless life, who gave to us the Holy Spirit to emulate His life. Jesus is the Christ, and we are the Christians. We are the offspring of the life of Christ. We are trying to be like Him, Jesus Christ, the greatest one that has ever lived.

How To Read And Teach The Bible

Hebrew Israelite adherents are taught that the Bible can't be read like a novel or book when reading the Bible's books, passages, chapters paragraphs, verses, and/or sentences. According to them, you must have *a precept* in order to understand what most intelligent people would call basic English structure with a given context. They have precepts for individual words; for example, "**world**" doesn't mean "**world**" and "**whosoever**" doesn't mean "**whosoever**" (more on this later in the book). According to the so-called **Hebrew Israelites**, they were endowed with the mystery of precepts by The Most-High, and Christians will never be able to understand the Bible. In short, it is *The Da Vinci Code* of *Hebrew Israelism.*

Hebrew Israelite adherents are trained: If A Christian reads a passage in the Bible that says "ABC...XYZ", here is *a precept* for it. They are taught to read the Bible irrationally. They are required to attend weekly classes and to learn how to "**cut**" (meaning to humiliate) Christians who don't know how to defend Scripture. Their usage of the word *precept* is designed to twist Scripture as if it supported and gave foundation to their doctrine of national identity.

The so-called **Hebrew Israelites** pull the word "*Precept*" from **Isaiah chapter 28 verses 9-10** and act as if the other verses above and below don't exist. If you were to ask them what the context of the passage is, their often response would be "show me the word **CONTEXT**" in the Bible.

One adherent of Hebrew Israelism tried to deflect from context by saying even King David, who was professing precepts said:

> "Through thy **precepts** I get understanding: therefore, I hate every false way." **Psalms 119:104 (KJV)**

First of all, Biblical Christians believe all Scripture is God Breathed **(2 Timothy 3:16-17)**. We receive all Scripture given in the context it was originally written with nothing added, taken away, or implied contrary to sound doctrine.

The Hebrew adherent said Christians read the Bible like reading a book (like a whole dialog) and that Christians can't just take the passage and pick it apart.

Hebrew Israelites adherents get confused and bewildered when Biblical Christians read the whole passage (and chapter when necessary) to properly exegete the text. They cry foul charging that we are covering a whole host of wisdom like the scholars taught us how to read, rather than relying on the precepts of The Most-High. They are not taught this in their nationality designed method of reading Scripture.

Sadly, many of them can't comprehend basic English (nouns, verbs, adverbs, adjectives, modifiers, parts of speech, prepositions/conjunctions (as, like)), idioms. I won't even mention Hebrew idioms, types, shadows, etc. Often to save face, adherents may begin to raise their voices to over talk a person or cut a person off with the use of foul language (another tactic they use).

BHI Adherents are taught and teach others that precepts were the system and order Moses taught to read Scripture and was passed down to the fathers face to face; showing that this is how you read Scripture. The **Hebrew Israelite** adherent then asked if that is not true why are precepts in Isaiah 28? if it is not teaching us that this is how to read the Bible? He asked why did Moses write "here a little and there a little" in the Scripture when he spoke to the fathers face to face? Perhaps, the so-called Hebrew Israelite classes didn't teach the books of the Bible, and Isaiah is a major prophet, and Moses was dead (absent from the body but present with the Lord) long before Isaiah wrote the Book of Isaiah. We will look at who Hebrew Israelism targets in the next Chapter.

However, when Isaiah Chapter 28 (please read the whole chapter) is properly studied, we learn:

DEFINITION OF PRECEPT:

> H6673. צַו **tsav** (846c); from H6680; perh. *command:—* command(1), order(8) [5]

COMMENTARIES ON PRECEPT:

> Isaiah 28:10 in mocking mimicry of Isaiah's words, and, Isaiah 28:13, of the unintelligible speech of foreign agents of judgment;

> Kimchi[6] says צו tsau, **precept**, is used here for מצוה mitsuah, **command**, and is used in no other place for it but here.

---

[5] Thomas, R. L. (1998). *New American Standard Hebrew-Aramaic and Greek dictionaries : updated edition*. Anaheim: Foundation Publications, Inc.
[6] https://www.britannica.com/biography/David-Kimhi (May 6, 2019

צ tsau signifies a little precept, **such as is suited to the capacity of a child**; see Isaiah 28:9.

ק kau signifies **the line** that a Mason stretches out to build a layer of stones by. After one layer or course is placed, he raises **the line** and builds another; thus, the building is by degrees regularly completed.

This is the method of teaching children, giving them such information as their narrow capacities can receive; and thus the prophet dealt with the Israelites. See Kimchi in loc., and see a fine parallel passage, Hebrew 5:12-14, by which this may be well illustrated.[7]

> **Hebrews 5:12** (NKJV) *"For though by this time you ought to be teachers, you need someone to teach you again the first principles of the oracles of God; and you have come to need milk and not solid food. 13 For everyone who partakes only of milk is unskilled in the word of righteousness, **for he is a babe**. 14 But solid food belongs to those who are of full age, that is, those who by reason of use have their senses exercised to discern both good and evil."*

The commentary helps us with the context as related to the usage of the word *precept* in **Isaiah chapter 28 (verses 7-13):**

7. Though Judah is to survive the fall of Ephraim, yet "they also" (the men of Judah) have perpetrated like sins to those of Samaria (Is 5:3, 11), which must be chastised by God.

erred … are out of the way—"stagger … reel." Repeated, to express the *frequency* of the vice.

priest … prophet—If the ministers of religion sin so grievously, how much more the other rulers (Is 56:10, 12)!

vision—even in that most sacred function of the prophet to declare God's will revealed to them.

---

[7] https://biblehub.com/commentaries/clarke/isaiah/28.htm (May 6, 2019)

judgment—The priests had the administration of the law committed to them (De 17:9; 19:17). It was against the law for the priest to take wine before entering the tabernacle (Le 10:9; Ez 44:21).

9, 10. Here the drunkards are introduced as **scoffingly** commenting on Isaiah's warnings: "Whom *will* he (does *Isaiah* presume to) teach knowledge? And whom will He make to understand *instruction?* Is it those (that is, does he take us to be) just weaned, &c.? For (he is constantly repeating, as if to little children) precept upon precept," &c.

line—a rule or law. [MAURER]. The repetition of sounds in *Hebrew. tzav latzav, tzav latzav, gav laqav, gav laquav,* expresses the scorn of the imitators of Isaiah's speaking; he spoke *stammering* (Is 28:11). God's mode of teaching offends by its simplicity the pride of sinners (2 Ki 5:11, 12; 1 Co 1:23). *Stammerers* as they were by drunkenness, and children in the knowledge of God, they needed to be spoken to in the language of children, and "with stammering lips" (compare Mt 13:13). A just and merciful retribution.

11. For—rather, "Truly." This is *Isaiah's reply to* the scoffers: Your drunken questions shall be answered by the severe lessons from God conveyed through the Assyrians and Babylonians; the dialect of these, though Semitic, like the *Hebrew,* was so far different as to sound to the Jews like the speech of *stammerers* (compare Is 33:19; 36:11). To them, who will not understand God will speak still more unintelligible.

12. Rather, "He (Jehovah) who hath said to them."

this ... the rest—Reference may be primarily to "rest" from national warlike preparations, the Jews being at the time "weary" through various preceding calamities, as the Syro-Israelite invasion (Is 7:8; compare Is 30:15; 22:8; 39:2; 36:1; 2 Ki 18:8). But spiritually, the "rest" meant is that to be found in obeying those very "precepts" of God

(Is 28:10) which they jeered at (compare Je 6:16; Mt 11:29).

13. But—rather, "Therefore," namely, because "they would not hear" (Is 28:12).

> **that they might go**—the *designed result* to those who, from a defect of *the will,* so far from profiting by God's mode of instructing, "precept upon precept," &c., made it into a stumbling-block (Ho 6:5; 8:12; Mt 13:14).
> **go, and fall**—image appropriately from "drunkards" (Is 28:7, which they were) who in trying to "go *forward* fall *backward.*"[8]

A proper reading of the chapter (even without my external evidence) debunked the so-called **Hebrew Israelites** claim that the Bible Teaches us to use *Precepts* for teaching in **Isaiah chapter 28**: "Precept upon precept and line upon line, here a little and there a little."

His comeback was that Jesus spoke to his people in **dark saying and parables** and he gave the following reference to prove *Precepts*" of **Isaiah 28:9-10**:

> "And the disciples came, and said unto him, Why speakest thou unto them in **parables**? [11] He answered and said unto them, Because **it is given unto you to know the mysteries** of the kingdom of heaven, but to them it is not given." **Matthew 13:10-11 (KJV)**

As you can see and judge for yourselves, the Doctrine of the so-called **Hebrew Israelites** is a "dangerous cancer." And sadly, many who are affected have a Bible in their hand.

---

[8] Jamieson, R., Fausset, A. R., & Brown, D. (1997). *Commentary Critical and Explanatory on the Whole Bible* (Vol. 1, p. 460). Oak Harbor, WA: Logos Research Systems, Inc.

PROBLEM TWO

THE IDENTITY CRISIS:

HAS THE CHURCH LOST ITS BIBLICAL MIND?

Note: *This section uses excerpts from a Facebook Live Stream teaching (Tuesday, May 7, 2019) titled The Ethnicity Distraction! "The Mass Infatuation with Hebrew Descent" by Elder Michael Holloway of Power Hope and Grace Bible Church*[9].

> "Then Peter opened his mouth and said: "**In truth I perceive that God shows no partiality**. 35 But in every nation **whoever fears Him and works righteousness is accepted by Him**." Acts 10:34-35 (NKJV)

There is a growing fascination with Hebrew Israelism not only from those within the ranks of their adherents but now from many black church pastors trying to prove Hebrew descendance. In other words, how we are the people of the Bible. Many Christian brothers and sisters are being infatuated with this.[10] [11] [12] It is becoming a distraction from the gospel of Jesus Christ and placing emphasis on ethnicity. This has infected a mass of individuals not only those outside of the body of Christ, but it has trickled over into the Church where there is now a striving to prove that we are the people of the book, the Hebrew descendants of the People of the Bible.

It is our responsibility, every born-again believer (every Christian) to preach the gospel of Jesus Christ to all people; Every Creature.

These are the words Christ said to His Disciples during His departure sermon; It was during His last message to His followers, and it was so important that before He left; He instructed them to preach the gospel to every creature.

> "And He said to them, "Go into all the world and preach the gospel **to every creature**. 16 He who believes and

---

[9] https://www.youtube.com/watch?v=YrXsXJHJxJQ May 10, 2019
[10] https://www.youtube.com/watch?v=sF39gw9JTIM May 9, 2019
[11] https://www.youtube.com/watch?v=mqZp-eMzEko May 10, 2019
[12] https://www.youtube.com/watch?v=sie5oZk1k8s May 10, 2019

The Identity Crisis:

is baptized **will be saved**; but he who does not believe will be condemned." Mark 16:15-16 (NKJV)

There is not a single person that the gospel of Jesus Christ cannot affect, or that the gospel cannot save.

But today from what has trickled into the body of Christ; men and women are being distracted, and now it has become more about who we are as a people, as an ethnicity, or culture than who is our Christ. Christology: The Person and His Works. It is a travesty, and it is causing many people to go astray. Now instead of our focus: as the body of Christ, as the church of the Living God who has been called to go into all nations to teach and preach the things concerning Him, Jesus Christ; The message has now changed from "preaching to every creature" to "**awakening our culture**." Hebrew Israelism is a very deceptive movement and satanically inspired to hinder us from the gospel that is to be preached to all people. Now, the urgency has been shifted to **awaking our culture**!

We can somewhat understand the mindset of many of the so-called Hebrew Israelite adherents fresh from the streets, gangs, jails, broken homes, parentless, system abused, etc. because they don't know the Jesus of the Bible and if anything, see Him only as some prophet. Of course, we love them, and we are to try to reach them with the gospel of Jesus Christ.

But what we can't understand is that some of the rhetoric that is spewed by many factions of the so-called **Hebrew Israelites** has now **oozed over into the body of Christ**. Those who have supposedly been washed by the blood of the Lamb and placed their faith in God: now zealously say **we got to awaken people of our culture, first!** That is a perversion of the gospel. If the church does not repent of this satanic delusion, it is going to cause many more people to go astray.

This awakening moves from awakening the Culture
- to why we were cursed in the first place.
- to we got away from keeping the Law.
- to getting back to keeping the Law.

Notice Christ has not been mentioned yet. It is a distraction.

The Identity Crisis:

Let us, brothers and sisters, who claim to have been washed by the blood of the Lamb,
- us that claim to believe in the divinity of Jesus Christ,
- us that understand that Christ is more than just a man,
- us that understand that He died and rose again on the third day

not be carried away and caught up in the false teachings of those who claim to be **Hebrew Israelites**.

It is a very shrewd trick of the devil to deter us. Churches are changing Sunday Service to Saturday Sabbath. Many of them have drank the false doctrine Kool-Aid of the so-called **Hebrew Israelites**, and it has trickled over into the church. If we don't get a handle on this, we will find ourselves in the same position as the church of Galatia were Paul had to come in and marvel at them because they were so soon removed into another gospel.

> *"**I marvel that you are turning away so soon** from Him who called you in the grace of Christ, **to a different gospel**, 7 which is not another; but there are some who trouble you and **want to pervert the gospel of Christ**. 8 But even if we, or an angel from heaven, preach any other gospel to you than what we have preached to you, let him be accursed. 9 As we have said before, so now I say again**, if anyone preaches any other gospel to you than what you have received, let him be accursed**."* Galatians 1:6-9 (NKJV)

So now, The Promises were just for us, the true Israelites. The Gentiles will be subservient to us (depending on the camp, some say the Gentiles were Israel).

When we read Revelation, we find that every elder took off their crown and laid it at His Feet:

> *"Whenever the living creatures give glory and honor and thanks to **Him who sits on the throne**, who lives forever and ever, 10 **the twenty-four elders fall down before Him who sits on the throne and worship Him who lives forever and ever, and cast their crowns before the***

The Identity Crisis:

> ***throne***, *saying: 11 "You are worthy, O Lord, To receive glory and honor and power; For You created all things, And by Your will they exist and were created."* **Revelation 4:9-11 (NKJV)**

The Bible is not about us or the so-called **Hebrew Israelites**. It is all about Jesus! **The Bible is not about Israel;** it is about Jesus Christ. Jesus Christ is the star of the story; He is the preeminent one. He is the one that our focus must be placed on, and not on your ethnicity. But this mass fascination on trying to determine who we are as a people has distracted many from the power of the gospel message of Jesus Christ. Brother and Sisters, we must bring this madness to a halt!

In this day and time, we can't be complacent but must take a biblical stand and proclaim that *Hebrew Israelism is false teaching*. It has infiltrated into the church. If we don't preach and expose it for the perversion that it is, it will affect all of us; our congregations and families.

> "And if you are Christ's, then you are Abraham's seed, and heirs according to the promise." **Galatians 3:29 (NKJV)**

> "But now the righteousness of God **apart from the law** is revealed, being witnessed by the Law and the Prophets, 22 even the righteousness of God, through faith in Jesus Christ, **to all and on all** who believe. For there is no difference;" **Romans 3:21-22 (NKJV)**

This has nothing to do with your ethnicity: nothing to do with whether you are a Jew or a Greek, Circumcised or Uncircumcised, Bearded or Shaven. The righteousness of God comes through faith in Jesus Christ to all and on all, apart from the Law. There is no difference **IF YOU BELIEVE**. Ethnicity is an ungodly focus, in the face of Christ and what He did for **ALL** on the Cross at Calvary.

Useless genealogy **(Titus 3:9-10)**: The promise given to Abraham was before circumcision and is bigger than the distinction between Israelites and Gentiles. Because the seed that God blessed to come through Abraham would not just bless Israel but all who would believe of every nation.

The Identity Crisis:

> "Now to Abraham and his Seed were the promises made. He does not say, "And to seeds," as of many, but as of one, "And to your Seed," **who is Christ**." **Galatians 3:16 (NKJV)**

We are **ALL** God's people **(John 3:16)**. Ethnicity limits our scope of the message of the gospel when we only focus on one ethnic group. God is the God of All people. And He desires that all men be saved **(1 Timothy 2:4)** and not wishing that any should perish **(2Peter 3:9).** Jesus is not just the atoning Sacrifice for Israel's sins only, but the whole world **(1 John 2:1-2)**. And to preach anything else is to preach not only another gospel but another Jesus **(2 Corinthians 11:4)**

> "For I am not ashamed of the gospel of Christ: for it is the power of God unto salvation to every one that believeth; to the Jew first, and also to the Greek." **Romans 1:16 (KJV)**

We must lose the ethnic focus. Why, because the focus of the gospel goes beyond ethnicity. **God is interested in saving souls, not ethnicities**, and every person (all men) has a soul. There are no white devils or black devils or Chinese devils etc.

Biblical Christians are not double minded: talking out of the side of their mouth and telling people, "I believe in Christ, but I am an Israelite. There is no such thing as a Christian Israelite. And we are the people of the Bible, and the promises were really to us, and we better get back to keeping the law." Stop with the foolishness. According to the Apostle Paul:

> "You have become **estranged** from Christ, you who attempt **to be justified by law**; you have **fallen from grace**." **Galatians 5:4 (NKJV)**

> "For if I build again those things which I destroyed, I make myself a transgressor." **Galatians 2:18 (NKJV)**

After Christ has made us free from a Law which you were incapable of keeping, why would you want to be entangled back again into the yoke of bondage? **You can't KEEP it!** And those who think they are keeping the LAW are not. Our focus should be on loving Jesus Christ and loving one another

(Galatians 5:14-15). The one another is not just black people or white people, but all people. This is the focus of the Gospel, which is to every creature **(Mark 16:15-16)**.

I USED TO BE A CHRISTIAN

In an interview: YouTube video titled, "Are Black People Cursed? Are Blacks the Real Jews? **Hebrew Israelites**!"[13] Malak and Yanni Yisrael of the California Hebrews, a black Hebrew Israelite group address questions about them formerly being Christians.

Malak Yisrael says he is a teacher/preacher. According to him, all the Hebrew Israelite groups are family, but everybody has their own little set. He says being a Hebrew Israelite is not a religion, but a birthright, a nationality. He says in the interview that you are considered a Hebrew Israelite if you are considered a so-called negro in America by blood. He says he used to be a Christian and that he woke-up around about fifteen years ago. He says he used to go to church every Sunday and that his testimony is interesting according to him.

He says he actually heard a voice from The Most-High leading him and guiding him. He says The Most-High took him to **Deuteronomy the 28th chapter** and showed him that the Bible is a history book and not a religious book. And that we are actually in the book and are the main characters. And that when he found out that he was a Hebrew Israelite, he was sad because the children of Israel had gone against The Most-High and that we got put under punishment. He says all this is in Deuteronomy the 28th Chapter.[14]

The wife, Yanni Yisrael says she also was a Christian and raised in a Baptist church growing up. And she became a Hebrew Israelite. When asked what the difference was from being a Christian and a Hebrew Israelite; She said the difference is with Christian those are all man-made religions; and like my husband Malak was saying, Hebrew Israelite is our culture, heritage, nationality. It is who we are as a people.

---

[13] https://www.youtube.com/watch?time_continue=82&v=xg97LQQF354 **(May 10, 2019)**
[14] https://www.youtube.com/watch?time_continue=12&v=Ud3MpK5G638 **(May 11, 2019)**

The Identity Crisis:

And according to the Bible and the Scriptures, we are the original Jews.

She says her life changed after becoming a Jew, rather than a Christian. She says that she changed everything, including her diet from what it was in the church. Although we read out of the same Bible, we were not following those laws that are written in that Bible. And that The Most-High God gives you the specific food that you are to eat. As a Christian, I was eating everything under the sun; foods that were an abomination.

Malak Yisrael says the white skinned people in Israel are not the Jews. He says they call themselves Ashkenaz and the Bible says in Genesis chapter 10 that Ashkenaz is the isles of the Gentiles. And that these are converts that came in and took our identity when we went into slavery. He says, being a Hebrew Israelite gave him his identity back. And that is what everybody in America is experiencing right now, is an identity crisis not knowing who they are.

He says they are walking around with amnesia. He says they were telling you we were Africans when we were brought here, and not telling you where we came from Africa. He holds a chart he calls the Negro-land. He says the Africans knew they were selling Jews to the Arabs. He says seeing himself as Jew (having his identity back) makes him feel better about himself because if you know where you came from you know where you are going. He says the Bible is really powerful because the whole Bible is about The **Hebrew Israelites**. He says the Most-High Himself called him out of his disobedience and led him into the Scriptures and showed him he was a Hebrew Israelite. And this is happening all over the world. He was asked about other **Hebrew Israelites** who wear warrior like clothes and that there seems to be a split (fighting amongst themselves) about who are the real **Hebrew Israelites**. But Malak insisted they all are one big family.

Yanni Yisrael steps in (to help Malak who is, was squirming in his seat for an answer); she replies, it is like your blood family, right? You may have disagreements, but you are still going to love your family. Malak Yisrael says anybody can be a Christian because it is a religion. But being a Hebrew Israelite is through the bloodline.

In another YouTube Video from the so-called Hebrew Israelite group called **The Gathering of The Church of Christ** (GOCC) titled, "Dispelling the Black Israelite Myths and Christian Discussion with an Israelite." [15]

The Hebrew Israelite says he grew up as a Christian, and as a Christian, he was always on guard and being in defense of Christ. He said, even in sin he loved himself some Jesus Christ, and that he didn't care what the brothers out on the corner would be teaching; If it was against Christ, he would have automatically refused to hear it.

But opposed to living in a world of ignorance and believing the lies he had been taught he at least left himself open for reasoning. He says, it wasn't that he was going to denounce his belief in Christ because he had a strong foundation going back to slavery and spirituality as far as having a Christian base; being raised in in a Christian family; and a long line of pastors in his family on his father's side, so there was no way some crazy guys on the corner was going to convince me to denounce Christ.

Continuing, he says you may wish to know what happens, since I who had grown up as a Christian with pastors in my family, singing in the choirs, you name it; Why did I decide to walk away from the Christian church? He says it was not because he didn't have any identity, or that he didn't have self-worth. He says no.1 He believed in Christ, and he was his foundation well before he had seen a so-called **Black Hebrew Israelite**, But I'm going to use that word "**Black**" loosely because Israelites don't really call themselves black Israelites. We are going to dispel that myth this evening, he says.

I'm not a black Israelite, and I don't even know what that is. That is just a dark term that they would like to put on Israelites or the awakening as a stigma.

---

[15] https://www.youtube.com/watch?v=13_u9asGk4s (May 11, 2019)

The Identity Crisis:

So, you used to be a Christian, then why did you choose to be an Israelite? No.1 Christ was about truth and fact. I found out through not only secular history but through Bible history that the blacks in America and the indigenous people that have been scattered throughout the earth, suffering colonialism, colonization fits the prophecies of the Israelite slaves in Egypt. Uncanny parallels! The prophecies concerning what happened to Israelites can only be related to us. He says he could not get that out of his mind. No.2 then he says he found out that this was well beyond the truth of us being Israelites or some black people in NY founding out that they were Israelites. I found out that the Jewish people and their so-called archeologists and historians researched "the **Igbo tribe**" who kept the customs of Israel in Africa for a thousand of years. And even the Jewish people could not denounce the "**Igbo**" which is another play on the word Hebrew. The "Igbo tribe of Africa., so you cannot tell me that white people came to get slaves out of Africa to bring to America and never knew there were black "**Igbo**" tribes in Africa.

He says, so we are dispelling the myth that people are just joining Hebrew Israelism because it is a new way of black people trying to self-identify. No more downplaying. First, they use dismissive tactics. And now they began to say it is an emotional sort of thing about them not knowing who they are; And that we are hopelessly just clinging onto what belongs to white people. I found beyond any shadow of a doubt that we're the children of Israel, And Christ prophesied that we would go into captivity in the books of Luke and Matthew. And that what we were suffering by the hands of white people, we have been looking at this totality wrong.

We have been examining this (those who have racist intent) by focusing on the white man and downplaying the prophecies of God written in the Bible. Downplaying this awakening and how great this is for us to finally be able to connect with our God outside of our influences, outside of our captive education, and outside of our theology taught in the Christian church.[16] [*To hear more of his rant, simply click on the cross-*

---

[16] https://www.youtube.com/watch?v=RL9QyhkjF4k&fbclid=IwAR1vvLYw7RM2nzxl72FfB5b-K54Q6WYt5M7bEFaPyqevsWUDMt0BaWjv8rw

reference link]. My point was that he said he used to be a Christian, but seemingly he is keeping the Christ part of it, now that he has gone through the Great Awakening.

THE PEOPLE WHO FOLLOW THE PIED PIPER

There has always been someone on a White Horse rising to the occasion for various reasons to save the so-called negro as if Christ was not enough and could not be used like a rabbit's foot. [17]

Noble Drew Ali:

In 1913, Timothy Drew [18] established the Moorish Science Temple of the United States in Newark, New Jersey. Embodying a variety of Islam, the movement spread throughout African American communities.

Mystery surrounds the origins of Drew's association with and knowledge of Islam, and various other belief systems.
Convinced that Christianity was the white man's religion, Drew offered a brand of Islam that blended traditional Islamic beliefs, biblical teachings, Orientalism, racial pride, Masonic influences, and mythology. [19]

He proclaimed that blacks were the descendants of "Moors," who had originally migrated from Asia and eventually settled in Africa, specifically Morocco. Declaring himself a prophet, he assumed the name Noble Drew Ali and wrote the Circle Seven Koran, an esoteric work, not to be confused with the Koran of orthodox Islam. [20]

Ali conferred "El" or "Bey" to the surnames of his followers, encouraged the adoption of Oriental garb, and directed his fellow "Moors" to follow strict moral and dietary guidelines.
The temple also issued "Moors" identification cards, or passports, proclaiming their new identity.
DREW ALI by the guiding of his father God, Allah; the great God of the universe. To redeem man from his sinful and fallen

---

[17] Anderson, Robert. Selling Something Nobody Needs: False Doctrine Cleaned Me Up! But God saved Me! (p. 79). Truth Seekers Read. Kindle Edition
[18] https://drive.google.com/open?id=0B5La9jT-2SAHQU9aOTh0bTFPMFU (May 13, 2019)
[19] http://www.apologeticsindex.org/278-moorish-science-temple-of-america May 13, 2019)
[20] http://hermetic.com/moorish/7koran.html (May 13, 2019)

stage of humanity back to the highest plane of life with his father God, Allah. The genealogy of Jesus with eighteen years of the events, life works and teachings in India, Europe, and Africa. These events occurred before He was thirty years of age. These secret lessons are for all of those who love Jesus and desire to know about his life works and teachings.

The reason these lessons have not been known is because the Moslems of India, Egypt and Palestine had these secrets and kept them back from the outside world, and when the time appointed by Allah, they loosened the keys and freed the secrets, and for the first time in ages have these secrets been delivered in the hands of the Moslems of America. All authority and rights of publishing of this pamphlet of 1927.
By the Prophet NOBLE DREW ALI[21]

ELIJAH MUHAMMAD:

It has been more than 40 years since **a Negro has appeared on the national horizon of racial leadership with a program for his people** as controversial and **as clear-cut as that of Elijah Muhammad**.[22] Not since the days of Marcus Garvey, the West Indian visionary back in 1920, has an "either or else" **plan of Negro salvation been placed before the people that is as sharply outlined as to consequences as that of Muhammad**.[23]

Allah (God) loves us, the so-called Negroes (Tribe of Shabazz,) so that He will give lives for our sake today. Fear not; you are no more forsaken. God is in person, and **stop looking for a dead Jesus for help,** but pray to Him whom Jesus prophesied would come after Him. **He who is alive and not a spook.**[24]

THE GODS OF ELIJAH MUHAMMAD: According to Elijah Muhammad (who claimed he learned it from Master Fard), the universe began seventy-eight trillion years ago when **God**

---

[21] https://drive.google.com/drive/folders/0B5La9jT-2SAHQU9aOTh0bTFPMFU?usp=sharing May 13, 2019
[22] https://drive.google.com/open?id=0B5La9jT-2SAHVHhrY0l1Mzhablk (May 13, 2019)
[23] Muhammad, Elijah. Message To The Blackman In America . Secretarius MEMPS Publications. Kindle Edition.
[24] Muhammad, Elijah. Message To The Blackman In America . Secretarius MEMPS Publications. Kindle Edition.

created Himself from a single atom which formed itself from nothing. Out of a universe of darkness, an "atom of life" appeared: "He was the only One in the whole entire dark Universe.

He had to wait until the atom of life produced brains to think what He needed. How long was that? I don't know, Brothers. **But He was a Black man, a Black man!. . The Black God produced Himself;** He's Self-created."[3] Not only that but "Allah (God) was created on the very earth that we are on today."[4] [25]

You must forget about ever seeing the return of Jesus, Who was here 2,000 years ago. Set your heart on **seeing the One that He prophesied would come at the end of the present world's time** (the white race's time).
- He is called the "Son of Man," **the "Christ,"** the **"Comforter."**
- **You are really foolish to be looking to see the return of the Prophet Jesus**. It is the same as looking for the return of Abraham, Moses, and Muhammad.[26]

In the Nation of Islam, both God and the devil are human beings. Elijah Muhammad identified the devil as the white man, the Caucasian race. According to Elijah, though the black race is many trillions of years old, the white race began a mere six thousand years ago with **Yakub, one of the Black Gods of this time cycle**

Elijah explained, "**The white race is not equal with darker people because the white race** was not created by the God of Righteousness. . . . They were made by **Yakub, an original Black Man**—who is from the Creator. Yakub, the father of the devil, made the white race, a race of devils—enemies of the darker people of the earth. The white race is not made by nature to accept righteousness".[27]

Elijah Muhammad taught that two thousand years after the coming of Moses, Jesus came to the Caucasian race to

---
[25] http://www.answering-islam.org/NoI/noi2.html May 13, 2019
[26] Muhammad, Elijah. Message To The Blackman In America . Secretarius MEMPS Publications. Kindle Edition.
[27] https://www.youtube.com/watch?time_continue=15&v=uD7ZVSX91fE May 13, 2019

reform them, but they rejected His rule. **Jesus was not miraculously born of a virgin**, as the Bible and the Qur'an teach. Rather, said Elijah, "The real truth that the Christians hate to confess is that **Joseph had gotten the child, Jesus, by Mary while he was married to another woman** and at that time had six children by the first marriage. So Master Fard Muhammad (God in Person) has taught me."[22]

Elijah also stated that the angelic prophecy, "He shall save His people from their sins" (Matt. 1:21), does not refer to Jesus of Nazareth saving His people (in Muhammad's mind, the white people) from sin. Rather, it refers to "a modern-day Jesus," **Fard Muhammad, who comes to save the black man**.[23] Much of the New Testament was not just reinterpreted by Elijah Muhammad, but totally rewritten.

He claimed that Jesus died, not by being crucified on a cross, but by being stabbed in the heart by a police officer in Jerusalem with a large hunting knife or small sword. Elijah claimed that Jesus was standing in a spread-eagle position, with His back to the wooden wall of a storefront. The Jewish authorities offered twenty-five hundred dollars in gold to anyone who brought Jesus to them dead and fifteen hundred dollars if He were brought in alive. The officer told Jesus, "They are going to kill you anyway, so why not let me kill you and make the twenty-five hundred dollars as I am a poor man and have a wife and family to care for?" Jesus agreed. He "knew that he would be killed but did not care."[24]

The sword blow through the heart literally pinned Jesus to the wall. The blood stopped circulating so quickly that Jesus' arms were frozen in the stretched-out position. Thus, Elijah corrects a popular misconception: Jesus "died in the form of a cross and not on the cross!"[25] Afterwards, His father Joseph (not Joseph of Arimathea) "mortgaged all of his little land and embalmed Jesus in a liquid in a glass tube. As long as the air does not get to him, he will be there just as he was the day he was killed two thousand years ago. He is buried in Jerusalem."[26] Any talk about Jesus' resurrection is dismissed by Elijah Muhammad as ignorant foolishness.

Elijah Muhammad, *The True History of Jesus as Taught by the Honorable Elijah Muhammad.*

LOUIS FARRAKHAN

In The past twenty-two years since Elijah Muhammad's death, Minister Farrakhan has been seemingly revising aspects of his predecessor's theology. Before different audiences, Minister Farrakhan will preach conflicting messages, which makes it more difficult to determine what he "really" believes. Yet overall, some sort of progress in his teaching can and should be charted.[28]

Louis Farrakhan has increasingly found acceptance before Muslim audiences and been recognized by several nations as a Muslim leader. He is familiar with the shahada, the Muslim confession of faith: "I witness that there is no God but Allah, and Muhammad is the Apostle [or Messenger] of Allah." Reciting this creed is all that is necessary to convert to Islam. When Muslims say this creed, the Apostle they mean is Muhammad ibn Abdullah of Mecca, the founder of Islam who died in A.D. 632

Twenty years ago, Louis Farrakhan taught "that there is no God but Master Fard Muhammad, Who is Allah, and that the Honorable Elijah Muhammad is His divine Messenger."[40] (To orthodox Muslims, this is crude blasphemy.)
If Farrakhan still believes this, he doesn't say it anymore, and when he quotes the shahada, he now uses the orthodox formula listed above.
[https://www.answering-islam.org/NoI/noi2.html]

Clarence 13X:

The Five-Percent Nation, sometimes referred to as NGE or NOGE, the Nation of Gods and Earths, or the Five Percenters, is a movement founded in 1964 in the Harlem section of the borough of Manhattan, New York City, by a former member of the Nation of Islam (NOI), Clarence 13X,[29] who was named Clarence

---

[28] http://www.answering-islam.org/NoI/noi2.html **May 13, 2019**
[29] https://drive.google.com/open?id=0B5La9jT-2SAHTDByN2RXaUZlZGM (May 13, 2019)

Edward Smith at birth, and who ultimately came to be known as Allah the Father.[30]

Allah the Father, a former student of Malcolm X, left the NOI after a dispute with Elijah Muhammad over Elijah's teaching that the white man was the devil, yet not teaching that the black man was God.

Allah the Father also rejected the assertion that Nation's biracial founder, Wallace Fard Muhammad, was Allah and instead taught that the black man was himself God personified.[31]

Spiritual Israel Church and It's Army

The organization, I eventually came out of was called "**The Spiritual Israel Church and It's Army**[32] *(founded in the 1920s long before there was a 1West)*". Although they didn't teach the Law aspect of Hebrew Israelism, notice the commonality of the twisted Scriptures with that of the camps.

Israel preached that our problem was that we, **the black people,** didn't know who we were.

> "The King of Israel would **say that he came after us, to get us, and to teach us who we really are by saying, "You are not negroes, niggers, darkies, spooks, jigaboos, or colored people.** Your nationality is Ethiopian, and **your spiritual name is Israel.**" Quoting Amos 9:7 'Are ye not as children of the Ethiopians" [Notice God didn't say any of these: niggers, jigaboos, negroes, spooks, darkies, colored people][33]

They taught, the reason you can't become to be a nation and have your right up under the sun is because **you are wearing another name and not the name that God gave you**[34]

It was taught in Israel that somebody beat us to our mailbox and got our letter (**the Bible**), but that it takes a man of

---

[30] https://en.wikipedia.org/wiki/Five-Percent_Nation May 13, 2019
[31] https://en.wikipedia.org/wiki/Five-Percent_Nation#Supreme_Mathematics May 13, 2019
[32] https://drive.google.com/open?id=0B5La9jT-2SAHZndCUU1QekZIWEk May 13, 2019
[33] Anderson, Robert. Selling Something Nobody Needs: False Doctrine Cleaned Me Up! But God saved Me! (p. 101). Truth Seekers Read. Kindle Edition.
[34] Ibn (p. 127).

understanding to draw it out. According to the doctrine of Israel, this man is **the King of Israel who was sent to wake us up from sleep as to who we are,** as found in:

> Proverbs 20:5 "*Counsel in the heart of man is like deep water; but **a man of understanding will draw it out**.*" [35]

The ministers in Israel would teach and defend that Jesus had to be black because the Bible **said his hair was "like wool;"** pulling the congregation into the error; he'd ask, "**who do you know besides the black man that has nappy wooly hair**;" quoting:

> Revelation 1:14 "*His head and his hairs were white like wool, as white as snow; and his eyes were as a flame of fire;*" [36]

THE ISRAELITE NATION WORLD WIDE MINISTRIES

This group is not affiliated with the camps and does not promote hate. However, when we examine their doctrine, we find the same method of superimposing of one's beliefs on Scripture. Although, their membership (according to their website) is open to all nations of people, white, etc., we still see the theme of Black nationality running through its core and the twisting of Scripture to support their doctrinal views. See their literature.[37]

> " Welcome to the Israelite Nation Worldwide Ministries![38] We hope that you enjoy your stay with us. I am proud to say that our Nation is not affiliated with any radical or militant group that may bear a similarity in name or other feature. We have no political agendas, nor do we make statements for political gain of favor. Our goal is to serve our God in the right way. We know' who we are and need not show' hostility or hate to anyone. This point is punctuated in the following scriptures:
> Mathew 28:19, Isaiah 56:3-8, Numbers 9:14".[39]

---

[35] Anderson, Robert. Selling Something Nobody Needs: False Doctrine Cleaned Me Up! But God saved Me! (p. 107). Truth Seekers Read. Kindle Edition.
[36] Ibn pp. 107-108
[37] •Shadrock, "The Truth, The Lie, and The Bible III," pp. 36-40, Fifth Ribb Pub., (1995).
[38] http://israelitenation.com/ (May 27, 2019)
[39] http://israelitenation.com/#iLightbox[b463d04de2639bf31341/0 (May 27, 2019)

"Why does the **I.N.W.W.M** include **white people** in their Congregation?

First, the mandate of the **I.N.W.W.M** is to teach ALL nations. Second, our forefathers helped to lay the foundation for Western European civilization, not only throughout the Americas, but Italy, Portugal, Spain, France, England, etc. Today, the complexion of our brothers and sisters may differ, but the spirit is the same. Third, we are proud to lead and not follow in the path of the oppressor, because the froward is an abomination to God, but his secret is with Abraham's Seed, **of whom we are descended**."

Hence, my usage of the term **Hebrew Israelism**.

THE BLACK HEBREW ISRAELITES - ABBA BIVENS — BHI:

A man called Bivens:[40] [41]

There is a song that Christians sang about Jesus that says, "Oh, oh, oh, what He's done for me, Oh, oh, oh, what He's done for me, Oh, oh, oh, what He's done for me, **I never shall forget what He done for me**,

"Sanctified Me Holy, that's what He's done for me, Sanctified Me Holy, that's what He's done for me, Sanctified Me Holy, that's what He's done for me, **I never shall forget what He DONE for me**, [42] [43]

But **Hebrew Israelites** seek to propagate a different song in the minds of the feeble. "I never shall forget **what they DONE to ME**."[44] [45]

The Christian song, with a focus on Jesus Christ, sets you free from the bondage of sin and changes lives.

The so-called Hebrew Israelite propaganda song has no freeing power, but rather keeps you entangled with bondage

---

[40] https://drive.google.com/open?id=0B5La9jT-2SAHdnpKdW9WRUVZZGM May 13, 2019
[41] https://www.youtube.com/playlist?list=PL-djiOgtDTUUcnJEvkUzdhx1U-gNRcFUD May 20,2019
[42] https://www.youtube.com/watch?time_continue=11&v=tkTEmbTXnxg May 9, 2019
[43] https://www.youtube.com/watch?time_continue=16&v=hMmzbhavwvU May 9, 2019
[44] https://www.youtube.com/watch?time_continue=2&v=D8u_9ZFlfHA May 9, 2019
[45] https://www.youtube.com/watch?time_continue=512&v=8dWx5adtaT8 May 10, 2019

on what the so-called Whiteman (so-called Esau) has done to you, and **you are determined never to forget what was done to YOU**. There will never be an end. There is no freedom on a sinking ethnicity ship with likeminded individuals, and Jesus Christ is not at the helm.

> "And upon a set day Herod, arrayed in royal apparel, sat upon his throne, and made an oration unto them. 22
> - And the people gave a shout, saying, **It is the voice of a god, and not of a man.** 23
> - And immediately the angel of the Lord smote him, **because he gave not God the glory**: and he was eaten of worms, and gave up the ghost" **Acts 12:21 (KJV)**.

Some of the things that attract people of color to the **Hebrew Israelites** are as follows:

Today, in truth, there are many ethnic distractions such as racism. People want to identify with something, *regardless of "the what,"* which makes them feel special, and they want to belong (wrong or right).

Racism does exist, and young men and women experience unarmed blacks being shot by cops. They see people of color disproportionally filling the prisons and jails. They feel that the system fails them from the White House to the poor house. They feel entrapped by economics and educational woes. They see the racial divide in our country. They blame the system for the drugs in the neighborhood. They feel the last to be hired, but the first to be fired. They blame the system for what we do to each other and ourselves. They are angry and mad at God; they feel that the Jesus that grandmama prayed to does not work for them.

Then to the rescue, you have misguided and manipulative people (with a hook), preaching do you know that you are the blessed people, the true people of the Bible, **Hebrew Israelites**, Jews, chosen by God. That's the reason they (**Esau and the nations**) are coming against you, our people. They discriminate against us because they know who we are. Therefore, you have been oppressed all these years because you didn't know who you are; and our people have been asleep.

Many **Hebrew Israelite** (BHI) groups believe and list the Twelve Tribes of Israel as follows:

1. **Judah** — **Black Americans (Negroes)**
2. Benjamin — West Indians
3. Levi — Haitians
4. Simeon — Dominicans
5. Zebulun — Guatemalans, Panamanians
6. Ephraim — Puerto Ricans
7. Manasseh — Cubans
8. Gad — Native American Indians
9. Reuben — Seminole Indians
10. Asher — Colombians, Uruguayans
11. Naphtali — Argentines, Chileans
12. Issachar — Mexicans

According to Vocab Malone in his book, <u>Barack Obama vs. The Black Hebrew Israelites: Introduction to the History & Beliefs of 1West Hebrew Israelism,</u> "The rise of Hebrew Israelism affects the global church of Christ. Hebrew Israelism doctrines especially affect Christians in large cities. The spread of Hebrew Israelism impacts families as well."[46]

They open the Bible to **Deuteronomy chapter 28** to the **Curses and Slavery**, and with their so-called method of precept teaching the trap is set. The white man, Transatlantic Slave Trade, and the negroes who are the real Jews. Masterfully and neatly wrapped with a ribbon and presented to many who are unlearned, uneducated and many who only had a superficial relationship with the Bible and Christ Jesus (if any); and others could care less one way or the other, they just want vengeance (on Esau) and are flowing with the crowd.

The message sounds good to the flesh. These false teachers, with a Bible in hand, tell them to **wake up** and **be identified with your roots,** your **nationality,** and turn back to **The**

---

[46] Malone, Vocab. Barack Obama vs The Black Hebrew Israelites: Introduction to the History & Beliefs of 1West Hebrew Israelism (pp. 7-8). Thureos Publishing / Lionhouse Publishing. Kindle Edition.

Most-High. You are a superior people, the **Hebrew Israelites**. Nations shall bow to you and be your servants.

SO-CALLED HISTORY ACCORDING TO THE BLACK HEBREW ISRAELITES

History: [47] [48]

1800 A literate blacksmith named **Gabriel Prosser** taught the slaves thru inspiration of the Bible that we were God's people and should rebel against the tyranny of America.

1831 A slave named **Nat Turner** was called The Prophet and raised a small slave rebellion based on Bible teachings and visions of war and blood he had. Many blacks today demonize this man who attempted to save them from oppression.

1896 William Saunders Crowdy in Lawrence, Kansas. Established "The Church of God and Saints of Christ," although he taught blacks were God's people, **he mixed a lot of Christianity in his teachings.**

1915 F.S. Cherry set up the "**Church of the Living God, the Pillar Ground of Truth for All Nations**." The group was founded in Chattanooga, Tennessee, and later moved to Philadelphia. Theologically, the Church of the Living God **mixed elements of Judaism and Christianity and the Talmud**.

1920 Wentworth A. Matthews established **the Commandment Keepers** in Harlem N.Y., he primarily based his learnings on so-called Jewish people. **He rejected all New Testament writings.**

1929 Israel ben Newman and **Mordecai Herman** established "The Moorish Zionist temple of the Moorish Jews" **They also followed white Jewish teachings**.

1930 Arnold Josiah Ford with a small group of Black Jews went to Ethiopia where they participated in the coronation of Emperor Haile Selassie, created a school and acquired 800

---

[47] https://www.youtube.com/watch?v=RL9QyhkjF4k&fbclid=IwAR1vvLYw7RM2nzxl72FfB5b-K54Q6WYt5M7bEFaPygevsWUDMt0BaWjv8rw May 13, 2019
[48] Anderson, Robert. Selling Something Nobody Needs: False Doctrine Cleaned Me Up! But God saved Me! (pp. 173-194). Truth Seekers Read. Publishing May 13, 2019

acres (320 ha) of land for the purpose of uniting Black Jews of the Diaspora with Ethiopians. He died there in 1935.

Near the end of the Civil Rights Movement, there were several prominent Israelite teachers; it was around this time the truth was being taught on a larger scale, and in more areas.

1960 Eber Ben Yamyan also known as **Abba Bivens** was initially taught he was an Israelite by an ex-slave some many many years earlier in the South. Bivens believed in **the Black Christ** and on his way to NY had visited many Indian reservations and came to the scriptural conclusion that **the so-called Indians were Israelites** as well. He then came to N.Y. and joined **the commandment keepers** under Matthews **but rejected Matthews teachings of old testament only**. Bivens founded **the Israeli school of Torah**[49]. He was the first to teach both the blacks and Indians of the Americas are **Israelites**.

1963 Ben Carter, also known as **Ben Ammi,** led 300 Israelites from Chicago to Liberia and then to Dimona, Israel. Established **"the African Hebrew Israelites"** He attempted **to deliver his group from the curses of Deuteronomy 28:15-68** under the oppressive hand of America but soon discovered that oppression followed him to Dimona. Due to lack of citizenship, they lacked the medical and dental capabilities to properly take care of one another, so he agreed to support the Jewish Israeli military allowing their young men to fight against the Palestinians in exchange for much-needed supplies for their camp.

1965 William A. Lewis taught a congregation in Grand Junction, Michigan.

1970 Hulon Mitchell Jr. aka Yahweh ben Yahweh established the **"Nation of Yahweh" proclaimed himself god, the Son of god.** He and many of his followers were arrested for murder, racketeering, arson, and many other crimes to establish themselves in various states. He was found guilty of these crimes in 1991 and died of colon cancer in prison.

---

[49] https://www.youtube.com/watch?v=TtdkhNqC4Ug (May 27, 2019)

1973 Moshe ben Chareem aka Masha, was chosen to carry on teaching in **Abba Bivens**[50] place with **Peter Sherrod aka Yaiqab**. They took over the Israeli School adding U.P.K.(**universal practical knowledge**). Later in the '70s, they were helped by five other brothers, and they were called **the 7**. They were offered several million dollars by the Rosicrucian's to teach a more Christian or Jewish message of unity' for all mankind as some of the other Israelite camps teach. Masha & Yaiqab refused. A Christian / Jewish message means negro will remain on the bottom of society- and the full truth will never be taught.

1977 Shadrock Porter formed the **Israelite Nation,** where a Christian message of love and unity for all races is taught.

THE BLACK HEBREW ISRAELITES

In the **Hebrew Israelite** camps, many are drawn to the attire of the camps, others to the rhetoric, others to power over others, ranks, etc. others are simply looking for a war with the white man (and even the Africans), for them the Bible is just a tool to justify their actions.

There are also those who say I used to be a Christian. Those who attended some church building, were on the deacon board, or sung in the choir, or ushered for years, but didn't know the books of the Bible. Didn't attend any type of Biblical classes (assuming the church had classes). They claim to know all about being a Christian, and it didn't teach them who they were. They say, now that I have come out of Christianity and came into "**Da Truth**," I know who I am.

When people are not grounded in the Scriptures as they should be, and they are not living for God, it is easy for them to go astray when a movement such as the **Hebrew Israelites** comes along.

The Hebrew Israelism caveat, You Must keep the Law as Yeshua Ha Mashiach did!

---

[50] https://www.youtube.com/watch?v=scPusOdvCMs (May 27, 2019)

The sad thing is that the adherents may now be learning more about Scriptures, but it is out of context and with twists and perversions (**Galatians 1:7, 2 Peter 3:16-17**).

Instead of getting wisdom, knowledge, and understanding of the Scripture. Hebrew Israelite adherents are taught to get wisdom, knowledge, and **understanding of their so-called Precepts** method used to teach Scripture and confound weak Christians in the word. Their doctrine is **a doctrine of nationality** and **a deceptive and wicked doctrine**. When the focus has changed
- from God to ethnicity,
- from Christ to culture,
- from preaching the gospel to every creature to awakening just our culture,

then we have gone astray. The gospel is not just to one ethnic group or one race; it is for all people.

Over the years we have moved through colored ~ Afro-Americans ~ Muslims (Black/and World) ~ "Black and I'm Proud" ~ "Black Lives Matter" ~ Hebrew Israelites (Black/and Not) ~ Christian Israelites ~ and those who don't know what to believe. But the Bible has not changed; it still proclaims:

> "**Jesus Christ the same** yesterday, and today, and forever. 9 Be not carried about with divers and strange doctrines...." **Hebrews 13:8-9 (KJV).**

BELIEFS NOT SHARED AMONG HEBREW ISRAELISM:

All of the Subgroups and Organizations of The **Black Hebrew Israelites DO Not** believe the same thing. Their beliefs and practices vary considerably:[51]
- Black Jews, who maintain a Christological perspective and adopt Jewish rituals.
- Black Hebrews, who are more traditional in their practice of Judaism.
- Black Israelites, who are most nationalistic and furthest from traditional Judaism.

---

[51] Anderson, Robert, Selling Something Nobody Needs, False Doctrine Cleaned Me Up! But God Saved me, pp173-195; TruthseekersRead Publishing (2016)

They who stumble over the "Whosoever."

Hebrew Israelism is not the only group that has swapped the Gospel of Jesus Christ for Black Activism. According to Bishop Nathaniel of **Israel United In Christ** (IUIC),[52] he says that we are witnessing the rebirth of the twelve tribes of the nation of Israel. The **Hebrew Israelites** teach nationality; The resurrection of a dead nation and that **they are the people** in the Holy Bible. He says he teaches prophecy and history.

But they use the same propaganda material used by the other camps to get into the minds of minorities who feel disenfranchised.
- The Truth About Slavery https://s3.amazonaws.com/iuic-prod-ws-repo/wp-content/uploads/2018/11/21111550/The-Truth-About-Slavery_eng_v4.pdf - May 8, 2019
- The True Image of Christ https://s3.amazonaws.com/iuic-prod-ws-repo/wp-content/uploads/2018/11/21111559/THE-TRUE-IMAGE-OF-CHRIST-ENG_1.pdf May 8, 2019
- Their Website, like the Jehovah Witnesses, practice date-setting and claiming prophecy for its existence. https://israelunite.org/brief-israelite-history/ - May 8, 2019

False doctrines could not flourish if they were not giving the illusion of fulfilling a need in people. What I have learned through talking to others and studying cults and false doctrines is that each lie is packaged with you in mind. You, the broken person, simply stepped up to the counter. It is difficult to sell people something they don't want or are not looking for. The truth of the matter is this, **there is a market for false doctrine, and the suppliers are many**.[53]

SHARED COMMON BHI BELIEFS CONCERNING THE EUROPEANS (WHITE-MAN) AND OTHER NATIONS

Most Black **Hebrew Israelites** (**BHI**) believe that the "The white man" (Europeans) are descendants of Jacob's (Israel's) **twin brother Esau (Edom)** (**Genesis 25:25**).
- White people are seen as conspirators who attempt to persecute the black people and hide their true identity as Israelites.

---

[52] https://www.youtube.com/playlist?list=PL-djiOgtDTUV0LNKAj9IRcqBJsQvPiDSI May 20, 2019
[53] IBN pp. 80-81.

- They also believe that The Most-High **has a stern punishment reserved for Esau's children**, at the end of days, for enslaving the **Hebrew Israelites**.
- They Believe **the White Man will be in heaven, but as slaves**. **BHI** teaches that according to **Isaiah 14: 1-2**, the white man is going to serve Israel as slaves in the kingdom of heaven.
- They teach that the "**The white man" (Europeans) are in their heaven now**, and they (the Caucasian) are the wicked that the earth was given to in **Job 9:24**.
  - People on this earth are in **the Caucasian heaven** right now since white people are dominating this world and subjugating black people.
- According to many **BHI** teachers, **Jesus only died and is coming back only for the twelve tribes of Israel. All other nations will be punished; there is no salvation plan for them**.
- **BHI** believes the Arabs(Ishmaelites), The Africans(Hamites) and the Europeans(Edomites) work together to enslave the House of Judah (Judah, Benjamin, Levi).

BASIC BELIEFS THAT MOST BHI INCONSISTENTLY PROFESS TO SUBSCRIBE:

- **Belief** in one God.
- **BELIEVE** that the Ten Commandments are immutable.
- **BELIEVE** that there is a resurrection(Reincarnation?).
- **BELIEVE** that heaven and hell are not geographical locations.
- **BELIEVE** that Judaism is not a race but a religion. Hence, we prefer the term "Israelite" in referring to members of our Congregation.
- **Believes** Jesus was a strict adherent to Judaism and a prophet sent by God.
- **DO NOT believe** that Jesus was God nor the son of God.
- **DO NOT believe** in Christianity.

THE DILEMMA OF A PEOPLE:

> *"O foolish Galatians, **who hath bewitched you**, that ye should not obey the truth, before whose eyes **Jesus Christ hath been evidently set forth**, crucified among you?"* **Galatians 3:1 (KJV)**

> *"But there were also **false prophets among the people**, even as there will **be false teachers among you, who will secretly bring in destructive heresies**, even denying the Lord who bought them, and bring on themselves swift destruction.*
> *2 **And many will follow their destructive ways**, because of whom the way of truth will be blasphemed.*
> *3 By covetousness **they will exploit you with deceptive words**; for a long time their judgment has not been idle, and their destruction does not slumber."* **2 Peter 2:1-3 (NKJV)**

Ethnicity Doesn't validate one's salvation. You can't hold on to nationality (ethnicity) and Jesus Christ and the Law at the same time. Two of these must go (**dung**), and only one of them saves. **(Philippians 3:2-10)**

> *"Therefore, if **anyone is in Christ, he is a new creation**; old things have passed away; behold, **all things have become new.*** **2 Corinthians 5:17 (NKJV)**

HIJACKING THE WORD BLACK IN THE BIBLE:

There are two types of ignorance:
1) Invincible ignorance:
   ignorance beyond the individual's control and for which, therefore, he is not responsible before God. Those who are ignorant of some truth through absolutely no fault of their own are in a state of invincible ignorance.

2) Vincible ignorance:
   Ignorance because of rejection of knowledge. The individual chooses not to know--chooses to be ignorant of knowable truth (hard-hearted). Those who

are ignorant through some fault of their own are referred to as having vincible ignorance.

BHI Do Not Believe All BLACK People Are Of The Tribe Of Judah:

Many so-called **Hebrew Israelites**[54] believe the American Negros are the descended of the Tribe of Judah who were exiled from Israel after the destruction of the Second Temple in 70 A.D. Black **Hebrew Israelites(BHI)** also known as Black Hebrews, or, Hebrew Israelites are groups of African-Americans situated mostly in the United States who claim to be descendants of the ancient Israelites.

- Not to be confused with African Hebrew Israelites, or Beta Jews (Ethiopian Jews) they claim that they are Alpha Israelites and that they are not Africans at all, but were merely sold into slavery from Africa.
- **Black Hebrew Israelites** believe that the term **Negros** can be used to define the descendants of the **Trans-Atlantic Slave Trade slaves** and can be used to distinguish them from the **Africans(Hamites).**
    - **BHI** makes the claim that **the real Jews are the Negros of America.**
    - **BHI** contend that The **Jews are one tribe of people** - Judah.
    - **BHI** believe that **you (the Negros)** along with the other tribes are the real Israelites.
- **BHI** claim **they are refugees** of the so-called "**First Jewish-Roman War**" avoiding the holocaust at Masada In 73 AD.
- **BHI** claim that in 70AD **they fled Judea into the interior of West Africa**, and sojourned there some 1,500 years.
- **BHI** claim that their Shemitic ancestors were:
    - sold by **Hamitic Africans**, to **Ishmaelite-Arabian slave traders**,
    - who (in turn) sold **them** to **European, Trans-Atlantic Slave Traders** in the early 1600s.

---

[54] http://www.religioustolerance.org/bhi.htm (May 27, 2019)

- They use many prophecies in the Hebrew Bible to show similarities to the predicted fate of the descendants of the Israelites in the "latter days." They most often cite **the 28th Chapter of the book of Deuteronomy** as proof that the predicted condition of the Israelites more closely matches their own, than that of today's Caucasian Ashkenazi, and Sephardic practitioners of Judaism.

So-called **Hebrew Israelites** believe and , as foretold in the Hebrew Scriptures, that the Nation of Israel was **"Scattered into the Four Corners of the Earth"** for sinning against the GOD of Israel and **for rejecting HIM** and **HIS Laws, Statutes, and Judgments. Leviticus 26th and Deuteronomy 28th Chapters** outline all the curses that would befall the Israelites and their descendants. These atrocities are the afflictions and sufferings that befell Blacks out of Africa, the very ones among those who endured the Slave Trade.

They teach that the "**African Slave Trade**" is the final fulfillment prophesied in **Leviticus 26th** and in **Deuteronomy 28th** Chapters concerning the Israelites going into captivity in the lands of other nations to serve them. And that while in these Gentile lands, The Hebrew Israelites would call to mind their sins and abominations against the GOD of Israel and think to return to HIS Righteous Way of Life, just as we are doing this very day. And also that we would seek to return to YEHOVAH the God of Abraham, Isaac, and Jacob, the God of our forefathers, with our whole heart, soul, and mind.

SO-CALLED HEBREW ISRAELITES BELIEF ABOUT JESUS CHRIST

So-called **Hebrew Israelites** believe Jesus was black, and all the prophets in the Bible were black. "Some Israelites do believe in the Messiah, and **some don't**. Even among the ones who don't there exist a slight separation of what they believe about the Messiah, this can also be found among the ones who do believe. **There isn't one**

universal belief about the Messiah among Hebrew Israelites.

There is no consensus on who the Messiah is: The true name of the Messiah in the New Testament is Yahshuah Ben Yah (Yahshuah the son of Yah). According to their website, there is no universal agreement regarding who the Messiah is. It is not a central component of what defines them as **Hebrew Israelites**.

Virgin Birth:
a) "Yahshuah the Messiah was an Israelite, but He had no earthly father, so what made him an Israelite? He was born through the womb of an Israelite woman."
b) Others teach that Joseph was Jesus Biological father.
c) And there are those who don't accept the New Testament as Scriptures.

Jesus Was A Black Man:

Hebrew Israelites cite the reference to wool as pointing to their hair type.

"*His head and his hairs were **white like wool, as white as snow**; and his eyes were as a flame of fire.*" **Revelation 1:14 (KJV)**

His head and his hairs were white **like** wool, **as** white **as** snow.

Exceedingly or perfectly white–

- the first suggestion to the mind of the apostle being that of wool,
- and then the thought is occurring of its extreme whiteness resembling snow–the purest white of which the mind conceives.

The comparison with *wool and snow* to denote anything peculiarly white is not uncommon.

The color white symbolizes His purity. It is not pointing out His race.

Isaiah 1:18 makes this clear unless we are to believe that sinners have sins of wool (afro-sins):

*"Come now, and let us reason together, saith the LORD: though your sins be **as** scarlet, they shall be **as white as snow**; though they be red like crimson, they shall be **as wool**"*

Hebrew Israelites cite that His feet are black.

*"**And his feet like unto fine brass**, as if they **burned in a furnace**; and his voice as the sound of many waters."* **Revelation 1:15 (KJV)**

Webster's 1828 Dictionary says that fine/burnished brass is *polished and glossy*. Burning/heating the brass in the furnace removes the impurities. It's not saying that they are burnt looking, as in black.

Bronze, on the other hand, speaks of judgment. The word translated "**brass**" in the King James Version would be more correctly translated **bronze.** In ancient Israel, there was no such metal known as brass. Bronze typifies the divine character of Christ who took upon Himself the fire of God's wrath, holiness, and justice by becoming a sin offering.

The exalted Jesus appeared in splendid form. John's vision of Jesus is similar to, but clearly outstrips Daniel's vision of a revealing angel (Dan. 10:5–6).

- The Gospels **nowhere describe the physical appearance of Jesus**; hundreds of artists have used their imagination to fill in the gap. Including so-called Hebrew Israelites.
- The current description is **symbolic, not literal**, for the picture becomes bizarre if, say, the sword coming from his mouth is literal.
- Note also the number of times **like** is used.
- No artist could paint what John described. The meaning of these symbols is not very difficult, as the discussion has made clear.

Jews/Israel Were Black People:

Job was a black Israelite[55]: **Job** himself said he was black:

> "***My skin is black upon me***, *and my bones are burned with heat.*" Job 30:30 (KJV)

Verse 30 unquestionably describes Job's diseased skin. It was "**black**" and "**peeled**," or literally, "My skin grows black from off me." In the second line, it was literally his "**bones**" that burned with fever. "**Skin" and "bones" both are metonymies for "body."** These last symptoms of Job's malady must be taken with others to complete the picture of his intense physical discomfort. [56]

Job was observing an odd condition caused by his infirmities: If Job was a black man, there would be no reason to proclaim that his skin is **black** during his suffering. The bones, in the Scriptures, are often represented as the seat of pain. The disease of Job seems to have pervaded the whole body (Job 2:7-8).

King Solomon was a black Israelite:

Solomon[57] himself said he was black. Referencing Song of Solomon 1: 1, 5, 6

> **Song of Solomon 1: 1** *The song of songs, which is Solomon's.* **5 I** *am* **black,** but comely, O ye daughters of Jerusalem,
> - as **the tents of Kedar,**
> - as **the curtains of Solomon**.
>
> **6** Look not upon me, **because I** *am* **black**, Because the sun hath looked upon me: **(KJV)**

However, when reading in the context of verses 1 through 6, we have a problem, Surely **Hebrew Israelites** are not suggesting that Solomon is feminine:

Song of Solomon 1: 2 Let **him**
- **kiss me** with the

---

[55] https://www.youtube.com/watch?v=zqj7VJMdQXA (May 7, 2019)
[56] Alden, R. L. (1993). Job (Vol. 11, p. 297). Nashville: Broadman & Holman Publishers.
[57] https://www.youtube.com/watch?v=Yki0qMl0Nwl (May 8, 2019)

> • **kisses of his** mouth: for thy love is better than wine.
> 4 Draw me, we will run after thee: **the king hath brought me into his chambers**: we will be glad and rejoice in thee, we will remember thy love more than wine: the upright love thee.

The Jews (Judah) Were Black:[58]

> "*Judah mourneth, and the gates thereof languish;* ***they are black unto the ground****; and the cry of Jerusalem is gone up.*" **Jeremiah 14:2 (KJV)**

The context: Judah's people lament on the ground. **Lament**. A general term encompassing various literary forms whereby the speaker appeals to God for aid in overcoming present calamity.[59]

Lamentation 4:7 "Her Nazarites *[princes]* were purer than snow, they were whiter than milk, they were more ruddy in body than rubies, their polishing *[beauty of their form]* was of sapphire: **8 Their visage *[faces]* is blacker than a coal *[soot]*; they are not known in the streets:** their skin cleaveth to their bones; it is withered, it is become like a stick *[as dry as wood]*." (KJV)

The Context of 4:7–8 Punishment fell on nobles and commoners. The language used here to describe the former and present state of the "princes" is a dramatic hyperbole. Their former impressive appearance (compared to snow, to the whiteness of milk, and to rubies and sapphires) would have attracted respectful attention wherever they went. Now they walked the streets indistinguishable from others. They suffered the same malnutrition and dehydration as the peasants (cf. **Job 30:30**).[60]

---

[58] https://www.youtube.com/watch?v=Yki0qMl0Nwl (May 8, 2019)
[59] Myers, A. C. (1987). In The Eerdmans Bible dictionary (p. 638). Grand Rapids, MI: Eerdmans. Myers, A. C. (1987). In The Eerdmans Bible dictionary (p. 638). Grand Rapids, MI: Eerdmans
[60] Huey, F. B. (1993). Jeremiah, Lamentations (Vol. 16, p. 481). Nashville: Broadman & Holman Publishers.

HEBREW ISRAELITES ARE BURSTING THROUGH THE DOORS OF CHURCHES

- More Hebrew Israelites kicked out churches
https://www.youtube.com/watch?v=XvvU2hQ_m6o (May 10,2019)
- Hebrew Israelites- Confront pastor's in the Christian church.
https://www.youtube.com/watch?v=IpuIpLoMMjk (May 10,2019)
- Texas Pastor Hands Over Chuch To Commanding General Yahanna - #ISUPK
https://www.youtube.com/watch?v=4zr-HJ2RBkc (May 10,2019)
- Hebrew Israelites put arrogant money pastor in his place after church service
https://www.youtube.com/watch?v=H6Bbm99Xzmg (May 10,2019)
- Hebrew Israelites INFILTRATING Church
https://www.youtube.com/watch?v=cqcX3hR5kUo (May 10,2019)
- Negro Coon Pastor kicks Hebrew Israelites out of his church
https://www.youtube.com/watch?v=ZfAQwv1mf3w (May 10,2019)
- Israelites Testify During Sunday Service !!
https://www.youtube.com/watch?v=B9b5pYqoJSg

DEUTERONOMY CHAPTER 28

RELATED QUESTIONS THAT MUST BE ADDRESSED BY BHI:

Who was The King of The Jews in the 15th or 16th century that went into captivity with them at the time of the Transatlantic Slave Trade?[61] [62]

> "The Lord **shall bring thee, and thy king** which thou shalt set over thee, **unto a nation** which neither thou nor thy fathers have known; and there shalt thou serve

---

[61] https://www.encyclopediavirginia.org/Transatlantic_Slave_Trade_The (May 27, 2019)
[62] https://www.youtube.com/playlist?list=PL-djiOgtDTUUtxwRWwgMkst4F7GR9h_tF (May 27, 2019)

other gods, wood and stone." **Deuteronomy 28:36 (KJV)**

Kings: As he did Manasseh, Joiakim, Zedekiah and others (2 Kings 17:4, 6; 24:12,14; 25:7,11; 2 Chronicles 36:1-21; Jeremiah 39: 1-9.

Hebrew exiles, with some honorable exceptions, were seduced or compelled into idolatry in the Assyrian and Babylonish captivities (**Jeremiah 44:17-19**). Thus, the sin to which they had too often betrayed a perverse fondness, a deep-rooted propensity, became their punishment and their misery.

When did Africa become the land of promise?

"And it shall come to pass, that as the Lord rejoiced over you to do you good, and to multiply you; so the Lord will rejoice over you to destroy you, and to bring you to nought; and **ye shall be plucked from off the land whither thou goest to possess it**." **Deuteronomy 28:63 (KJV)**

When did the Jews (Israel) conquer the land of Ethiopia (Africa) between 70AD and the 15th Century?

According to Matthew Salih, in his book, <u>Christians/Hebrew Conversations: For Spouses and Loved Ones Volume One</u>, "Black **Hebrew Israelites** believe that since these curses in the 28th chapter only speak of happening to Israel, it must mean that it identifies God's people by the oppression that matches the curses from past to present. It should be noted that Deuteronomy 28 is a conditional covenantal chapter, not prophetic. Therefore, it cannot be applied to scattered Israelites who exist AFTER the new Covenant, especially since Deuteronomy 28 is old Covenant conditions." [63]

"The Bible repeatedly affirms that God, who is not flesh and not made in our image, is the rightful God of all people whatever their nationality or complexion. Thus, we dare not seek to deny him to others, but rather we intend to refute

---

Salih, Matthew. Christian/Hebrew Conversations: For Spouses and Loved Ones Volume One (Kindle Locations 211-214). Kindle Edition.[63]

Deuteronomy Chapter 28

implicit claims by some others which would deny him to us or imply that we are at best secondary heirs of his kingdom. As stated before, the first non-Jewish Christian was an African court official (**Acts 8:26-39**). God and the early church did not share the modern world's fixation with color boundaries but had they done so, Africans would not have been the ones excluded. Jewish Christians initially had problems with Gentiles, but their biggest recorded problems with Gentile Christians were with Greeks and Romans-the Bible's closest cultures to Europeans."[64]

YouTube Video from Israel United In Christ (IUIC) titled, **The Israelites: The Curses That Identifies The Children Of Israel**.[65]

Notice the BHI adherent dialog with a young man of color on the street corner: **BHI** asked him what is your nationality? The young man replied, **supposedly African American**. The **BHI** adherent tells the young man that he is glad that he put the *supposedly* on there because *supposedly* that is what *they* gave us. And that *they* gave us all these by-words and that they were put on us for a reason.

The **BHI** adherent tells the young man that, if he has the time, they (**BHI**) will show him *who he is* according to the Bible. They invite him to step closer to look at the poster signs so they can show him *who his forefather was*. The **BHI** adherent asked him, do you see yourself on the sign (Twelve Tribes Chart)? The young man pointed to **Judah – American Blacks** on the chart.

He asks the young man did he know that Christ descended from the line of Judah and that Christ was a Black man? See that is not what you are going to learn in the church. He asked the young man did he go to church. He replied sometimes. **BHI** asks/replies, what you came up out of that bunch of foolishness, huh; a bunch of lies. He tells the young man that Christian pastors have been taught by the

---

[64] Glenn Usry; Craig S. Keener. Black Man's Religion: Can Christianity Be Afrocentric? (Kindle Locations 959-963). Kindle Edition.
[65] https://www.youtube.com/watch?v=knxTxmnydoc (May 13, 2019)

Deuteronomy Chapter 28

oppressors in seminary schools. How can a people that beat me and hang me on trees teach me about the Bible? He says to the young man, right now our people are rebellious; but that he (**BHI**) tells people what the Bible says and hopefully it will agree with your spirit. He has the reader read:

> *"O Lord, righteousness belongeth unto thee, but unto **us confusion of faces**, as at this day; to the men of Judah, and to the inhabitants of Jerusalem, and unto all Israel, that are near, and that are far off, through all the countries whither thou hast driven them, because of their trespass that they have trespassed against thee."* **Daniel 9:7 (KJV)**

The **BHI** adherent says to the young man that **confusion of face is given to us because we break the Most-High commandments**; We don't know who we are, and our people are lost and confused, but today you are going to get some understanding. Today you are going to learn who you are and that the Bible is going to bear witness with your spirit.

> *"The Spirit itself beareth witness with our spirit, that we are the children of God:"* **Romans 8:16 (KJV)**

The '**Spirit itself**' is '**this the Bible**.' It is a spiritual book. This book, The Most-High sent from His prophets to be written by the prophets to give you a message. It is a book of prophecy; I am going to show you some prophecies that happen and some that didn't happen yet.

This the only book on the earth that will show you the beginning, middle, and end of time. It shows you **what happened to you** back when under Moses and **what is happening to you** today in America. Today is the day that you have been waiting for your hold life brother; to find out that you are not Africa America. Before I came into "**Da truth,**" I waited for 30 years before I heard this. This is going to show you how to get salvation and that having blond hair is a curse in the Bible, but our people want to follow after the oppressor ~ the white man. Our men want to follow

Deuteronomy Chapter 28

after the white man, and they are Esau according to the Bible. The **BHI** reader reads:

> "*For thou art an **holy people** unto the Lord thy God, and the Lord hath chosen thee to be **a peculiar people** unto himself, **above all the nations that are upon the earth**.*" **Deuteronomy 14:2 (KJV)**

The **BHI** devotee tells the young man that he is separate from the Africans and that we are NOT African Americans; We are not from Africa, but we are from Israel. He points to the posters with men (black) with yokes of iron on them at Auction blocks and tells him that this did not happen to Africans.

Another **BHI** adherent reads from the Zondervan Compact Dictionary the definition of **Ham** to show the young man, who is listening diligently, that Ham is **the progenitor of the dark races** (Africans) and not the negros.

The BHI adherent says to the young man, just because we are the same color doesn't mean we are the same people. The **BHI** reader reads:

> "*But against any of **the children of Israel** shall not a dog move his tongue, against man or beast: that ye may know how that the Lord doth **put a difference between the Egyptians and Israel**.*" **Exodus 11:7 (KJV)**

BHI expounds, see right here it is showing you that The Most-High doesn't have NO Respect to the other Nations. He created all people of the earth, but He had one people He chose above every nation that He created. And put a difference between us and the Egyptians and the Africans. We just read in the Zondervan that Ham is the forefather of the Africans. **BHI** reader reads:

> "*Moses commanded us **a law**, even the **inheritance of the congregation of Jacob**.*" **Deuteronomy 33:4 (KJV)**

Deuteronomy Chapter 28

> "*He sheweth his word unto Jacob, **his statutes and his judgments unto Israel. 20 He hath not dealt so with any nation:** and as for his judgments, **they have not known them**. Praise ye the Lord.*" **Psalms 147:19-20 (KJV)**

The **BHI** adherent explains that Moses, our forefather, gave us the law. The inheritances were the laws, statues, and commandments. Jacob makes up the twelve tribes of Israel. The Bible is redundant; it says the same thing repeatedly. He is talking to the Children of Israel. And if they don't do these things, certain things are going to happen to them. No other nations had His laws, statutes, and commandments. And because they didn't get them, we are the only ones held accountable for keeping His laws, statutes, and commandments. The other nations are NOT held accountable. The covenant He made was with Abraham, Isaac, and Jacob; the Children of Israel. He didn't make it with the other nations, but with us. And we are going to prove these things in the Bible. This is the reason why we are out here today; to show you the curses you are living under right now. And why we are at the bottom of society and don't own any of the building around here. **BHI** reader reads:

> "*Yea, **all Israel have transgressed thy law**, even by departing, that they might not obey thy voice; **therefore the curse is poured upon us,** and the oath that is written in the law of Moses the servant of God, **because we have sinned against him**.*" **Daniel 9:11 (KJV)**

He says that all Israel have transgressed God's law, and he refers to 1 John 3: 4 to show **Sin is the transgression of the law.** And this is what our people are doing. But we, the **Hebrew Israelites**, have come back to The Most-High's statutes and commandments. We keep them today, the Sabbath day holy. **BHI** reader reads:

> "*Hear this word that **the Lord hath spoken against you, O children of Israel, against the whole family** which I brought up from the land of Egypt, saying, 2 **You only have I known of all the families of the earth**: therefore I will punish you for all your iniquities.*" **Amos 3:1-2 (KJV)**

Deuteronomy Chapter 28

BHI expounds saying that The Most-High said I'm going to punish you: Blacks, Hispanics, and Native Americans for all your iniquities. He tells the young man that during our captivity, we have rebelled against The Most-High. **BHI** reader reads (Deuteronomy 28:15):

> *"But it shall come to pass, if thou wilt not hearken unto the voice of the Lord thy God, to observe to do all his commandments and his statutes which I command thee this day; that all these curses shall come upon thee, and overtake thee:" Deuteronomy 28:15 (KJV*

He explains that the curses didn't happen in Moses day, but came to pass in 1619 [66] [67] and throughout. He goes through the curses to the young man.

> *"And the Lord shall bring thee into Egypt again with ships, by the way whereof I spake unto thee, Thou shalt see it no more again: and there ye shall be sold unto your enemies for bondmen and bondwomen, and no man shall buy you."*
> **Deuteronomy 28:68 (KJV)**

He tells the young man that it was us who were making straw in Egypt to build the Pyramids, and because of the curses, we went back into Egypt again with ships.

The young man asked him about the ships; **BHI** says, **no we didn't go back to Egypt on ships**. **BHI** adherent (erroneously) explains to him that what it means is that we would go back into slavery *(pointing out it is synonymous with bondage)* again in, America. He asked the young man; you do know that we did come here on ships, right? **BHI** pulls up another poster to show the young man of people stuffed in a ship like sardines. **BHI** says that is what the Most-High God did to us because we broke his laws and commandments

Many **Hebrew Israelites** say it is incorrect to say they all believe the same thing. My response, they may not **ALL** teach the same thing, but they are **ALL** in the same error "Jesus

---

[66] https://www.smithsonianmag.com/history/misguided-focus-1619-beginning-slavery-us-damages-our-understanding-american-history-180964873/ (May 13, 2019)
[67] https://www.history.com/topics/black-history/slavery (May 13, 2019)

Christ + PLUS XY." They may not teach hate, but they teach that Jesus only came for Israel and some good white folks may get into the Kingdom. They'll teach that you must keep the law, but NOT one of them have KEPT it. The purpose of this book is not to try and expose every nook and cranny of the erroneous teachings of Hebrew Israelism, but rather to provide enough sampling across the board for the reader (biblical or otherwise) to judge the tree for the apples that are on it.

Many of the **Hebrew Israelite** adherents are regurgitating the same regurgitation of Satan's anti-Christs who preach Nationalism with a deflection away from the truth of the gospel.

Below are a few more of their different camps teachings about the curses. And notice the foul language that many of them have no problem using on the streets as they talk about the one they call The Most-High with a Bible in their hand:

- **SICARII BHI** camp: YouTube titled "**Edify On The Curses That Have Befallen Blacks & Hispanics.**"[68]
- **GMS BHI** camp: YouTube titled **GMS Produce Curses Pt2**[69]
- **ISUPK BHI** Camp: YouTube titled "ISUPK – Curses In The Bible Proves Blacks & Hispanics Are The Real Israelites – Hebrew Israelites."[70]
- **GOCC BHI** Camp: YouTube titled "GOCC ~Curses That Came With 'Fallen Ones'"[71]
- **H.O.I BHI** Camp : YouTube titled H.O.I. H.O.I. : Paul Only Taught The Law/The Curses Are About Us! [72]
- **SonsofYahawah BHI** Camp: titled "Deuteronomy 30:7 God will put curses and judgment on Esau pt2."[73]
- **Alpha Omega Clan BHI** Camp: YouTube titled "A.O.C. Israelites Classics General HaShar Schools A Young ROYAL Know It All"[74]

---

[68] https://www.youtube.com/watch?v=jvk6esIRR9I (May 13, 2019)
[69] https://www.youtube.com/watch?v=2_aGGUzSvC8 (May 13, 2019)
[70] https://www.youtube.com/watch?v=7V7-Q5Ly9uQ (May 13, 2019)
[71] https://www.youtube.com/watch?v=DZmNvzTo5IE (May 13, 2019)
[72] https://www.youtube.com/watch?v=s6kM9clMiwQ (May 13, 2019)
[73] https://www.youtube.com/watch?v=xxBIzh7WRuU (May 13, 2019)
[74] https://www.youtube.com/watch?v=wnJ2CQAIKB4&t=1726s (May 13, 2019)

ISRAEL UNITED IN CHRIST: What's In The Name?

- **FWOI BHI** camp: YouTube titled "FWOI-Will Ye Hear."[75]
- **H.O.D.C. BHI** Camp: YouTube titled "H.O.D.C. CAMP - Esau Your Time Is Up!!!"[76]
- **Watchmen For Israel BHI** camp: YouTube Titled "So Called Black Woman and Edomites Get Cut Up."[77]

ISRAEL UNITED IN CHRIST: WHAT'S IN THE NAME?

Most camps are just raw with lies. But IUIC advocates are shrewd with their lies and brilliance to their lies through professional advertisement and Marketing skills of Satan. They make their lie sellable to even unlearned and novice Christians; IUIC tactic is like that of the new Farrakhan who promotes one thing behind the scene and the cleaned-up version of the lie on the scene.

"The prophets prophesy falsely, and the priests bear rule by their means, and my people love to have it so: and what will ye do in the end thereof?" **Jeremiah 5:31 (KJV)**

Think of them as a professional gang with marketing skills:

IUIC Commercial: Tamir Rice, Sandra Bland, Philando Castile. Wake Up Israel!!![78]

Black Israelites - The Shocking TRUTH About Hebrew Israelites REVEALED[79]

Out Of The Mouth Of Babes[80]

IUIC 365: Out of the Mouth of Babes Jesus is Black[81]

Bishop/Elder Nathanyel Is the Top Official in THE IUIC.

Web BIO:

---

[75] https://www.youtube.com/watch?v=i0TFWmJJjO8 (May 13, 2019)
[76] https://www.youtube.com/watch?v=YPff1_oXeFc (May 13, 2019)
[77] https://www.youtube.com/watch?v=eBRPqbpB7ak (May 13, 2019)
[78] https://www.youtube.com/watch?v=oeWCDZBHitU (May 16, 2019)
[79] https://www.youtube.com/watch?v=tQrjYOzMnuw (May 14, 2019)
[80] https://www.youtube.com/watch?v=maAmkFVcWr0 (May 14, 2019)
[81] https://www.youtube.com/watch?v=g7OISoa-tXI (May 14, 2019)

ISRAEL UNITED IN CHRIST: What's In The Name?

"I've been in this truth for over twenty years and learned at the feet of the 7elders of Israel. I've seen many things in this walk, great things and bad things, but they all played a part in molding me into who I am today. I've seen world scholars confounded by this truth,[82] I've seen gangs of drug dealers either change or moved out the way, I've seen men on the bottom rise and become unrecognizable to who they once were.

I've seen greed, lust, hate, and money tear a movement apart or so some thought... This movement is according to prophecy; it can't be stopped one man falls, and two will rise in his place. The Most-High used me to establish "Israel United in Christ," but this movement is not about any organization but rather **the resurrection of a nation**; The 12 Tribes of the Nation of Israel.[83]

My mission is to take this truth on a higher level and as professional as possible[84]. I struggled in teaching this truth for a long time, and one day, brothers and sisters sought me out, guided by the Spirit of the Almighty.[85] [86]

They wanted to know what I know to see what I see in the word of God to make a difference, to make a change. I told them as I tell you all, you want the Most-High to use you come to learn but know that the Lord will try you, he will make a man out you a woman out of you that will do our Israelite ancestors proud.

Like I said The Most-High is going to test you to make you into an Israelite indeed. But if you aren't built for this: you too weak, too evil then leave, goodbye. Hide behind a computer or set up your own thing. You must be a living example for the rest of our people. I won't say it's easy, but what revolution is ever easy?

---

[82] https://israelunite.org/the-biblical-image-of-christ/ (May 14, 2019)
[83] https://israelunite.org/category/12-tribes-of-israel-today/?doing_wp_cron=1557813491.2833049297332763671875 (May 14, 2019)
[84] https://www.youtube.com/watch?v=oeWCDZBHitU (May 14, 2019)
[85] https://israelunite.org/camp-flyers/ (May 14, 2019)
[86] https://israelunite.org/the-biblical-christians/ (May 14, 2019)

This revolution is transforming boys into men, deadbeats into fathers and players into husbands. **This revolution changes the Black and Hispanic man into the Israelite leader** he is meant to be."[87]

ISRAELITE SCHOOL OF PRACTICAL KNOWLEDGE: ISUPK

It appears that one thing you better NOT do in the camps "*is asking for evidence.*" [88] You just take it on faith say many of the **BHI** adherents. They even attempt to use **Matthew 16:17** to show that you didn't have to read it in a book to know that Mashah, their leader, was King David reincarnated, but if the Spirit reveals it to you it was from the Most-High. In the YouTube clip titled "'Hebrew Israelite' Leader Said to be King David Reincarnated!" the **GMS** adherent says that back in the day they made everybody swear that Mashah was King David reincarnated and if you said differently you would be banished. He says it was Ahryah himself who taught it to us. This belief was promoted by the school and is still believed today.

Reportedly, [89] High Priest, **General LAHAB**[90] [91] was the #4 man of the seven heads of the original ISUPK at 1 West 125th Street. He was personally responsible for the Military Mindset of ISUPK, the boots, the studs, the berets, all that came from **LAHAB**. Elder TAHAR, Elder Nathanyel Ben Israel, and General YAHANNA all served directly under LAHAB in the original **ISUPK**.

Lahab says the way things were (he was there about 18 to 20 years) when he joined was that they were dealing with the Pharisaical order (Old Testament). But in his studying, the Spirit led him into the study of the Gospel. So Christ enters into the picture of his life on a higher level of consciousness. He began to see that Christ was the King of Israel and not no other Israelite. He sees that Moses represents the old, but

---

[87] https://israelunite.org/elder-nathayel-bio/ (May 14, 2019)
[88] https://www.youtube.com/watch?v=2vYjyUQiUBI (June 2, 2019)
[89] https://www.youtube.com/watch?v=mwgLN-WtbfY (June 2, 2019)
[90] https://www.youtube.com/watch?v=5alatV9A1rU (June 2, 2019)
[91] https://www.youtube.com/watch?v=3WXeFNnVwvk (June 2, 2019)

the Father says, hear ye him the Son during the transfiguration.

Lahab says he began to question things in the organization (*Note: listen to the interview*). How could **Mashah**, the leader in **ISUPK**[92] be above **Jesus Christ**? He says he realized that he was really serving men. The concept of Mosha being the King (David) was being brought forth by Ahryah on a serious level a few years before he left. He says they wanted people to swear an oath to that fact. Lahab said when they brought that to him to swear an oath under him that he was king, by this time he, Lahab, was well established in the gospel. He says he went back and taught the gospel in his classes and they videoed it. He says they called him the next day and told him not to come back. They saw him teaching that Christ was the King and preaching the gospel and he says it offended them.

Of course, we get a different story from Tahar of **GMS** who also split from **ISUPK** and started the Great Millstone camp.[93] He even discussed those gangs planning to murder leaders related to power struggles (gang like control). It would appear that there is a lot of hate and bad blood among the different camps that claim to represent the Most-High. I've provided links demonstrating these men cannot be representatives of God.[94][95][96]

Rebuttal: Lahab story reminds me of my similar story (assuming he is telling the truth and has no agenda). But here is the issue, it is called **baggage**. He came into the knowledge of the gospel, but he is still promoting Israel (The replacement theology of who he believes to be Israel). I too made that mistake in the beginning. He has come into the knowledge that many of the things he previously believed and taught were wrong according to the Bible. We will pray for Lahab that Jesus Christ will continually open his eyes to the whole truth and that he will understand that he must burn the baggage, all of it.

---

[92] https://isupk.com (May 14, 2019)
[93] https://www.youtube.com/watch?v=PfMO6DOD0wU (June 2, 2019)
[94] https://www.youtube.com/watch?v=Un-hm4mP5FU (June 2, 2019)
[95] https://www.youtube.com/watch?v=scA2LimZMRE (June 2, 2019)
[96] https://www.youtube.com/watch?v=U6iAQiL4YVI (June 2, 2019)

The Story:
The **ISUPK** was established in 1969. Ever since we have been teaching Blacks. Hispanics. and Native Indians their true identity according to the Bible.

Commanding General Yahanna is the **"Head of the ISUPK"** and the **"Nation of Israel" second only to Christ**; come and learn the TRUTH from **the Man the Most-High and Christ has ordained** to gather and rebuild the 12 Tribes of the Nation of Israel...

About Us:
In the **ISUPK**, we are educating Blacks, Hispanics, and Native Indians about their true heritage; which is **comprised of the laws, statutes, and commandments of the Bible**. Once our people begin to follow the laws in the Bible, God, or Yahawah in the Hebrew, will look down from heaven and have mercy on us. He will also send Christ to free us from our oppression. Using the Bible, **the ISUPK will fix all the problems in the Black, Hispanic, and Native Indian communities**. Turning a lawless and immoral people, into a law-abiding righteous people. **The true nationality of the Negroes, Hispanics, Native Indians, and West Indians of North, Central, and South America are the true decedents of the Lost 12 Tribes of the Nation of Israel, and Jesus Christ is their King**.

What we do...
The Israelite School of Universal Practical Knowledge is a nonprofit, faith-based, community organization that responds to the plagues of poverty-stricken, urban American's through programs such as Education (Adult & Youth); Food Distribution: Rehabilitation (Drug & Alcohol): Mentoring. Counseling & Spiritual support the organization whose purpose is to teach so-called African Americans, Hispanics. and Native American Indians, the true history of their people as it pertains to the Bible.

The **ISUPK's** belief and experience is that the true knowledge and understanding of the core, fundamental values, and teachings of the **'"King James Version"** of the

The Gathering of Christ Church (GOCC) Provides Some BHI History Background.

Holy Bible can conquer the ills of society that plague urban American's of low-income that are under-educated and poverty-stricken. By bridging the biblical knowledge of the past with the present, we can advance the spiritual, mental, and physical strength of our demographic to produce stable, non-government system dependent persons.

Originally founded in 1969. the **ISUPK** Nonprofit began in December 2006: incorporated in February 2007. and received its tax-exempt status in May 2008. **Only the ISUPK has the understanding and truth, using the "King James" version of the Bible, to awaken the lives of African Americans**. Hispanics. and Native American Indians, that are broken by hunger; drug addiction: and homelessness (to name a few).

There is **HODC BHI** camp YouTube video where reportedly, All of 1 west knows Yahanna plotted to kill the elder of Israel for power and money. With a warning to beware of these guys."Yahanna (ISUPK) Plotted To Kill His Elder For Power and Money (Facts) ISUPK." [97] They accuse Yahanna of conspiring to murder Mashah (King David) with Lahab, Ahryah, and others.

THE GATHERING OF CHRIST CHURCH (GOCC) PROVIDES SOME BHI HISTORY BACKGROUND.

GOCC BHI camp in a video titled "GOCC Bible Teachings – The Reincarnation Deception." [98] The leader, Elder Rawchaa, talks about how they came up through the **ICUPK** school until he found Christ. He says the majority of what we see today (such as the star of (Moloch) David, the cussing, reincarnation, etc.) coming from the new adherents (camps) has trickled down from the original teachers (125th Street) long before there was a YouTube. In the video clip, he points out who those original leaders were and what was their agenda. He says that because they were under the Star (of Moloch) which was witchcraft, it will make you believe things that are

---

[97] https://www.youtube.com/watch?v=Dzi-wl9qRkl (June 2, 2019)
[98] https://www.youtube.com/watch?v=-ru6hqk7cic&list=PLfQEBSys1uQRM8JWfEE9QutOZ7l9o60sZ (June 3, 2019)

The Gathering of Christ Church (GOCC) Provides Some BHI History Background.

not true because it is magic. Elder Rawchaa admits it (Black Hebrew Israelism) was built on a lie starting with believing that Abba Bivens was Elijah (**Malachi 4:5**); Mashah was Moses (and then King David); Ahryah was Daniel and John the Revelator. He says that if you can teach this and get people to believe; you can persuade people to give you money, etc. They will give you everything they have.

But there was a trick behind all this: Elder Rawchaa of **GOCC** says, all these brothers that he is mentioning (the seven heads) before the mid-eighties they did not even follow Christ. When they got near the nineties, they started adding Christ to their doctrine. What they should have done was shut everything down and build on Christ. He says they were trying to cover themselves and keep the reincarnation doctrine and bring forth Jesus Christ also. They were also teaching that there was no hell; but that souls went back to the Father and comeback every third and fourth generation. Elder Rawchaa says they started teaching that even Jesus Christ came here himself over four times and people in the camp believed it. If they could teach this and have people believe that Christ was reincarnated, then they could slide themselves into the book, having people believe that they also are someone reincarnated.

He points out that one of the dangers of teaching the reincarnation doctrine is seen when the school began to split for various reasons. if it would have never been taught by the original leaders, Tazadaqyah[99] could have never claimed to be **The Comforter ~ The Holy Spirit incarnated in a man**. Keep in mind; the original leaders did not believe in Christ, so they were adding Christ as they went along. It was like I have a doctrine, and I will fit Christ in there anywhere I want

---

[99] https://www.nj.com/bergen/2018/04/black_hebrew_israelite_leader_jermaine_grant_arres.html (June 4, 2019)

IS THE SO-CALLED HEBREW ISRAELITES (BHI) A RACIST GROUP?

Speaking with a forked tongue, they would say that they are not racist:
- **Black Hebrew Israelites practice separatism** instead of **racism.**
- **BHI** don't judge based on the color of one's skin, **but whether you are part of the Twelve Tribes of Israel or not.**
- **BHI** has **no intention of uniting with the other nations under Jesus Christ** because they believe the Bible instructs them to separate from the other nations.

So-called **Hebrew Israelites** use and call the Apocrypha inspired writings. They teach that God divided the nations and separated the sons of Adam from the children of Israel:

> "When the Most-High divided to the nations their inheritance, when he separated the sons of Adam, he set the bounds of the people according to the number of the children of Israel." **Deuteronomy 32: 8 (KJV).**

They use **2 Esdras 6:54 -56** to show that all came from Adam, but God only chose Israel, and the other nations he said was nothing to him, but like spit:

> **2 Esdras 6:54** "And after these, **Adam also, whom thou madest lord of all thy creatures:** of him come we all, and the people also whom thou hast chosen. 55 All this have I spoken before thee, O Lord, because thou madest the world for our sakes" 56 "**As for the other people**, which also come of Adam, **thou hast said that they are nothing**, but be like unto spittle: and hast likened the abundance of them unto a drop that falleth from a vessel."

SO-CALLED HEBREW ISRAELITES BELIEF ABOUT GRACE

BHI teaches that Christ only died for the Israelites. Grace is only extended to the Israelites. According to their doctrine:

GRACE PERIOD: a period officially allowed for payment of a sum due or for compliance with a law or condition, especially an extended period granted as a special favor.

So when we are under grace, **it is only allotted to us to return to the laws, statutes, and commandments** since we have all fallen away from the truth and the will of The Most-High. The time we have been allotted to do that is now. Before he returns. [**Romans 3:23; Romans 6:23**]

<u>**Some BHI groups explain GRACE like this**</u>:
"Grace is what God is giving the Israelites. It is the time period for the Israelites to get themselves together and **start keeping the law** if they don't when Jesus Christ returns; he is going to kill them.

PROBLEM THREE

THE BIRTH OF CHRIST – THE SEED

A Christian should know what they believe and should be able to give a sound Biblical answer as to why they believe what they do. What is the evidence for what you believe?[100]

THE VIRGIN BIRTH

MARY:[101] [102]

Hebrew Israelites teach the word "**virgin**" in Luke does not mean pure but means **young girl (maiden) of marriageable age;** Mary had intercourse with Joseph and he was Jesus biological father. **Luke 1:26-27**[103].

They teach a marriage arrangement (espouse) was made with Mary's family for Joseph to marry Mary, but Mary was unaware of the marriage arrangement.[Luke 1:34]

Strongs #	Hb/Gk Word	Pronunciation	English Equivalent
Old Testament (Hebrew) for "virgin"			
H1330	bĕthuwlah	beth·ü·lä'	virgin, maid, maiden

Virgin: Strong's Number G3933 matches the Greek παρθένος (parthenos), which occurs 2 times in 1 verses in 'Luk' in the Greek concordance of the KJV
https://www.blueletterbible.org/lang/Lexicon/Lexicon.cfm?strongs=G3933&t=KJV

Luk 1:27	To a virgin G3933 espoused to a man whose name was Joseph, of the house of David; and the **virgin's** G3933 name *was* Mary.

Outline of Biblical Usage []
I. a virgin
    A. a marriageable maiden
    B. a woman who has never had sexual intercourse with a man
    C. one's marriageable daughter

---

[100] Norman L. Geisler, The Essentials of the Faith (CD) Powerpoint 2006
[101] https://www.youtube.com/watch?v=ddfd_d_viog&t=8s (May 20, 2019)
[102] https://www.youtube.com/playlist?list=PL-djiOgtDTUXBem6ZMoYf7Se27gf6iYlj (May 20, 2019)
[103] https://www.youtube.com/watch?v=ddfd_d_viog (May 8, 2019)

The Virgin Birth

    II. a man who has abstained from all uncleanness and whoredom attendant on idolatry, and so has kept his chastity
        A. one who has never had intercourse with women.

HOLY GHOST:

Hebrew Israelites teach that the Holy Ghost which overshadowed Mary is referring to **The Law**.

> "And the angel answered and said unto her,
> - **The Holy Ghost shall come upon thee,**
> - **and the power of the Highest shall overshadow thee**:
>
> therefore also **that holy thing** which shall be born of thee shall be called the Son of God." **Luke 1:35 (KJV)**

They somehow merge as a precept for explanation Luke 1:35 with Acts 7:51-53.

> "*Ye stiffnecked and uncircumcised in heart and ears, ye **do always resist the Holy Ghost**: as your fathers did, so do ye. 52 Which of the prophets have not your fathers persecuted? and they have slain them which shewed before of the coming of the Just One; of whom ye have been now the betrayers and murderers: 53 **Who have received the law by the disposition of angels, and have not kept it**.*" **Acts 7:51-53 (KJV)**

    a) Meaning the word is going to be fulfilled in Mary. They say the "**Holy Ghost**" was "**the spirit of the Law**" **that came upon Mary, which the fathers had resisted and not kept**.
    b) Meaning that **Mary would fulfill the law**.
    c) The power of the Highest that would overshadow Mary **was the instructions according to the law to direct Mary on what to do**.

JOSEPH:

Hebrew Israelites teach that Joseph also lived in the city of Juda as did **Zacharias and Elisabeth**. They say Mary left Galilee to go to the City of Juda to be with Joseph.

"Then Mary said, "Behold the maidservant of the Lord! Let it be to me according to your word." And the angel departed from her. 39 Now Mary arose in those days and went into the hill country with haste, to a city of Judah," **Luke 1:38-39 (NKJV)**

They teach that Mary stayed about three months in the same area where Joseph lived and that you must be able to connect the dots.

*"And Mary abode with her **about three months**, and returned to her own house. 57 Now Elisabeth's full time came that she should be delivered, and she brought forth a son."* **Luke 1: 56-57 (KJV)**

PROBLEM WITH HEBREW ISRAELISM BIRTH ASSUMPTION

Mary Said: "Then Mary said to the angel, "How can this be, **since I do not know a man?"** Luke 1:34 (NKJV)

Before They Came Together we are informed: "*Now the birth of Jesus Christ was as follows: After His mother Mary was betrothed to Joseph, **before they came together, she was found with child of the Holy Spirit.**" Matthew 1:18 (NKJV)*

BHI teach their adherents that this verse confuses Christians, and Christians will say that Mary and Joseph had not had sex. They teach their adherents to always ask Christians what were the Jewish customs and laws regarding marriage? The following is a list **BHI** use to prove the customs of marriage with an attempt to use them on the passage: Luke 14:8, John 2:1-3, Judges 15:1, and

The Virgin Birth

> Tobit 6:12-13, Tobit 7:13-18, Tobit 8: 1-4,19-20; 2 Esdras 10, Deuteronomy 22:13-19. [104]

They teach the verse (Matthew 1:18) proves that Joseph and Mary had sex before marriage; What the Christians call fornication. But what Joseph and Mary did is not fornication according to the Bible. It destroys that argument.

Many of their camps teach that if you don't know about marriage custom and law, you already have the white man's Jesus on the brain, you're done. It is an example of why you must have **precept upon precept**. **BHI** teaches verse 18, "before they came together" means:

- Mary and Joseph had already had sex.
- Before the wedding feast, before the wedding chamber, and before the tokens of virginity had been taken, Mary was already pregnant.

BHI teach that Mary was found pregnant according to the law: Notice that they changed the verse from "she was found with child of the Holy Ghost." [Matt 1:18][105]

> **Joseph Thoughts:** *"Then Joseph her husband, being **a just man**, and not wanting to make her a public example, was minded **to put her away secretly**.* **Matthew 1:19 (NKJV)**

They argue, because they had already had sex, and Mary was pregnant; this would have **caused great embarrassment**. You did not get pregnant and was not (legally) married.[Husband and wife joined together]
According to **BHI,** verse 19 says "**husband;**" And It is letting you know that Joseph is the daddy of Jesus. But the reason Joseph is thinking along these lines (v.19) is that he is now ashamed *because he had already jumped the gun and had sex with Mary before the wedding ceremony*. How would he explain this to her parents? Joseph was thinking, what can I do to get out of this mess I caused.

---

[104] https://www.youtube.com/watch?time_continue=197&v=uZcalkPe8vw **(May 8, 2019)**
[105] https://www.youtube.com/watch?v=qz4qhUFdZl8 **(May 8, 2019)**

The Virgin Birth

In their doctrine, they changed the verse to mean "for that which is conceived in her is according **to prophecy and is of the law."** They imply this is what the angel is really saying to Joseph. **BHI** labors the point that the angel did not say "**fear not to take unto thee Mary thy virgin**" because the angel knew that they had already had intercourse (**Matthew 1:20**).

If as the **so-called Hebrew Israelites** claim with no evidence, that Joseph had already had sexual intercourse with Mary before the wedding ceremony:
1. Why would he be surprised to find her pregnant with his child?
2. And why would "**a just man**" as the Bible called him be thinking about putting his wife away, being that he was responsible for the pregnancy?

The Angel informs him: *"But while he thought about these things, behold, an angel of the Lord appeared to him in a dream, saying, "Joseph, son of David, **do not be afraid to take to you Mary your wife, for that which is conceived in her is of the Holy Spirit.**"* **Matthew 1:20 (NKJV)**

The Bible clearly informs us that Joseph and Mary did not Consummate their marriage until after Jesus was born:

*"Then Joseph, being aroused from sleep, did as the angel of the Lord commanded him and took to him his wife, 25 **and did not know her till she had brought forth her firstborn Son**. And he called His name Jesus."* **Matthew 1:24-25 (NKJV)**

Notice the text does not say **"their"** firstborn, **but it says "her"** firstborn (verse 25).
BHI teach that when it says that Joseph did not sleep (have sex) with Mary until after Christ was Born (Matthew 1:25), It simply means that he had to wait (7+33) 40 days according to the law (Leviticus 12).

Page 75

The Virgin Birth

Hebrew Israelites teach that the parenthesis was added later (Luke 3:23); and in the original text, there was no (**as was supposed**) in the verse of Scripture.

> *"And Jesus himself began to be about thirty years of age, being **(as was supposed)** the son of Joseph, which was the son of Heli,"* **Luke 3:23 (KJV)**

BHI teach their followers there is no parenthesis in the following verses, and people knew Jesus daddy, pointing out that It didn't say, stepson.

> *"And all bare him witness, and wondered at the gracious words which proceeded out of his mouth. And they said, Is not this **Joseph's son**?"* **Luke 4:22 (KJV)**

> *"And they said, **Is not this Jesus, the son of Joseph**, whose father and mother **we know**? how is it then that he saith, I came down from heaven?"* **John 6: 42 (KJV)**

> *"Philip findeth Nathanael, and saith unto him, We have found him, of whom Moses in the law, and the prophets, did write, Jesus of Nazareth, **the son of Joseph**."* **John 1:45 (KJV)**

> *"**Is not this the carpenter's son**? is not his mother called Mary? and his brethren, James, and Joses, and Simon, and Judas? 56 And his sisters, are they not all with us? Whence then hath this man all these things?"* **Matthew 13:55-56 (KJV)**

The **Hebrew Israelites** teach that **Luke 2:48** proves that Mary knew who the father of Jesus was, and infers this is my **husband's son.** [106]

> *"And when they saw him, they were amazed: and his mother said unto him, Son, why hast thou thus dealt with us? **behold, thy father** and I have sought thee sorrowing."* Luke 2:48 (KJV)

Rebuttal: This does not imply biological father. Why didn't **BHI** go to the 49th verse? Notice what Jesus replied:

The Virgin Birth

> *"And He said to them, "Why did you seek Me? **Did you not know that I must be about My Father's business**?" 50 But they did not understand the statement which He spoke to them."* **Luke 2:49-50 (NKJV)**

Hebrew Israelites teach that one word for the spirit of anti-Christ is **Christianity**.

> *"And every spirit that confesseth not that **Jesus Christ is come in the flesh** is not of God: and this is that spirit of antichrist, whereof ye have heard that it should come; and even now already is it in the world."* **1 John 4:3 (KJV)**

They teach that you must confess that:
1. Christ came of the seed of man (Leviticus 15:16),
2. and Joseph is his earthly father and Mary, his mother, then you are not of God.

THE LINEAGE OF CHRIST

Luke traced **David's line through Nathan**, whereas Matthew traced it through **Solomon**. Following Shealtiel's son, Zerubbabel, the lists once again differ until both lists unite at Joseph whom, Luke noted, was "thought" to be the father of Jesus. Little doubt exists that Matthew's genealogy traced the kingly line of David—**the royal legal line**.[107]

The two branches of descent from David, by **Solomon and Nathan**, being thus united in the persons of **Mary and Joseph**, Jesus the son of Mary reunited in himself all the blood, privileges, and rights, of the whole family of David, in consequence of which he is emphatically called "the Son of David."

Luke related Jesus not only to Abraham but all the way back to Adam and to God. This is an indication of the universal offer of salvation, which is common to his Gospel—that Jesus came to save all people—Gentiles as well as the nation of Israel (cf. Luke 2:32).[108]

---

[107] Martin, J. A. (1985). Luke. In J. F. Walvoord & R. B. Zuck (Eds.), *The Bible Knowledge Commentary: An Exposition of the Scriptures* (Vol. 2, p. 212). Wheaton, IL: Victor Books.
[108] Martin, J. A. (1985). Luke. In J. F. Walvoord & R. B. Zuck (Eds.), *The Bible Knowledge Commentary: An Exposition of the Scriptures* (Vol. 2, p. 213). Wheaton, IL: Victor Books.

The Virgin Birth

Scholars widely believe that this is the Lord's genealogy through Mary for the following reasons:

1. The most obvious is that **Joseph's family line is traced in Matthew's Gospel (1:2–16).**
2. In the early chapters of Luke's Gospel, **Mary is more prominent than Joseph**, whereas it is the reverse in Matthew.
3. Women's names **were not commonly used** among the Jews as genealogical links. This would account for the omission of Mary's name.
4. In Matthew 1:16, it distinctly states that **Jacob begot Joseph**. Here in Luke, it does not say that Heli begot Joseph; it says **Joseph was the son of Heli**. *Son* may mean *son-in-law*.
5. In the original language, the definite article (*tou*) in the genitive form (*of the*) appears before every name in the genealogy *except one*. **That one name is Joseph**. This singular exception strongly suggests that Joseph was included **only because of his marriage to Mary**.[109]

Examine the genealogy in detail; we note several important points:

1. This list shows that Mary was of the linage of **David** through his son **Nathan** (v. 31). In Matthew's Gospel, **Jesus inherited the *legal* right to the throne of David through Solomon**.

    As legal Son of Joseph, *the Lord fulfilled that part of God's covenant with David, which promised him that his throne would continue forever*. But Jesus could not have been the real son of Joseph **without coming under God's curse on Jechoniah**, which decreed that no descendant of that wicked king would prosper (Jer. 22:30).

    As the real Son of Mary, *Jesus fulfilled that part of the covenant of God with David, which promised him that his seed would sit upon his throne forever*; and by

---

[109] MacDonald, W. (1995). *Believer's Bible Commentary: Old and New Testaments*. (A. Farstad, Ed.) (p. 1379). Nashville: Thomas Nelson.

lineage from David through Nathan, **He did not come under the curse which was pronounced on Jechoniah.**

2. **Adam** is described as **the son of God** (v. 38). This means simply that he was created by God.

3. It seems obvious that the Messianic line ended with the Lord Jesus. *No one else* **can ever present a valid legal claim to the throne of David.**[110]

THE SEED

Hebrew Israelites teach that genealogy relates and implies sperm. They'll read through all the "**begats**" in Matthew 1:1 through verse 16. However, when they get to Joseph, they ignore the change from "**begat**" to "**born**" as it relates to Jesus.

1. They ask if Christ only came by Mary, why would the verse mention Joseph?
2. They ask if Christ just popped-up in Mary what is the significance of Joseph being in the verse?

BHI teach their adherents that Christians are willfully ignorant and want to be stupid. **BHI** goes through great pain to prove that Joseph was Jesus biological father and was of black lineage of whom they, today, are descendants.

> "And **Jacob begot Joseph** the husband of Mary, **of whom was born** Jesus who is called Christ.
> 17 So all the generations from Abraham to David are fourteen generations, from David until the captivity in Babylon are fourteen generations, and from the captivity in Babylon until the Christ are fourteen generations."
> **Matthew 1:16-17 (NKJV)**

They teach that the reason that Matthew mentions verse 17 is because the Jews were in Captivity: Medes-Persian, Greeks, and now Rome. And in verse 21, Jesus is going

---

[110] MacDonald, W. (1995). *Believer's Bible Commentary: Old and New Testaments*. (A. Farstad, Ed.) (p. 1379). Nashville: Thomas Nelson.

The Virgin Birth

to save His people from captivity, **and that excludes all other races.**

> *"And she will bring forth a Son, and you shall call His name Jesus, for **He will save His people from their sins**.*" **Matthew 1:21 (NKJV)**

Matthew's genealogy (generation of Jesus Christ):

The son of David:
- Matthew proves the Saviour to be the son of David on account of the promise that he should, as David's son, sit on David's throne (Luke 1:32, Isaiah 9:6-7) in fulfillment of the Davidic Covenant.

The son of Abraham:
- Matthew proves the Saviour to be the son of Abraham as "**the seed of Abraham in whom all nations of the earth should be blessed**" (Genesis 17:5, Galatians 3:16, Romans 4:16) in fulfillment of the Abrahamic Covenant.

Luke in his genealogy:
- establishes our Saviour to be the son of Man (Luke 3:23; Luke 3:38)
- to prove him "**the Seed of the Woman**" (Genesis 3:15),
- the "Second Adam" (1Corintians 15:47),
- the Redeemer of man, and the restorer of his lost inheritance (Psalms 8; Hebrew 2:5-8)

The so-called **Hebrew Israelites** teach their followers to use these Scriptures to demonstrate that when it says "**seed**" it is talking about "**sperm**" and that copulation is sexual intercourse.[111]

> *"Speak unto the children of Israel, saying, If a woman have conceived **seed**, and born a man child: then she shall be unclean seven days; according to the days of the separation for her infirmity shall she be unclean. 3 And in*

---
[111] https://www.youtube.com/watch?v=wNUJZezA8Ck **May 8, 2019**

> the eighth day the flesh of his foreskin shall be circumcised." **Leviticus 12:2-3 (KJV)**

> "And if any man's **seed** of copulation go out from him, then he shall wash all his flesh in water, and be unclean until the even." **Leviticus 15:16 (KJV)**

> "Concerning his Son Jesus Christ our Lord, which was made of the **seed** of David according to the flesh;" **Romans 1:3 (KJV)**

BHI teach their adherents to understand Galatians 4:4, you must first look at what the law said about childbirth." made under the law." The "fulness of time" is ten months. They labor to point out that nowhere in the Law do you find **immaculate conception**.

> "But when the fulness of the time was come, God sent forth his Son, made of a woman, made under the law," **Galatians 4:4 (KJV)**

- **BHI** reference Wisdom of Solomon 1: 1-7 that explains the "fulness of time."
- They reference Leviticus 15:16 to explain the seed.
- **BHI** reference Leviticus 12: 2-3 to show for a woman to conceive seed, a man must (ejaculate) release sperm in the woman.
- They know that if she is pregnant the law says depending on the child boy or girl, she can't have intercourse for X-Days. Leviticus 12: 2-8

They teach their followers that **EVERY TIME** you see "**seed**" in Scripture, You want to hit **Leviticus 15:16** to explain **sperm (seed of copulation)**. They are told to keep **Leviticus 15:16** in their hip-pocket for those "**seed**" Scriptures to shut Christians down. [112]

> "Hath not the scripture said, That Christ cometh of the seed of David, and out of the town of Bethlehem, where David was?" **John 7: 42 (KJV)**

---

[112] https://www.youtube.com/watch?v=XUjJ-pd03pQ (May 8, 2019)

"*Of this man's seed hath God according to his promise raised unto Israel a Saviour, Jesus:*" **Acts 13:23 (KJV)**

"*Remember that Jesus Christ of the seed of David was raised from the dead according to my gospel:*" **2 Timothy 2:8 (KJV)**

"*Therefore being a prophet, and knowing that God had sworn with an oath to him, that of the fruit of his loins, according to the flesh, he would raise up Christ to sit on his throne;*" **Acts 2:30 (KJV)**

THE COMFORTER (HOLY SPIRIT) IS A BLACK MAN

ICGJC BHI camp YouTube video titled "Tazadaqyah- The Comforter- The Truth about." [113]

The Holy Apostle and Chief High Priest Tazadaqyah say he is "The God Sent Comforter of the Nation of Israel." [114]

> "But **the Comforter, even the Holy Spirit**, **whom the Father will send in my name**, he shall teach you all things, and bring to your remembrance all that I said unto you." **John 14:26 (ASV)**

He says now that is not going to go well without some explaining, because you have people that are going to be upset saying how can you *being a man*, especially a black man be **the Comforter**. As the reader reads the verse, Apostle & Chief High Priest Tazadaqyah (Jermaine Grant) **RE-DEFINING** the text of John 14:26:

John 14:26 But the Comforter, which is the Holy - **STOP!!!!**

Tazadaqyah expounds,
- A BLACK MAN Can Never Be **HOLY**
- A BLACK MAN Can Never Be **SPIRITUAL**
- "HOLY" ~ "SPIRITUAL."
    - ➢ HOLY SPIRIT
    - ➢ **A Man Is The HOLY SPIRIT**!!!!!!

---
[113] https://www.youtube.com/watch?v=XwvVmi-JBzI (May 22, 2019)
[114] https://www.youtube.com/watch?v=QE2XRo38Mgc (May 22, 2019)

The Comforter (Holy Spirit) Is A Black Man

Tazadaqyah proclaims,

- **I AM THE HOLY SPIRIT,**
- **I AM THE COMFORTER**

THAT GOD HAS SENT.

He says, The Holy Spirit was manifested In the flesh the same as Jesus, and the Holy Ghost is a man.

Rebuttal: Tazadaqyah has a big problem here:

> "And I will pray the Father, and he shall give you another Comforter, **that he may be with you foreve**r, 17 even the Spirit of truth: whom the world cannot receive; for it beholdeth him not, neither knoweth him: ye know him; for he abideth with you, **and shall be in you**." **John 14:16-17 (ASV)**

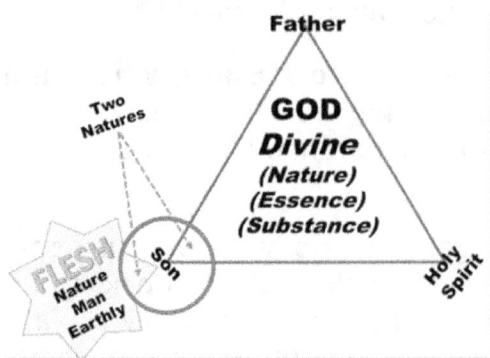

Tazadaqyah does not abide forever (**Hebrew 9:27**), and as a man, he can not be in the people. He is not the Spirit of truth or a man of truth (**Romans 3:4**).

He also has another problem: Tazadaqyah of the ICGJC arrested for embezzling $5.3 Million Live Coverage Of The FBI:CIA Raid On The Comforter's Hebrew Israelites Headquarters [115] [116]

THE COMFORTER ~ COUNSELOR (14:15–31)

John's Gospel pays much attention to **the Holy Spirit**. This is the first of several passages that teach about the nature and role of the **Holy Spirit** in the life of the church and the individual believer (15:26; 16:7–15).

---
[115] https://www.youtube.com/watch?v=E6w62vYSAtY (May 22, 2019)
[116] https://www.youtube.com/watch?v=g7gcC1vAfXA (May 22, 2019)

Here the **Holy Spirit** is referred to as the "Counselor" who will be with the disciples forever (14:16). Note that **Jesus called the Holy Spirit "another" Counselor**, suggesting **that the work of the Holy Spirit would take the place of His role in their lives**. The word "Counselor" is a legal term that goes beyond legal assistance to that of any aide given in time of need (1 John 2:1).

The Greek word is **Paraclete**, which suggests adviser, encourager, exhorter, comforter, and intercessor. The idea is that the Spirit will always stand alongside the people of God. The Holy Spirit is also referred to as the "Spirit of truth" (14:17). [117]

---

[117] White, J. E. (1998). John. In D. S. Dockery (Ed.), Holman concise Bible commentary (pp. 483–484). Nashville, TN: Broadman & Holman Publishers

PROBLEM FOUR

THE IMMACULATE CONCEPTION IS NOT THE VIRGIN BIRTH

Biblical Christians do not hold the view or teach the Immaculate Conception. There is no evidence that the Jews hold to the virgin birth nor the Immaculate Conception.

The Immaculate Conception is commonly confused with the Virgin Birth of Jesus.
- Jesus's birth is covered by the Doctrine of Incarnation,
- while the Immaculate Conception deals with the conception of Mary, not that of her son.

The Immaculate Conception, according to the teaching of the Roman Catholic Church (apostate), **is the conception of the Blessed Virgin Mary free from original sin by virtue of the merits of her son Jesus Christ**.

The Catholic Church teaches that **God acted upon Mary in the first moment of her conception, keeping her "immaculate."**

Although the belief that **Mary was sinless**, or **conceived without original sin**, has been widely held since Late Antiquity, the doctrine was not dogmatically defined until 1854, by Pope Pius IX in his papal bull Ineffabilis Deus.[2]

The Catholic Church celebrates the Feast of the Immaculate Conception on December 8; in many Catholic countries, it is a holy day of obligation or patronal feast, and in some a national public holiday. [118] [119] [120] [121]

- **BHI** teach that the immaculate conception is a Jewish fable, it is a lie,
    - and it is a commandment of men because the white man taught the thing,
    - Christianity taught that thing.

---

[118] https://en.wikipedia.org/wiki/Immaculate_Conception (May 8, 2019)
[119] http://www.vatican.va/archive/ccc_css/archive/catechism/p122a3p2.htm (May 8, 2019) Catechism of the Catholic Church, 490-493
[120] http://www.bbc.co.uk/religion/religions/christianity/beliefs/immaculateconception.shtml (May 8, 2019)
[121] https://en.wikipedia.org/wiki/Ineffabilis_Deus (May 8, 2019)

- o And it turns you from the truth; It turns you from the law.

> "*Not giving heed to Jewish fables, and commandments of men, that turn from the truth*. 15 Unto the pure all things are pure: but unto them that are defiled and unbelieving is nothing pure; but even their mind and conscience is defiled." **Titus 1:14-15 (KJV)**

- They teach using Hebrew 2:16 to show that **Jesus was not born of an angel, meaning he was not immaculately born.** [122] [123] [124] [125] [126]

> "*For verily he took not on him the nature of angels; but he took on him the seed of Abraham.*" **Hebrews 2:16 (KJV)**

- They focus on the seed (**sperm**) of Abraham.
- **BHI** use Deuteronomy 18:18 to show **like unto his brethren** and **showing that Moses was not immaculately born**, but he had a biological mother and father.

> "*I will raise them up a Prophet from among their brethren, like unto thee*, and will put my words in his mouth; and he shall speak unto them all that I shall command him." **Deuteronomy 18: 18**

- **BHI** teach their followers to drive this point home to show that Jesus was also not immaculately born, and he had a biological mother and father.

Their premise does not make sense. The virgin birth is not the Immaculate Conception. Angels are not born; they were created Spiritual beings. **Hebrews 1: 5-6**. And Jesus has two natures, fully God and fully man.

The so-called **Hebrew Israelites** teach that this is Solomon talking about himself and that this chapter in the **Wisdom of**

---

[122] https://www.youtube.com/watch?v=ddfd_d_viog (May 8, 2019)
[123] https://www.youtube.com/watch?v=ImC3dr5ynFk (May 8, 2019)
[124] https://www.youtube.com/watch?v=XUjJ-pd03pQ (May 8, 2019)
[125] https://www.youtube.com/watch?v=wNUJZezA8Ck (May 8, 2019)
[126] https://www.youtube.com/watch?v=6WjU04fMOEI (May 8, 2019)

Solomon 1: 1-7,17-19 can be used to smash the immaculate conception garbage: **BHI** compares these verses with Jesus Christ **to show that his birth was not immaculate**:

- I was nursed in swaddling clothes
- For there is no king that had any other beginning of birth

Rebuttal: The Wisdom of Solomon or Book of Wisdom is not Scripture (God Breathed). It is a Jewish work composed in Alexandria (Egypt) around the **1st century CE**, with the aim of bolstering the faith of the Jewish community in a hostile Greek world. [127]

The early church rejected the authorship of Solomon; an ancient manuscript known as the Muratorian fragment refers to the Wisdom of Solomon as having been written by "the friends of Solomon in his honor." It is widely accepted today, even by the Catholic Church, that Solomon did not write the book, which dates back to the 1st or 2nd century BC, many centuries after the death of Solomon. [128]

RELIGION IS BIBLICAL

BHI claim that being a **Hebrew Israelite** is not a religion, but according to blood. And it is not like Christianity and Judaism which are both religions.

- Many **BHI** groups **do not say they are Jews**, but that **they are the tribe of Judah.**
- So-called **Hebrew Israelites don't consider themselves to be Jews** in the modern sense of the term as associated with Orthodox, Reformed, Conservative, or Hasidic Judaism.
- However, oxymoronically, they will say they are not Jews in one breath and then argue themselves as the Jews of the curses in another breath.

Hebrew Israelites have hit the nail on the head. They are not a Biblical religion or Biblically religious based on James

---

[127] https://en.wikipedia.org/wiki/Book_of_Wisdom (May 8, 2019)
[128] https://www.gotquestions.org/Wisdom-of-Solomon.html (May 8, 2019)

Religion Is Biblical

writings to the church. They are false, un-pure, defiled, and ungodly as it relates to both words; religion and religious.

It is not Hebrew Israelism, Buddhism, Hinduism, Mormonism, Islamism, Roman Catholicism, etc. that James has in mind, but they who would be followers of the Biblical Christ; The Body of Christ.

RELIGION: The word **thrēskeia** translated in the NT, occurs three times, and means outward religious service (see Acts 26: 5; James 1: 26-27). [129]

The word '**religion**' came into Eng. from the Vulg., where *religio* is in a 13th-century paraphrase of Jas. 1:26f.
In Acts 26:5, it denotes Judaism (cf. Gal. 1:13f.).
Here and in the Apocrypha, **thrēskeia** refers to **the outward expression of belief**, not the content, as when we contrast the Christian religion with other false doctrines.

RSV uses the word, however, in something approaching this sense in **1 Timothy 3:16**, to translate Gk. **eusebeia** (AV '**godliness**'), and in **2 Timothy 3:5**, where again our instinct would be to use the word 'Christianity' which Hebrew Israelites oppose.

Because of the association of **thrēskeia** with **Judaism**, James' use is probably ironical. The things which he calls the elements of '**thrēskeia** that is **pure** and **undefiled**' would not in the view of his opponents, who restricted it to ritual, have counted as **thrēskeia** at all.

Regardless of how others with hesitance use the word '**religion**', today, whether in reference to the content of the Christian faith or in reference to its expression in worship and service, **Christianity is not simply one conviction among many religions: but differs from all others in that**
- its content is divinely revealed,
- and its outward expression by believers is not an attempt to secure salvation but a thank-offering for it. [130]

---

[129] Unger, Merrill F.. The New Unger's Bible Dictionary (p. 1072). Moody Publishers. Kindle Edition.
[130] Job, J. B. (1996). Religion. In D. R. W. Wood, I. H. Marshall, A. R. Millard, J. I. Packer, & D. J. Wiseman (Eds.), New Bible dictionary (3rd ed., p. 1007). Leicester, England; Downers Grove, IL: InterVarsity Press.

BHI says they don't believe in a religion and that they are a nation of people. **(IUIC)** [131] They say the Bible is about heritage, not religion. **(GMS)**[132] Some will say that their religion is God's Law. What the Hebrew Israelites fail to biblically understand is that religion is not who you, but what you do biblically, And it is done religiously. Wholeheartedly and not having a form of godliness or pure religion:

> "*If any man among you* **seem to be religious**, *and bridleth not his tongue, but deceiveth his own heart,* **this man's religion is vain**." **James 1:26 (KJV)**

But notice what the practice was that is not pure religion and of God, but only a form of godliness and pureness:

> "*For ye have heard of my conversation in time past in* **the Jews' religion**, *how that beyond measure*
> - **I persecuted the church of God,**
> - **and wasted it**: *14 And profited in the Jews' religion above many my equals in mine* **own nation**,
> - *being more* **exceedingly zealous** *of the traditions of my fathers.*" **Galatians 1:13-14 (KJV)**

> "*They shall put you out of the synagogues: yea*, **the time cometh, that whosoever killeth you will think that he doeth God service.**" **John 16:2 (KJV)**

They that perform the service of God, biblically, can be defined by it religiously.

The truly religious (a) cares for the things of God, (b) loves what God loves, and (c) receives Him that God sent.

> "*Now when the congregation was broken up*, **many** *of the* Jews *and* **religious** *proselytes* **followed** *Paul and Barnabas: who, speaking to them,* **persuaded them to continue in the grace of God**." Acts 13:43 (KJV)

Christians are to keep our selves "from being polluted by the world"—part of what constitutes "pure and faultless" religion:

---

[131] https://www.youtube.com/watch?v=dKscgPH69RU (May 17, 2019)
[132] https://www.youtube.com/watch?v=YmaE-0G7lZ4 (May 17, 2019)

> "*Pure religion* and *undefiled* before God and the Father is this, **To visit the fatherless and widows in their affliction, and to keep himself unspotted from the world.**" **James 1:27**; (*Matthew 25:35-40*)

HEBREW ISRAELITES CREATE THEIR OWN HEBREW LANGUAGE

The language **Lashawan Qadash** reportedly was created by **Ahrayah** [133] [134], who was a high priest in the old Israeli Church of Universe Practical Knowledge (1-West). He was one of the original leaders from which all these splinter groups sprang. His proof text for creating this so-called language is

> "For at that time **I will change the speech of the peoples to a pure speech**, that all of them may call upon the name of the Lord and serve him with one accord. 10 From beyond the rivers of Cush my worshipers, the daughter of my dispersed ones, shall bring my offering. **Zephaniah 3:9-10 (ESV)**

> "For then will I turn to the people a pure language, that they may all call upon the name of the Lord, to serve him with one consent. 10 From beyond the rivers of Ethiopia, my suppliants, even the daughter of my dispersed, shall bring mine offering." **Zephaniah 3:9-10 (KJV)**

Others say the language was created by Abba Bivens.

"**The Moreh**, a former member, was asked:

(1) LASHAWAN QADASH. Did it originate strictly with Ahrayah? as most seem to think, or did it go back to Abba Bivens as one person claimed to me a while back?
Answer: It started with Ahrayah, and he even promoted a cursive form of Lashawan Qadash called "Ahrayah Script" (now you are making me crack my stash, or is it a stash of crack you decide)
This is page 1 of lesson 5 of the ICUPK Curriculum (circa 1992-93)

---

[133] https://www.youtube.com/watch?v=scPusOdvCMs (May 27, 2019)
[134] https://www.youtube.com/watch?v=KkUpFQyMc-s (May 27, 2019)

Hebrew Israelites Create Their Own Hebrew Language

At the top, it states the name of the "Language" is Lasawan Qadash, not the glyphs themselves.

At the bottom of the page, it says that the name of the writing is 'AH-RA-YA-MA-SHA'

Now I always took this to mean that the cursive style of writing at the immediate right side was what they were referring to until I found out that the cursive form was called 'Ahrayah' Script.

As you can see a system of "connectors," and "separators" (that do not appear on any ancient cuniform artifacts) was also invented by Ahrayah None of this came from Bivens, but the actual ancient glyphs which were common to the hand scribed Jewish Torah's of Biven's day

You can see the Kabbalistic influence of Jewish Mysticism on the numerical equivalents which is a form of Gematria

I have no problem providing clarity to matters of academia; I just despise gossip

Moreh: Qanaa Ben Yehudah
Har* Tziyon, 1088 Nostrand Avenue Brooklyn, NY 11225
Shariat, Ahriyah Ben Gad: Spiritual Leader Azriel Ben Levi: Kohen" https://www.youtube.com/watch?v=I3UelqGnRTY

Lashawan Qadash (HOLY TONGUE) : The ISUPK **BHI** camp has online classes for this Pig Latin (I mean supposed Hebrew) holy language.

GMS BHI camp also teaches this **1-West** invented so-called Hebrew language. [135]

"Over the past few years there has been a growing number of people who are re-creating the Hebrew alphabet and claiming that the Hebrew pronunciations used today are not Hebrew, but Assyrian and each Ancient Hebrew letter was a syllable; a, ba, ga, da, ha, etc.
They call this "alphabet" the "Lashawan Qadash," their pronunciation of the Hebrew phrase Lashon qodesh meaning

---

[135] https://www.youtube.com/watch?v=31BxJslk6TU (May 27, 2019)

"holy tongue," or "holy language. To illustrate their pronunciation of the Lashawa Qadash, let's look at Genesis 1:1.

According to the Masoretic Hebrew text this verse is pronounced; B'reshiyt bara elohiym et hashamayim v'et ha'arets.

But according to this group, the original pronunciation was; Barashayat bara alahayam at hashamayam wat harat.

There are several problems with this "re-creation" of the alphabet. If you attempted to speak Hebrew to someone who knows Hebrew, you would be completely unintelligible and probably mocked for your pronunciation. Those who are making this claim have no evidence to support the claim. The evidence from ancient texts suggests that the pronunciation of the Masoretic text is correct, or at least more correct than this new theory of pronunciation.

Let's take the name Israel as an example. In Hebrew, this word is pronounced Yis'ra'eyl, but they believe that this was originally pronounced yasharala.

While there is no evidence to support this new style of pronunciation, there is evidence to refute it.

Here is the name Israel from the Masoretic Hebrew Bible, which dates to about 1,000 AD.

יִשְׂרָאֵל

The first letter is a yud with a "y" sound. This is the vowel pointing for the letter "I." This is the letter sin, identified by the dot on the left of the letter, and pronounced with an "s," as opposed to the letter shin, with a "sh" sound, when the dot is on the right. This is the vowel sh'va, which is silent. Here is the letter resh with an "r" sound. Here is the vowel qamats representing the "a" vowel. This is the letter aleph, which is silent. This is the vowel tsere representing the vowel pronunciation "ey." And lastly, the letter lamed with an "l" sound.

However, these vowel pointings were created by the Masorites a thousand years ago, and prior to this; this is how this word would appear. Those who teach the Lashawan Qadash are making the claim that this would be pronounced Yasharala.

So how do we know if this was originally pronounced yisra'eyl or yasharala? I can't tell you how it was pronounced 3,000 years ago, but I can tell you how it was pronounced 2,000 years ago.

2,000 years ago, the Jews translated the Hebrew Bible into Greek. This Greek translation of the Bible is called the **Septuagint**. But when it came to names the translators transliterated the names into Greek, which help us to learn how Hebrew was pronounced 2,000 years ago. In the Greek Septuagint, the name Israel was written like this and is pronounced Isra'eyl. It is not Yasharala
Ισραηλ

Nowhere, in any ancient document, do we find evidence supporting the Lashawan qadash, but we find ample proof supporting the pronunciations found in the 1,000-year-old Masoretic Hebrew Bible." Article by **Jeff A. Benner**[136]

"An introduction and small refutation of the faulty claims made for the fraudulent Hebrew dialect promoted by various 1 Wester (ISUPK, GMS, GOCC, Sicarii, etc) and non-1 Wester Hebrew Israelite groups (Torah Knights, etc.) alike." Refutal Article by **Faithful to God**[137] [138] [139]

"Vocab Malone asks fellow SHIELD SQUAD CREW affiliate Abu Khamr the hard questions about the invented language of the 1West "Hebrew Israelites" and those groups who use Lashawan Qadash, such as GMS and the Torah Knights. This video is a response to the claims 1Westers make about LQ and biblical Hebrew." Refutal Article by Vocab Malone[140]

---

[136] https://www.youtube.com/watch?v=Tijr-vCQmE4 (May 27, 2019)
[137] https://www.youtube.com/watch?v=-x8sSFh54B0 (May 27, 2019)
[138] https://www.youtube.com/watch?v=l3UelqGnRTY (May 27, 2019)
[139] https://www.youtube.com/watch?v=nZjXLqL_zHs (May 27, 2019)
[140] https://www.youtube.com/watch?v=mXZJqYfyO5M (May 27, 2019)

The reality is that Ahrayah is the one who created Lashawan Qadash, and there are many who remember when he foisted this innovation onto the school at 1 West 125th street in Harlem. This is why some former members of the ICUPK now reject Lashawan Qadash. [141] [142]

THE FALSE SO-CALLED HEBREW ISRAELITE PROPHET AHRAYAH

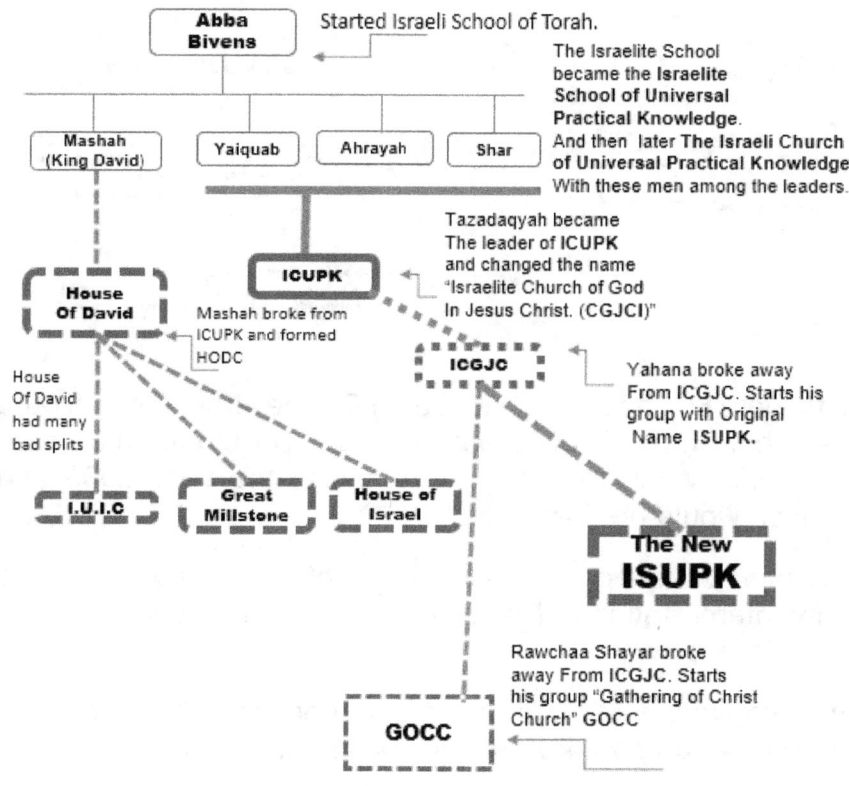

---

[141] https://www.youtube.com/watch?v=JpzVFWQfnUk (May 27, 2019)
[142] https://www.youtube.com/watch?v=LNjRSe--Y38 (May 27,2019)

The False So-Called Hebrew Israelite Prophet Ahrayah

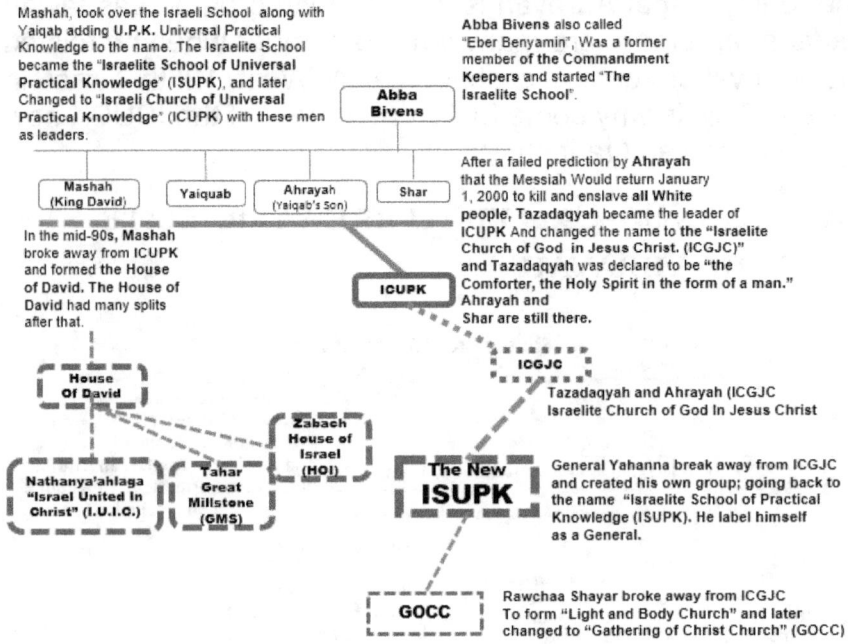

"In the late 80s and throughout the 90s, the Israeli School (and later Church) of UPK and others who split from them claimed that Christ would return by (or before) the year 2000 and America would be destroyed.

This was based on so-called chief high priest **Ahrayah**'s faulty Interpretation of **Hosea 6:2**, which was regurgitated by all parties involved.

This despite Christ's warning about predicting the date of his return in **Matthew 24:36** and **Mark 13:32**.

Along with the warning passages against false prophesies in **Deuteronomy 18:20-22**, which not only exposes the doctrine itself, but also the lack of discernment of those involved for not questioning such an obviously false teaching."

Ahrayah, the false prophet, is the same person that gave the camps the so-called holy language **Lashawan Qadash**. Many splits from the ISUPK after the false prophecy of **DOOM's Day 2000 for America**, came and went. But the former adherents carried the baggage (*the core of ISUPK doctrine*) along with them. **ISUPK** was still the foundation of the newly created camps. Even Ahrayah had a new group **ICGJC** formed by his trained blasphemous student, Tazachayah, who claims that he is **the God Sent Comforter ~ The Holy Spirit**.

In a **HODC** YouTube video titled, "'THE HOT SEAT' Truth about Mashah and The House of David."[143] In the video, you have Barak, Banyamyan, Mayakaalahba, and Ash addressing frictions with other Hebrew Israelite camps. My concern is not with the frictions, but the opportunity to understand and report an inside view (from people who were there in the beginning) on what was actually believed and taught within the camps.

The originate **1-West** was very much into the belief of reincarnation.[144] [145] Mashah was one of the seven heads of UPK school. Ahrayah had dubbed him the reincarnated **King David**. According to a former member Chadash, Mashah also had several reincarnations: he was Moses, the Apostle Peter, and the Apostle John. Ahrayah, himself, was John the Revelator.

The original **1-West** faction within the **Hebrew Israelite** movement taught that **Mashah was King David reincarnated**. This was based on their false doctrine of reincarnation. It was said that Abba Bivens was Elijah. Barak from the House of David (**HODC**), said brothers were going to camps teaching that Bivens was Elijah. Barak said they were taught to go to the streets and tell people that **the twelve apostles** were at our school. Barak says you had some of everybody that was in the Scriptures at 125th Street. Matthew and everybody was there. This was one of many false beliefs promoted by the school which is still believed by certain former members to this day, including those in GMS.

---

[143] https://www.youtube.com/watch?v=zuy90FWU3bQ (May 27, 2019)
[144] https://www.youtube.com/watch?v=LBa0i_0YkvU (May 27, 2019)
[145] https://www.youtube.com/watch?v=jVxWvVnTXfk (May 27, 2019)

PROBLEM FIVE

CHRISTIANS

BEFORE JOINING A CHURCH:

Before joining a church, ask immediately to see the church doctrinal statement. This is a statement of beliefs. Contrary to popular belief, it is not how good the choir sings, how good the preacher can moan and groan with smooth rhetoric, or how friendly the people there seem to be. First on the list is what are the teachings of the church, their beliefs. If you are already a (Biblical) Christian, you should already be aware of the **essentials of the faith** and would know if their doctrinal statement lines up with Christian orthodoxy.

Now if you are a new convert, assuming you don't know the Bible, this might be a little rough for you because you are in the learning stage. You may not know what to look for in the doctrinal statement. Don't simply go by what the members of the church tell you. Often, they are not aware of the church doctrinal statement and what defines "**Sound Doctrine**." The goal of this book is to provide you with insight on what should be looked for and what should be avoided. It is never too late to leave a church that teach false doctrine. Once you become aware that you are in a church teaching false doctrine, you should immediately leave that organization.

No one will continue to shop at a grocery store that stocks and sells rotten meat no matter how nice the merchant smiles at you: you'll exit quickly. The same thing applies when it comes to your local church. Your loyalty should be to Jesus Christ, and whatever helps you to be of service to Him. You can't do that in a church that is teaching false doctrine. Sound Doctrine is essential to the spiritual growth and health of the members of a church. This does not mean that you agree on everything. There can be things in Orthodoxy that we differ over but are not divided over. When it comes down to the teaching of Christianity the truth can never be compromised. It is every Christian's responsibility. It is non-negotiable. Did I know the truth and continue to follow error or did I follow after the truth of God? You will be judged by God based on walking in the truth or in error.

REGENERATION IS NOT REINCARNATION:

Biblical Christians Believe In "The Bodily Resurrection":

At death, the soul separates from the body (2 Cor. 5: 6,9) and is reunited at the voice of the Son of God (John 5:28-29) to its new, immortal, resurrected body by a divine miracle.

> *"Therefore we are always confident, knowing that, whilst we are at home in the body, we are absent from the Lord,"* **2 Corinthians 5:6 (KJV)**

> *"We are confident, I say, and willing rather to be absent from the body, and to be present with the Lord."* **2 Corinthians 5:8 (KJV)**

> *"Verily, verily, I say unto you, The hour is coming, and now is, when the dead shall hear the voice of the Son of God: and they that hear shall live."* John 5:25 (KJV)

> *"Marvel not at this: for the hour is coming, in the which all that are in the graves shall hear his voice, 29 And shall come forth;* **they that have done good, unto the resurrection of life***; and* **they that have done evil, unto the resurrection of damnation***."* John 5:28-29 (KJV)

> *"And many of those who sleep in the dust of the earth shall awake,* **Some to everlasting life***,* **Some to shame and everlasting contempt***."* **Daniel 12:2 (NKJV)**

This is the Christian view. This view, the supernatural resurrection of the body rather than the natural immortality of the soul alone, is the only version of life after death in Scripture. It is dimly prophesied and hoped for in the Old Testament, but clearly revealed in the New. [146]

---

[146] https://www.biblestudytools.com/dictionaries/bakers-evangelical-dictionary/resurrection.html May 8, 2019

The concept of **reincarnation** is completely without foundation in the Bible, which clearly tells us that we die once and then face judgment (Hebrews 9:27).

> *"And as it is appointed unto men once to die, but after this the judgment."* **Hebrews 9:27 (KJV)**

The Bible never mentions people having a second chance at life or coming back as different people or animals. Jesus told the criminal on the cross, "Today you will be with me in paradise" (Luke 23:43), not "You will have another chance to live a life on this earth."

Matthew 25:46 specifically tells us that believers go on to eternal life while unbelievers go onto eternal punishment.

Reincarnation has been a popular belief for thousands of years, but it has never been accepted by Christians or followers of Judaism because it is contradictory to Scripture.[147]

Belief in reincarnation is an ancient phenomenon and is a central tenet within the majority of Indian religious traditions, such as Hinduism, Sikhism, and Jainism. Many modern Pagans also believe in reincarnation as do some New Age movements, along with followers of spiritism. For the Christian, however, there can be no doubt: reincarnation is unbiblical and must be rejected as false.

Ten Refutations of Reincarnation

The whole thrust of the Bible opposes reincarnation. It shows that man is the special creation of God, created in God's image with both a material body and an immaterial soul and spirit. He is presented as distinct and unique from all other creatures—angels and the animal kingdom alike. The Bible teaches that at death, while man's body is mortal, decays and returns to dust, his soul and spirit continue on either in a place of torments for those who reject Christ or in paradise (heaven) in God's presence for those who have trusted in the Savior.

---

[147] https://www.gotquestions.org/reincarnation.html (May 8, 2019)

Ten Refutations of Reincarnation

Borrowed from A Handbook of Christian Apologetics by Peter Kreeft and Ronald Tacelli. (InterVarsity Press, Downers Grove). - **Christianity rejects reincarnation for ten reasons (listed below are eight):** [148]

1. It is contradicted by Scripture (**Hebrews 9:27**).

2. It is contradicted by orthodox tradition in all churches.

3. It would reduce the Incarnation (referring to Christ's incarnation) to a mere appearance, the crucifixion to an accident, and Christ to one among many philosophers or avatars. It would also confuse what Christ did with what creatures do: incarnation with reincarnation.

4. It implies that God made a mistake in designing our souls to live in bodies, that we are really pure spirits in prison or angels in costume.

5. It is contradicted by psychology and common sense, for its view of souls as imprisoned in alien bodies denies the natural psychosomatic unity.

6. It entails a very low view of the body, as a prison, a punishment.

7. It usually blames sin on the body and the body's power to confuse and darken the mind. This is passing the buck from soul to body, as well as from will to mind, and a confusion of sin with ignorance.

8. The idea that we are reincarnated in order to learn lessons we failed to learn in a past earthly life is contrary to both common sense and basic educational psychology. I cannot learn something if there is no continuity of memory. I can learn from my mistakes only if I remember them. People do not usually remember these past "reincarnations."

---

[148] https://bible.org/question/what-does-bible-say-about-reincarnation

HEBREW ISRAELITES AND REINCARNATION:

Israelite School of Practical Knowledge (ISUPK): In a YouTube video titled, "Reincarnation is Real, If Not, then Jesus Christ Is Dead - Hebrew Israelites."[149]
In this video, two **BHI** camp members are out on the street, supposedly teaching from the text of **1 Corinthians chapter 15**.

One is the speaker who is expounding, and the other is the reader (out loud):

The **BHI** speaker asked the following question of listeners, "**How can you say Christ rose from the dead and you don't believe in reincarnation**"? He asks, are you insane? and he replies with another question, what's wrong with Black people?

The speaker goes on to say the Lord is going to bring you back, **looking like somebody else** and punish you in a hellish condition. He then instructs the reader to read.

The reader eisegeted the text and inserts reincarnation where resurrection should have been.

> "Now if Christ be preached that he rose from the dead, how say some among you that there is **no reincarnation** of the dead?" **1 Corinthians 15:12 (KJV)**

Some yelled, asking him to read it one more time. And again **the reader** says (while reading):

> "Now if Christ be preached that he rose from the dead, how say some among you that there is **no reincarnation** of the dead?" **1 Corinthians 15:12 (KJV).**

The speaker says if Christ said he rose from the dead, how in the H-E-L-L are you going to say there is **no reincarnation**? He then asked the listeners, oh you don't believe in Lazarus? He then asked, so you don't believe in Elijah? where he prayed for a woman's dead son and his spirit came back into

---
[149] https://www.youtube.com/watch?v=xPskup5A7Ws&t=137s May 8, 2019

the boy. You gonna tell me it's not real and there is no reincarnation? When it is all over the Bible.

The speaker instructs **the reader** to read on. **The reader** says:

> "But if there be no reincar…"

This time **the reader** catches himself and then reads (verse 13) correctly:

> *"But if there be no resurrection of the dead, then is Christ not risen:* **1 Corinthians 15:13 (KJV)**

But the **BHI** speaker not hearing the correction still says to the listeners, you said that **reincarnation** ain't real.

SICARII another **Hebrew Israelite camp.** has a YouTube video post titled, "REINCARNATION IS CLEARLY IN THE BIBLE."[150]

In a **BHI** members table discussion, the reader reads:

> *"For all the prophets and the law prophesied until* **John**. *14 And if ye will receive it,* **this is Elias, which was for to come**." **Matthew 11:13-14 (KJV)**

The teacher in the group expounding on the text says that Messiah out of His own mouth just told you that **John the Baptist was the reincarnation of Elijah.** He says that is plain and simple.

Great Millstone (GMS) another Hebrew Israelite camp. has a YouTube video post titled, "REINCARNATION - GMS BREAKDOWN."[151]

WILL THE REAL CHURCH PLEASE COME FORTH?

According to the so-called **Hebrew Israelites**: Biblical Israel left the church of Jesus Christ In **The Wilderness** (where they had previously worshiped a Golden Calf while headed to the Promised Land.

---

[150] https://www.youtube.com/watch?v=6oCL3fWjjMA (May 8, 2019)
[151] https://www.youtube.com/watch?v=XhBSSaR05gY (May 8, 2019)

> "Now when the people saw that Moses delayed coming down from the mountain, the people gathered together to Aaron, and said to him, "Come, make us gods that shall go before us;" **Exodus 32:1 (NKJV)**

> "And he received the gold from their hand, and he fashioned it with an engraving tool, and made a molded calf. Then they said, "This is your god, O Israel, that brought you out of the land of Egypt!" **Exodus 32:4 (NKJV)**

Jesus says:
> "And I also say to you that you are Peter,
> - **and on this rock**
> - **I will build My church,**
>
> and the gates of Hades shall not prevail against it." **Matthew 16:18 (NKJV)**

Rebuttal: The question Hebrew Israelism should be asking is, *what is* **the ROCK;** According to Jesus? And is this **Chur**ch that He is referring to something new or did it already exist?

By carefully examining the text in the context of the surrounding verses, Scripture gives us the answer: [152]

a) Jesus had asked His Disciples, who are the folks proclaiming that the Son of man Am (v.13).
  - Disciples reply something like; some say this, some say that, and the others say something else. (v.14)
b) Then Jesus asked His Disciples, but who do you proclaim that **I Am**? (v.15).
  - Peter says, **Thou art the Christ, The Son of the living God**. (v.16)
c) Jesus tells Peter it was **His Father** in Heaven who revealed **this truth** to him. (v.17)
d) Jesus says upon **the statement of confession** (truth) proclaimed through Peter, which declared who He, Jesus, is; He **WILL** build **His Church**. (v. 18)

---

[152] https://www.youtube.com/playlist?list=PL-djiOgtDTUWi20Fylzb9IQVWM8ZG5roI (May 8, 2019)

The **Rock** is the confession statement that "**Jesus is the Christ the Son of the living God.**" And His Church Would be built on this FACT (Rock).

ISRAEL IS NOT THE CHURCH THAT JESUS BUILT:

In a Facebook dialog with a so-called **Hebrew Israelite Jediah Ben Judah**, he argues the first assembly was in the wilderness. **Israel is the church**. To be saved, you must be grafted into Christ and follow the Laws of Israel given by God. Also, **everyone in the wilderness was black**, and interesting historical side note. Other than that, it's the same God leading the same people.

Acts 7:38 (KJV) 38 "This is he, that was in **the church in the wilderness** with the angel which spake to him in the mount Sina, and with our fathers: who received the lively oracles to give unto us:" **Acts 7:38 (KJV)**

Congregation h5712. עֵדָה ' êḏâ; feminine of 5707 in the original sense of fixture; a stated assemblage (specifically, a concourse, or generally, a family or crowd): — **assembly, company, congregation, gathering, multitude**, people, swarm.

- **Exodus 12:3 (ESV)** Tell all the **congregation** of Israel that on the tenth day of this month every man shall take a lamb according to their fathers' houses, a lamb for a household

- **Genesis 28:3 (KJV)** And God Almighty bless thee, and make thee fruitful, and multiply thee, that thou mayest be **a multitude of people**;

- Genesis 28:3 (NKJV) "May God Almighty bless you, And make you fruitful and multiply you, That you may be **an assembly of peoples;**

- **Genesis 35:11 (NKJV)** Also God said to him: "I am God Almighty. Be fruitful and multiply; a nation and **a company of nations** shall proceed from you, and kings shall come from your body.

- **Genesis 35:11 (NIV 1984)** And God said to him, "I am God Almighty; be fruitful and increase in number. A nation and **a community of nations** will come from you, and kings will come from your body.

  - **Genesis 49:6 (KJV)** O my soul, come not thou into their secret; unto **their assembly**, mine honour, be not thou united: for in their anger they slew a man, and in their selfwill they digged down a wall.

> **Genesis 49:6 (ESV)** Let my soul come not into their council; O my glory, be not joined to **their company**. For in their anger they killed men, and in their willfulness they hamstrung oxen.

None of the above Old Testament Scriptures alludes to the "**My Church**" which Jesus Christ would build on **a Rock** in the New Testament.

Definition of **Conflate**: combine (two or more texts, ideas, etc.) into one:

Similarity DOES NOT EQUATE Actuality: The Word Church

G1577 ekklēsía
(from 1537 /ek, "out from and to" and 2564 /kaléō, "to call")

– properly, people called out from the world and to God, the outcome being the Church (the mystical body of Christ) – i.e., the universal (total) body of believers whom God calls out from the world and into His eternal kingdom.

[The English word "**church**" comes from the Greek word Kyriakos (G2960), "belonging to the Lord" (kyrios). 1577 /ekklēsía ("**church**") is the root of the terms "ecclesiology" & ecclesiastical."] https://biblehub.com/greek/1577.htm

Promises Related To The Promised Land Do Not Equate To Promises Made To The Church

Israel in the Promised Land is never Prophesied To Be (called) a New Testament church.

In the wilderness, Israel was a true church
  (G. ecclesia {ekklēsía}= **called-out assembly**),

> but in striking contrast with the New Testament ecclesia {ekklēsía}.

Israel was truly called out of Egypt.

Assembly: H6951- **Congregation,** company, crowd, horde
Congregation: H5712 - **Assembly**, band, company, herd, swarm

> **Exodus 12:6 (KJV)** And ye shall keep it up until the fourteenth day of the same month: and **the whole assembly of the congregation of Israel** shall kill it in the evening.
>
> **Leviticus 4:13 (KJV)** And if **the whole congregation of Israel** sin through ignorance, and the thing be hid from the eyes of **the assembly**, and they have done somewhat against any of the commandments of the Lord concerning things which should not be done, and are guilty; 14 When the sin, which they have sinned against it, is known, then **the congregation** shall offer a young bullock for the sin, and bring him before the tabernacle of **the congregation**.

The New Testament Church of Jesus Christ was never Instructed to Keep The Passover:

> **2 Chronicles 30:2 (KJV)** For the king had taken counsel, and his princes, and **all the congregation** in Jerusalem, to keep the passover in the second month.
>
> **Luke 22:19 (NKJV)** And He took bread, gave thanks and broke it, and gave it to them, saying, "This is My body which is given for you; **do this in remembrance of Me**."
>
> **1 Corinthians 11:25** (NKJV) In the same manner He also took the cup after supper, saying, "This cup is the new covenant in My blood. This do, as often as you drink it, in **remembrance of Me."**
> 26 **For as often as** you eat this bread and drink this cup, **you proclaim the Lord's death till He comes**.

Congregation translates ekklēsía **Act 7:38** as in **Hebrews 2:12** for **a congregation of Israel**, but normally translated **church**; The term is used in the secular sense for an **assembly**.

- "This is he, that was in **the church in the wilderness** with the angel which spake to him in the mount Sina, and with our fathers: who received the lively oracles to give unto us:" **Acts 7:38 (KJV)**

- "This is he who was in **the congregation in the wilderness** with the Angel who spoke to him on Mount Sinai, and with our fathers, the one who received the living oracles to give to us," **Acts 7:38 (NKJV)**

- ❖ "Saying, I will declare thy name unto my brethren, in **the midst of the church** will I sing praise unto thee." **Hebrews 2:12 (KJV)**

- ❖ "saying: "I will declare Your name to My brethren; In **the midst of the assembly** I will sing praise to You." **Hebrews 2:12 (NKJV)**

- ❖ "I will declare thy name unto my brethren: in **the midst of the congregation** will I praise thee." **Psalms 22:22 (KJV)**

Moses - Assembly – Wilderness:
- **Ruler and Deliver** (Acts 7:35)
- **The Head** - Moses a Sinner (Num. 20:1-13)
- **Called Out** of Egypt (Hosea 11:1)
- **A Nation** (A People)
- **No Indwelling** of The Holy Spirit
- Assembly Cursed 40 Years (Numbers 14: 23-35)
- **Wife** (Isaiah 54:5; Jeremiah 3:14)
- **Worshipped a Golden Calf** (Exodus 32:8)
- **Punished** for Disobeying God (Deut. 28:15-68)
- **The Nation** Will Not Be Raptured (Dan. 9:20-27)
- **The Mosaic Law** (John 1:17)
- **Moses Did Not Die for The Sins of The Assembly** (Deut. 32: 48-52; 34:5-8)
- **Ask that A Man** (Numbers 27:14-17)

Christ - Assembly - Church (Believers)
- **Lord and Christ** (Acts 2:36)
- **The Head - Christ** Sinless (2 Cor. 5:21, Col 1:17-18)
- **Called Out of Darkness** (1 Peter 2:9)
- **Individuals** (Follow Me)
- **Indwelling** of The Holy Spirit
- **No Curse for The Church**- (Gal. 3:13)
- **Bride** (Revelation 19:7-9; Ephesians 5:25-27)
- **Worshipped Jesus Christ** (Matt 2:11; 28:9; John 20:28)
- **Persecuted** For Christ Sake (1 Tim. 4:10; Acts 9:1)
- **The Church** Will Be Raptured (1 Thess. 4:16-18)

- **Grace and Truth** (John 1:17; Galatians 6:2)
- **Christ Died For All** That Would Believe (Church) (John 8:24; 1 John 2:2; 1 Peter 3:18)
- **Prays That The Holy Spirit** (John 14:16-18)

Moses - Assembly - Wilderness	Christ - Assembly - Church(Believers)
• Ruler and Deliver	• Lord and Christ
• The Head - Moses a Sinner	• The Head - Christ Sinless

We normally use the **verb WILL** to speak about the future. It is always combined with another verb.

"And I also say to you that you are Peter, and on this rock I **will build** *My church, and the gates of Hades shall not prevail against it."* **Matthew 16:18 (NKJV)**

"And He is before all things, and in Him all things consist. 18 And **He is the head of the body, the church**, *who is the beginning, the firstborn from the dead, that in all things He may have the preeminence."* **Colossians 1:17 (NKJV)**

"And He put all things under His feet, and gave Him to be head over all things to **the church**,*"* **Ephesians 1:22 (NKJV)**

"But I want you to know that the head of every man is Christ, the head of woman is man, and **the head of Christ is God**.*"* **1 Corinthians 11:3 (NKJV)**

WHAT DEFINES A CHRISTIAN:[153]

What or who defines a Christian? The simple answer is not us! The Bible defines, and we simply observe the fruit that grows on trees (including our own tree).

However, this doesn't mean we look at a pig and call it a possum or look at an apple and call it an orange. We simply pray the pig will recognize it is a pig and do what a pig does. We also pray the apple should be flushed red, with apple seeds, a black stem, and a green leaf or two attached to the stem. We won't condemn either of them if they don't; but I will

---

[153] https://www.youtube.com/playlist?list=PL-djiOgtDTUWDfaxbvIJC-hWa6Ally7g (May 20, 2019)

acknowledge that whatever they may be, they don't have the characteristics of any pig or apple that I ever came across.

The word "Christian" is used three times in the New Testament (**Acts 11:26; 26:28; 1 Peter 4:16**). Followers of Jesus Christ were first called "Christians" in Antioch (**Acts 11:26**) because their behavior, activity, and speech were like Christ. The word "Christian" literally means, "belonging to the party of Christ" or a "follower of Christ."

CHRISTIANS ARE NOT THE ISRAEL OF GOD

In a Facebook dialog with Elder L. Lewis, he argues that Christians are **the Israel of God**. We are Christians, which makes us the real **Israelites**, children of the promise. God's people that is what **Israel symbolically** is, *so the church is Israel,* also **the Israel of God.**

Wrong! The Scripture clearly teaches," A little leaven leaveneth the whole lump." **Galatians 5:9 (KJV)** He is affirming pure Replacement Theology. But to the contrary, the church **has not** replaced Israel **nor merged** into Israel.

Sadly, we have a misguided Christian endorsing Replacement Theology which is no different than a so-called Hebrew Israelite that endorses Historical Revisionism.

- The Term "**True Israel of God**" Is Not Found (Nor Taught) In Scripture.
- The Term "**Spiritual Israel**" Is Not Found (Nor Taught) In Scripture.
- The Term "**Spiritual Israelites**" Is Not Found (Nor Taught) In Scripture.
- The Term "**Spiritual Hebrews**" Is Not Found (Nor Taught) In Scripture.
- The Term "**Spiritual Jews**" Is Not Found (Nor Taught) In Scripture.

Symbolically:
1. purely in terms of what is being represented or implied:" the words are to be taken both literally and symbolically."

2. as or by means of a symbol or symbolism:" the household symbolically represented a nation or homeland."

The Body of Christ and The Nation of Israel are Two different Entities:
1. Israel **Does NOT** represent the **Church.**
2. The Church **Does NOT** represent **Israel.**
3. Israel **Does NOT** represent **Jesus Christ.**
4. Jesus Christ **Does NOT** represent **Israel**.
5. Israel **Is NOT** the Body of Christ (**Church**).
6. The Church **Does NOT** replace **Israel**.
7. Israel **Does NOT** replace the **Church**.

The Question of Who?
A. Who Did Jesus represent? (John 6:38; 8:28-29)
B. Who Does the Church represent? (Matt 28:19; 10:16; 2 Cor. 5:20)
C. Who is Raptured Up? (1 Thes. 4:16-18; 1 Cor 15:51-53)
D. Who is Going Through the Tribulation? (Dan. 9: 20-27

Neither Gentiles nor Jews Morph into any of The Above. But as Believers (Gentiles and Jews), we are Born Again New Creatures In Christ. (John 3:7; 2 Corinthians 5:17-19)

BHI Camps are Void of Biblical Love

They frown on loving others whom they consider not to be fellow so-called Hebrew Israelites. Jesus taught,

> "**But if you love those who love you**, what credit is that to you? For **even sinners love those who love them**. 33 And **if you do good to those who do good to you**, what credit is that to you? **For even sinners do the same**." **Luke 6:32-33 (NKJV)**

So-called Hebrew Israelites by their own admission don't want to forgive Esau (so-called White Man) for what they did to people of color (So-called Black man). But we could learn from the wisdom of Joseph

> "Joseph said to them, 'Do not be afraid, for am I in the place of God? 20 But as for you, **you meant evil against me; but God meant it for good,** in order to bring it about as it is this day, to save many people alive. 21 Now therefore, do not be afraid; I will provide for you and your little ones.' And he comforted them and spoke kindly to them." **Genesis 50:19-21 (NKJV)**

They even hate people of their own skin color. [154] [155] [156] [157]

SUFFERING AS A CHRISTIAN:

The new convert (and seasoned Christians) should understand what the Bible says about suffering, important Bible teaching which has been watered down and overshadowed by the pursuit of blessings and material gain in many of today's sermons.

The Bible clearly teaches that Christians are going to suffer. Suffering is a consistent doctrine of the Christian faith. You cannot read through the New Testament without finding suffering mentioned in so many places where it happened. Our Salvation was not free. It cost Jesus His life and every drop of His blood to redeem us. Those that followed Him in obedience lost their lives in service to Him that we might have His gospel in our hands.

Jesus comforts and warns:

> "*These things I have spoken unto you, that in me ye might have peace. **In the world ye shall have tribulation**: but be of good cheer; I have overcome the world.*" (**John 16:33**)

> "*Blessed are ye, when men shall **revile you**, and **persecute you**, and shall **say all manner of evil against you falsely, for my sake***." (**Matthew 5:11**)

In Peter's writings, he discusses suffering. In fact, Peter was writing this to the Church during the time of persecution:

---

[154] https://www.youtube.com/watch?v=UXv3vKZl2Vs (June 3, 2019)
[155] https://www.youtube.com/watch?v=ttOJ5lpN34I (June 3, 2019)
[156] https://www.youtube.com/watch?v=sRu52kgAi0s (June 3, 2019)
[157] https://www.youtube.com/watch?v=_StP0LsP8DY (June 3, 2019)

> *"Forasmuch then as Christ hath suffered for us in the flesh, **arm yourselves likewise with the same mind**: for **he that hath suffered in the flesh** hath ceased from sin;"* (**1 Peter 4:1**)

Peter says that suffering brings us closer to God. It shows when you suffer for God. It helps you to be more sanctified and holy.

> *"**Yet if any man suffer as a Christian**, let him not be ashamed; but **let him glorify God on this behalf**."* (**1 Peter 4:16**)

Paul encourages:

> *"29 For unto you it is given in the behalf of Christ, not only to believe on him, **but also to suffer for his sake**;"* (**Philippians 1:29**)

Just as Jesus suffered for us, we will suffer for His name's sake. We don't hear this in churches today because many are not preaching the gospel. Instead, many preach things which tickle the congregation's ears, things that are pleasing to people rather than preaching the truth of the gospel.

Notice in **Acts 14** how certain of the Jews incited the people and stoned Paul for preaching the gospel of Jesus Christ and left him for dead. Even so, Paul and the others returned again, preaching the gospel:

> *"Confirming the souls of the disciples, and exhorting them to continue in the faith, and that **we must through much tribulation enter into the kingdom of God**."* (**Acts 14:22**)

Suffering and tribulation are, most definitely, part of the Christian faith. These so-called "feel good" and "seeker friendly" churches are bad because they don't tell people the straight-out truth of Scripture, but rather things people want to hear. It is comparable to marketing's supply and demand. There is a demand for "feel-good-messages," and there are many churches ready to meet the supply. But the Scriptures are clear about the subject of suffering, for it is mentioned all through the Bible.

Notice how easy it is to find these passages, assuming you don't skip over them.

Some want to use these verses "by His stripes we are healed" as if just to say they produce a miraculous result for you. But that is not really what the Bible tells us. In fact, the Bible tells us something else. **Romans chapter 8:**

Paul tells us we must suffer with Jesus to be glorified with Him.
"^{17} *And if children, then heirs; heirs of God, and joint-heirs with Christ;*
- *if so be that **we suffer with him**, that*
- ***we may be also glorified together***.

Paul says there is suffering in this present time. Yes, even today, there is suffering in this present time. People are being slaughtered in other countries for having Bibles in their possession and for identifying with Christ as Christians.

^{18} For I reckon that **the sufferings of this present time are not worthy to be compared with the glory which shall be revealed in us**." **(Romans 8:17-28)**

Notice the verse above does not say, "you can name-it, claim-it, or speak-it away." But, it causes us to realize that suffering here cannot be compared to the glory which we shall receive afterward.

"^{19} *For the earnest expectation of the creature waiteth for the manifestation of the sons of God.* ^{20} *For the creature was made subject to vanity, not willingly, but by reason of him who hath subjected the same in hope,* ^{21} *Because the creature itself also shall be delivered from the bondage of corruption into the glorious liberty of the children of God.* ^{22} **For we know that the whole creation groaneth and travaileth in pain together until now**. ^{23} *And not only they,* **but ourselves also**, *which have the firstfruits of the Spirit, even we ourselves groan within ourselves, waiting for the adoption, to wit, the redemption of our body."* **(Romans 8:19-23)**

Why you might ask in a book that is supposed to be simple and about essentials, would I include a section on suffering? The answer is simple. It's Biblical.

> *"I tell you that he will avenge them speedily. Nevertheless when the Son of man cometh, **shall he find faith on the earth**?"* (**Luke 18:8**)

Paul had infirmities:

> *"8 For this thing I besought the Lord thrice, that it might depart from me. 9 And he said unto me, My grace is sufficient for thee: for my strength is made perfect in weakness. Most gladly therefore will I rather glory in my infirmities, that the power of Christ may rest upon me. 10 Therefore I take pleasure in infirmities, in reproaches, in necessities, in persecutions, in distresses for Christ's sake: for when I am weak, then am I strong."* (**2 Corinthians 12:8-10**)

The Law:

PROBLEM SIX

THE LAW:

Shared Common BHI Beliefs About The LAW:

- **They believe you must keep** the Ten Commandments **and** Observe Jewish dietary laws and circumcision.
- **They believe the law** was **NOT** abolished (fulfilled). Quoting: **Romans 3:23; 6:23; 1 John 3:4** "Whosoever committeth sin transgresseth also the law: for sin is the transgression of the law." **Romans 6:1-2**.
  - They say the Messiah said: **Matthew 5:17**. "Think not that I am come to destroy the law, or the prophets: I am not come to destroy, but to fulfill."
    - Therefore this means the Law is not destroyed... The Law still stands... The Most-High does not change: **Malachi 3:6** "For I [am] the LORD, I change not; therefore ye sons of Jacob are not consumed."

THE LAW VS. COMMANDMENT

There are many who if possible, would trouble you as regards to the law[158]. This will require us to ask them what do they mean, why they believe it, and the evidence for believing it as related to the law.

> *"For* **Christ is the end of the law** *for righteousness to every one that believeth."* **Romans 10:4 (KJV)**

> "And whatsoever we ask, we receive of him, because **we keep his commandments**, *and do those things that are pleasing in his sight. 23 And* **this is his commandment, That we should believe on the name of his Son Jesus Christ, and love one another, as he gave us commandment. 24 And he that keepeth his commandments** *dwelleth he in him, and he in him. And hereby we know that he abideth in us, by the Spirit which he hath given us".* **1 John 3:22-24 (KJV)**

---

[158] Essentials Simple But Biblical (2017) By Robert Anderson & Pastor Emery Moss Jr., Detroit MI, pg. 114. TruthSeekersRead Publishing

The Law:

> *"He shall not fail nor be discouraged, till he have set judgment in the earth: and the isles* **shall wait for his law**.*"* **Isaiah 42:4 (KJV)**

> *"Bear ye one another's burdens, and* **so fulfil the law of Christ**.*"* **Galatians 6:2 (KJV)**

Hebrew Israelism falsely states that Christians don't keep God's commandments. Does the question become, what are God's commandments? The commandment to the church (the believers) is to love God and to love one another on this hang **all the Law and the prophets**.

> *"On these two commandments hang all the Law and the Prophets.*** " Matthew 22:40 (NKJV)**

1) Love God. (Matthew 22:37-38)

- Commandments 1 thru 4.

2) Love thy neighbor (others). (Matthew 22:39)

- Commandments 5 thru 10.

The Commandments of God transcends time; they don't have a start and ending point. They are not about
- Feasts
- Sabbath days
- Customs
- Fringes
- Unshaven beards
- Polyester – wool – cotton blending
- Etc.

The commandments of God are about the moral righteous character of God, and biblical Christians keep the commandments of God when they are lead by the Spirit of God **(Galatians 5:16, 18)**.

> "But the fruit of the Spirit is love, joy, peace, longsuffering, kindness, goodness, faithfulness, 23 gentleness, self-control. **Against such there is no law**." **Galatians 5:22-23 (NKJV)**

The Law:

There is no law that can force you to do these. The law only condemns you for failing to keep them. The law says you need a savior and points you to Jesus Christ. The law caused you to realize that you must be born again.

Those led by the Spirit of God are not legalistically bound to any of the ceremonial or sacrificial laws that were included under the Mosaic covenant. All these things have their fulfillment in Christ Jesus; He has made us free.

Biblical Christians don't (Galatians 5:19-21 (NKJV):
- Practice Adultery,
- Practice fornication,
- Practice uncleanness,
- Practice lewdness,
- Practice idolatry,
- Practice sorcery,
- Practice hatred,
- Practice contentions,
- Practice jealousies,
- Practice outbursts of wrath,
- Pursue selfish ambitions,
- Promote dissensions,
- Teach and Promote heresies,
- Practice envy,
- Practice murder,
- Practice drunkenness,
- Practice revelries, and the likes

Why? Because **it would violate the Royal Law:**
"*For all the law is fulfilled in **one word**, even in this: "You shall **love** your neighbor as yourself."* **Galatians 5:14 (NKJV)**

> "*If you really **fulfill the royal law** according to the Scripture, "You shall **love** your neighbor as yourself," you do well;*" **James 2:8 (NKJV)**

THE BAIT AND SWITCH TACTICS OF THE HEBREW ISRAELITES

The Law:

Hebrew Israelites deceptively claim that Christians teach that the law was done away with (destroyed). **BHI** adherents love to go to **Matthew 5:17** pointing out that Christ himself said, he didn't come to destroy the law.

> "*Do not think that I came* **to destroy the Law** *or the Prophets. I did not come to destroy but to fulfill* ." **Matthew 5:17 (NKJV)**

They teach that Jesus meant that **you should keep the law**. And that He didn't come to do away with the prophets either.

Hebrew Israelites from **Israel United In Christ (IUIC)** were in the streets dialoguing with a Christian; they asked what did Christ fulfill?

The Christian replied that he agreed that Jesus **did not come to destroy the law**, but rather **to fulfill the law and the prophets** because they all pointed to him **(Luke 24:44)**.

Sarcastically, **BHI** ask, so he destroyed it after he fulfilled it?

The **BHI** reader then reads:
> "*And he said unto them, These are the words which I spake unto you, while I was yet with you,* **that all things must** *be fulfilled,* **which were written in the law of Moses**,"

- ➢ The **BHI** Speaker exclaims these that were written in should be fulfilled, **not the law itself**. The things that were written in it. Somethings written in it **can't be fulfilled**.

The **BHI** reader reads:
> "*and in the prophets*,"

- ➢ The **BHI** Speaker exclaims things in the prophets that the prophets wrote Jesus came to fulfill.

The **BHI** reader reads:
> "and in the psalms, concerning me." **Luke 24:44 (KJV)**

- ➢ The **BHI** Speaker says the Christian said Jesus came to fulfill the law. But I don't know what he means. But

The Law:

> it doesn't mean Jesus did it, but y'all don't have to keep it. The speaker asked hypothetically what exactly did he fulfill? He has the reader read Isaiah 53:3-

The **BHI** reader reads **Israel 53: 3-**

- ➢ The **BHI** Speaker extrapolates from the text the "us" ~ "our" ~ "we" in his attempt to prove this was ONLY for Israel. He was wounded for our transgression(v5) Half dialoguing (but not) He asks the Christian what is iniquity? (he replied Sin).
  - o He has the reader go to **1 John 3: 4** to point out "sin is The Transgression of the law."
  - o Not allowing any dialog, he has the reader go to **Psalm 147:19** to pull the law was given to Israel through Moses. He again stresses that Christ only died for the sins of Israel. Of course, he brings up the curses of Deuteronomy chapter 28 as he expounded.
- ➢ Still not allowing the Christian to ask a question or to comment, he has the reader read **Romans 9:4** as he paints his picture of so-called Hebrew Israelites by reading themselves into the text. Finally, he yields the floor to the Christian, who reminds him that **we did not finish the law part** (smile).
- ➢ The **BHI** Speaker is going back to **Luke 24:44**. He says to the Christian now you're thinking He fulfilled the law and now we don't have to keep the law. I'm trying to prove to you exactly what in the law He fulfilled. He did not fulfill the law (613), but He fulfilled the prophecies in the law pertaining to Him. He has the reader read **Acts 3:18**. He did not fulfill the law.
- ➢ The Christians confirm that he agrees with all Scriptures **2 Timothy 3:16**. Yes, He **indeed fulfilled the prophecies written about Him, and He also fulfilled the Law**. He reminds them of the text they read in Matthew

> *"Think not that I am come to destroy the law, or the prophets: I am not come to destroy, **but to fulfil**. 18 For verily I say unto you, Till heaven and earth pass,*

The Law:

> *one jot or one tittle* **shall in no wise pass from the law, till all be fulfilled.**"**Matthew 5:17-18 (KJV)**

➢ **BHI** Speaker said that the Apostle Paul doesn't speak normal and that he was speaking a hold another language. Paul spoke in such a way that he made **the heathens want to be Israelites**. And Paul was very slick in his words and how he put things. **He wanted to confuse people, that was his goal**. He wanted to confuse people that are not learned. If you don't learn this book (Bible), you are going to be confused. He tells the reader to read **Romans 7:14,** referring to the law being spiritual. He says keeping the laws of God is what makes you spiritual.

➢ **BHI** Speaker says we're trying to wake our people up to what the Bible is really saying. The Bible says **to KEEP the laws** AND **have faith in Christ** or **DIE**. That is what it says. It is about the nation of Israel and keeping God's Laws and having faith in Christ. That is the end of everything in this book (Bible). But the Christian church makes it vague, he says. Unlearned Christians want to wrestle with Paul's writings; as the reader read **2 Peter 3:16**. He says once you read Paul's epistles and get his writing confused, now you get the rest of the Bible confused and all out of proportion. He says when Paul is talking about the schoolmaster (**Galatians 3:24-25**) that he is not talking about **the whole law**, but *the sacrificial law*.

➢ Finally, the Christian is allowed to get in a word; he points out that Peter makes it clear in **2 Peter 3** the things which were hard to be understood were the **end-times** (verses 10-16) concerning the last days and not the things concerning the law when reading in context. And in Romans 7:14 where it was referring to the law being spiritual, you must read that in context: key verse

> *"Wherefore, my brethren,* **ye also are become dead to the law by the body of Christ**; *that ye should be* **married to another**, *even* **to him** *who is*

The Law:

> *raised from the dead, that we should bring forth fruit unto God."* **Romans 7:4**

We are not married to the law, but we are to be married to Christ. We have become dead to the law. This is not talking about the sacrificial law, but the whole the law. Christians are not against the laws of God; Christians simply understand that under Christ that we are no longer legalistically bound to Mosaic laws (**John 1:17**).

➢ Then strangely, the **Hebrew Israelite** speaker asks the Christian, who is more important Paul or Christ (smile). And when did Christ ever say don't keep the laws of God?

Then the **Hebrew Israelite** said **part of the law had been done away with**.

The Christian reminds the **Hebrew Israelite** of his own previous words from **Matthew 5:18** "….one jot or one tittle shall in no wise pass from the law, till all be fulfilled." So how can you say **part of the law has been done away with**?

The **Hebrew Israelites**, playing cat and mouse, asks what does the "all be filled" mean? He answers himself saying, it is referring to the prophecies. He says you can only fulfill prophecies; **You do and keep the law, but you fulfill prophecies**. The other Hebrew Israelite adherents chime in, That's Right!

THE LAW VS. FAITH:

It Is **NOT the Law** that makes A Person a **New Creature In Christ**, And Abraham didn't look forward to the Day of the Law, But he looked forward to the day of Christ.

> "Your father Abraham rejoiced to see my day: and **he saw it,** and was glad." **John 8:56 (KJV)**

> "Therefore, if anyone is in Christ, **he is a new creation;** old things have passed away; behold, all things have become new." **2 Corinthians 5:17 (NKJV)**

The Law:

We Are **NOT Ambassadors of the Law**, but of Christ who did what the law could not do.

> "Now then, **we are ambassadors for Christ**, as though God were pleading through us: we implore you on Christ's behalf, be reconciled to God. 21 For He made Him who knew no sin to be sin for us, that we might become the righteousness of God in Him." **2 Corinthians 5:20-21 (NKJV)**

The works of the law were the attempts of the Jews to think that salvation could be obtained by the keeping of the law. They are ignorant of God's righteousness and seek to establish their own righteousness by overlooking the fact that Christ is the end of the law described by Moses

In Romans 10:3-13, Paul contrasts **law** and **faith**:
- the righteousness which is of the law
  - debtor to keep the whole law and live by it.
- the righteousness which is of faith
  - Acknowledge **Christ is the end of the law (10:4)**. **He did what we could not do**. Christ fulfilled the righteousness of the law (**Matthew 5:17**).
  - **Confess Jesus Christ with the mouth** and **believe with the heart**.
  - **Call** on Christ (**Romans 10:13**), **live** in Christ (**Philippians 1:21**), **Walk**-in Christ (**Colossians 2:6**).

However, we are not lawless, but rather under the law of Christ.

> "Brethren, if a man be overtaken in a fault, ye which are spiritual, restore such an one in the spirit of meekness; considering **thyself, lest thou also be tempted**. ² Bear ye one another's burdens, and so **fulfil the law of Christ**." (**Galatians 6:1-2**)

> "A new commandment I give unto you, That ye love one another; as I have loved you, that ye also love one another." (**John 13:34**)

The Law:

We are under **the law of Christ**[159], understanding He did for us what the Old Testament could not do. But the Old Testament did its job:
- of pointing us to Christ.
- Continuously pointing out our sins, which should lead us to Christ.

The Purpose of the Law:

"*What shall we say then? Is the law sin? God forbid. Nay, I had not known sin, **but by the law**: for I had not known lust, **except the law had said**, Thou shalt not covet. 8 But sin, taking occasion by the commandment, wrought in me all manner of concupiscence. **For without the law sin was dead**.*" (**Romans 7:7-8**)

Keeping the Law could never save:

"*Is the law then against the promises of God? God forbid: **for if there had been a law given which could have given life**, verily righteousness should have been by the law.*" (**Galatians 3:21**)

"*But when the fulness of the time was come, **God sent forth his Son**, made of a woman, made under the law, 5 **To redeem them that were under the law**, that we might receive the adoption of sons.*" (**Galatians 4:4-5**)

Christ did what the righteousness of the Law could never do:

"*2 For **the law of the Spirit of life in Christ Jesus** hath made me free from the law of sin and death. 3*
- ***For what the law could not do**, in that it was weak through the flesh,*
- ***God sending his own Son** in the likeness of sinful flesh, and for sin, **condemned sin in the flesh**: 4*

---

[159] http://www.biblestudytools.com/dictionaries/bakers-evangelical-dictionary/law-of-christ.html (May 15, 2017)

The Law:

- ***That the righteousness of the law might be fulfilled in us**, who walk*
  - *not after the flesh,*
  - *but after the Spirit.*" **(Romans 8:2-4)**.

God gave Israel **a single law** which included **the Ten Commandments**.

[**2 Chronicles 31:3** ....as it is written in the law of the Lord..]

[**Nehemiah 8:2, 3, 8** ...the people were attentive unto **the book of the law**]

[**Nehemiah 8:14,15,18** .... And **they found written in the law** which the Lord had commanded by Moses, that the children of Israel should dwell in booths in the feast of the seventh month:....]

[**Psalms 19:7 The law of the Lord** is perfect, converting the soul:....]

a. The Ten Commandments **were given to the Israelites at Sinai (Exodus 20:1-17)**.

b. Israel was commanded to **obey the Law of Moses**; the law included **the Ten Commandments**.

[**Malachi 4:4** Remember ye the law of Moses my servant, which **I commanded** unto him in Horeb for all Israel, with the **statutes** and **judgments**.]

  i. Someone keeping one part of the law **must keep the whole law**.

  " ***For as many as are of the works of the law are under the curse:***
  for it is written,
  - *Cursed is every one that **continueth not in all things which are written in the book of the law to do them**.*" **(Galatians 3:10)**.

  ii. Someone keeping the Ten Commandments **must keep the entire Mosaic Law**.

The Law:

> "Behold, I Paul say unto you, that if ye be circumcised, **Christ shall profit you nothing**. 3 For I testify again to every man that is circumcised,
> - *that he is a debtor to do the whole law.* 4
> - ***Christ is become of no effect unto you***, *whosoever of you are justified by the law;* ***ye are fallen from grace***." **(Galatians 5:2-4)**

c. No one is justified by the works of the law.

> Jesus said, "*For verily I say unto you, Till heaven and earth pass*, **one jot or one tittle shall in no wise pass from the law**, *till all be fulfilled.*" **(Matthew 5:18)**

The BAD News:

Neither the Jews nor the Gentiles could keep the law or fulfill the law.

The GOOD News:

"*But the scripture hath concluded* **all under sin**, *that the promise by faith of Jesus Christ might be* **given to them that believe**. *23* **But before faith came**, *we were kept under the law, shut up* **unto the faith which should afterwards be revealed**." **(Galatians 3:22-23)**

a. **Jesus** came to **fulfill the law.**
   "*Think not that I am come to destroy the law, or the prophets: I am not come to destroy,* **but to fulfil**." **(Matthew 5:17)**
b. **Christ is the end of the law** for righteousness to everyone who believes (**Romans 10:4**).
c. Christ is the end of the law because he nailed it to the cross (**Colossians 2:11-14**)

The Law:

    d. Since Jesus fulfilled the law, we can be saved in Christ
- "**Neither is there salvation in any other**: for there **is none other name under heaven** given among men, **whereby we must be saved**." (**Acts 4:12**)
- "**Being justified freely by his grace** through the redemption that is in Christ Jesus:" (**Romans 3:24**)
- "Know ye not, **that so many of us as were baptized into Jesus Christ** were baptized into his death?" (**Romans 6:3**)
- "For as many of you as have been baptized into Christ have **put on Christ**." (**Galatians 3:27**)
- "Thou therefore, my son, **be strong in the grace that is in Christ Jesus**." (**2 Timothy 2:1, 10**)

    e. Now we can walk according to the Spirit

"There is therefore now no condemnation to them which are in Christ Jesus, who walk not after the flesh, **but after the Spirit.** 2
- **For the law of the Spirit of life in Christ Jesus** hath made me free from the law of sin and death. 3
- **For what the law could not do,** in that it was weak through the flesh,
  - **God sending his own Son in the likeness of sinful flesh**, and for sin, **condemned sin in the flesh**:
  - 4 <u>**That the righteousness of the law**</u> might be **fulfilled in us, who walk not after the flesh, but after the Spirit**." (**Romans 8:1-4**)

    f. Anyone attempting to be justified by law **has fallen from grace**.(**Galatians 5:4**).

    g. The **law was a tutor** (schoolmaster). **Since faith has come, we are no longer under the tutor** (i.e., we are no longer under the law). (**Galatians 3:24-25**).

The Law:

- h. The commandments that were written on stone (i.e., **the Ten Commandments**) brought death. Today we must obey the epistle of Christ, which is written on our hearts (**2 Corinthians 3:7-11**).
- i. The law was changed. We no longer live under the Ten Commandments or any other part of the Mosaic Law.

    *"For **the priesthood being changed**, there is made of necessity **a change also of the law**."* (**Hebrews 7:12**)

    God does not change in his nature. He is omnipotent, omniscient, and omnipresent. But God's actions do change.
    - In the Old Testament, there was animal sacrifice, but not in the New Testament.
    - In the Old Testament, there is a priesthood, but not in the New Testament in the same sense.
    God can change His plans, but that does not mean it changes who He is. He is still the same loving and merciful God, full of judgment as it says in **Exodus 34**. He says, "*I change not*" (**Malachi 3:6**). But definitely, He changes in His dispensations and in the fulfillment of His plans.

    We see a change as it relates to the Sabbath (which was a part of the Ten Commandments). However, the Sabbath is also fulfilled. See section on Sabbath.

- j. Jesus could not be our High Priest **until God changed the law (Hebrews 7:12-15, 8:4)**
- k. Christ came to earth to take away the first covenant (law) and establish the second covenant (law).

    *"Above when he said, Sacrifice and offering and burnt offerings and offering for sin thou wouldest not, neither hadst pleasure therein; **which are offered by the law**; 9 Then said he, **Lo, I come to do thy will, O God. He taketh away the first, that he may establish the second**. 10 By the which will we are sanctified through the offering of*

The Law:

> the body of Jesus Christ once for all." (**Hebrews 10:8-10**)

Apostle Paul writes:
> "*5 Now **the end of the commandment is charity** out of a pure heart, and of a good conscience, and of faith unfeigned: 6 From which some having swerved have turned aside unto vain jangling; 7 **Desiring to be teachers of the law; understanding neither what they say, nor whereof they affirm**.* (**1 Timothy 1:4-11**)

Jesus said:
> "***On these two commandments hang all the law and the prophets***." (**Matthew 22:40**)

1) Love God. (**Matthew 22:37-38**)

- Commandments **1 thru 4**.

2) Love thy neighbor (others). (**Matthew 22:39**)

- Commandments **5 thru 10**.

There is no law that can force you to do these. The law only condemns you for failing to keep them. The law says you need a savior and points you to Jesus Christ. The law caused you to realize that you must be born again.

Jesus said and demonstrated what the law could not say and do. The law could not forgive or love, so it could never demonstrate forgiveness or loving another. For the Christian, what was written on tablets of stone, Christ writes these in our hearts[160].

> "***A new commandment I give unto you***,
> - *That ye **love one another**;*
> - ***as I have loved you**,*
> - *that ye **also love one another***.
> *35 By this shall all men know that ye are my disciples, if ye have love one to another.*" (**John 13:34-35**)

---

[160] http://thelawofchrist.info/index_files/Comparison_of_Law_of_Moses_with_Law_of_Christ.htm (May 15, 2017)

The Law:

There is an old saying; misery loves company. People want to put a yoke on the necks of others that they can't carry themselves. Why on earth would anyone consider returning to that which Christ has redeemed us from? In the face of so many Scriptures, why would anyone consider following the want-to-be law keepers? What if they are wrong? You can't serve two masters: the law and Christ.

Of course, as Christians, we submit ourselves to the law of Christ, acknowledging that God did not change his mind about sin and that grace is not a license to sin. It is ludicrous to imply such foolishness and demonstrates one's lack of understanding sound doctrine. Apostle Paul responds:

- "What then? shall we sin, because we are not under the law, but under grace? **God forbid.**" (**Romans 6:15**)

- "For **if we sin wilfully after that we have received the knowledge of the truth**, there remaineth no more sacrifice for sins, 27 But a certain fearful looking for of judgment and fiery indignation, which shall devour the adversaries. 28 He that despised Moses' law died without mercy under two or three witnesses: 29 **Of how much sorer punishment, suppose ye, shall he be thought worthy, who hath trodden under foot the Son of God**, and hath counted the blood of the covenant, wherewith he was sanctified, an unholy thing, and hath done despite unto the Spirit of grace? 30 For we know him that hath said, Vengeance belongeth unto me, I will recompense, saith the Lord. And again, The Lord shall judge his people. 31 **It is a fearful thing to fall into the hands of the living God**." **(Hebrews 10:26-31.**"

The Law:

	The Old Covenant. 10 Commandments. (Done away, nailed to the cross)	The New Covenant. The Law of Christ.
1	No other gods beside me.	Brought forward into New Covenant (**I Thess. 1:9**).'Ye turned to God from idols to **serve** the living & true God
2	No graven images.	Brought forward into New Covenant (**Galatians 5:20**). 'works of the flesh . . . idolatry.'
3	Don't take God's name in vain.	Brought forward into New Covenant (**I Timothy 1:20**). 'That they may learn not to blaspheme.'
4	Six days shall you work, but the 7th day is the Sabbath.	**Still nailed to the cross (Colossians 2:14-17). Never brought forward. No NT command to keep Sabbath. We rest in Jesus Christ.**
5	Honor your father and mother.	Brought forward into New Covenant (**Ephesians 6:1-3**). 'Honour thy father and mother.'
6	Don't kill.	Brought forward into New Covenant. (**Galatians 5:21**). 'Works of flesh . . . murders.'
7	Don't commit adultery.	Brought forward into New Covenant. (**Galatians 5:19**). 'works of the flesh . . . adultery.'
8	Don't steal.	Brought forward into New Covenant. (**Ephesians 4:28**). 'Let him that stole steal no more, let him work to **give.'**
9	Don't bear false witness.	Brought forward into New Covenant. (**Ephesian 4:25**). 'Putting away lying, speak every man the **truth.**'
10	Don't covet.	Brought forward into New Covenant. (**Ephesians 5:5**). 'Nor covetous man who is an idolater.'

In Summary, "The Ten Commandments were essentially **a summary of the entire Old Testament law**. Nine of the Ten

Commandments are clearly repeated in the New Testament (all except the command to observe the Sabbath day). Obviously, if we are loving God, we will not be worshipping false gods or bowing down before idols. If we love our neighbors, we will not be murdering them, lying to them, committing adultery against them, or coveting what belongs to them. The purpose of the Old Testament law is to convict people of our inability to keep the law and point us to our need for Jesus Christ as Savior (Romans 7:7-9; Galatians 3:24) The Old Testament law was never intended by God to be the universal law for all people for all eternity." [161]

DID THE APOSTLES KEEP THE LAW?

ISUPK BHI camp YouTube video titled "Christ, His Disciples, and Paul All Taught That We Should Keep The Law, Christians are liers - ISUPK.." [162]

The **BHI** adherent speaks much about lacing up in your black (ISUPK colors). He reads Romans 6:1

> "What shall we say then? Shall we continue in sin, that grace may abound?" **Romans 6:1 (KJV)**

The so-called **Hebrew Israelite** says **grace is a time period to allow them a chance (opportunity) to get themselves (things) in order**; their people (nation) back in order according to the law. He reads:

"For if we have been planted together **in the likeness of his death**, we shall be also in the likeness of his resurrection:" **Romans 6:5 (KJV)**

He says that in the likeness of His death means our King sacrifice for us to come back to these laws, statues. And commandments; and to uphold these principles and to come together as a nation. He says just switch-on your TV, and you will see that some white man has put some black person to death because we are not upholding these Law, statues, and commandments. Through much rambling on (and off the

---
[161] https://www.gotquestions.org/Crihstian-law.html (May 15, 2017)
[162] https://www.youtube.com/watch?v=-T-iJNKG5R0 (June 6, 2019)

video topic), he says the black Christian Church must be destroyed.

Rebuttal:

Paul kept the Mosaic Law (The Covenant), and Paul Himself tells us why he did it; He did it for the purpose of evangelizing the Jews; while he was teaching the Gentile Church the **gospel of the New Covenant.**

> "For though **I am free** from all men, **I have made myself a servant to all**, that I might win the more; 20
> - and to the Jews **I became as a Jew**, that I might **win Jews**;
>   - to those who are **under the law**, as **under the law**, that I might **win those who are under the law**; 21
> - to those who are **without law**, as **without law** (not being without law toward God, but under law toward Christ), that I might **win those who are without law**; 22
> - to the weak **I became as weak**, that I might **win the weak**.
> - I have **become all things to all men**, that I might **by all means save some**. 23
>
> Now **this I do for the gospel's sake**, that I may be partaker of it with you." **1 Corinthians 9:19-23 (NKJV)**

However, **Paul did not teach the Gentile Church (Jews and Gentiles) to keep the Law.** Concerning the Law he taught the Gentile Church (Jews and Gentiles):

- **Romans 6:14** says Christians, "you **are not under the Law.**"
- **Romans 7:6** says Christians, "we are **released (delivered) from the Law.**"
- **Romans 10:4** says Christians, "**Christ is the end of the Law.**"
- **Ephesians 2:15** the word for "**abolishing**" is used elsewhere by Paul when discussing the Law being "**set aside**" (e.g. 2 Corinthians 3:7; Romans 7:2, 6).

- **John 1:17** says Christians,
    - "**the law was given through Moses**;
    - **grace and truth came through Jesus Christ**."

The **grace** was in **contrast** to the condemnation of **the law**, the **truth** was the exact opposite to the shadowy outline of the types and ceremonies.

"**The law** and **the prophets** were **until John**.
- Since that time **the kingdom of God has been preached, and everyone is pressing into it**. Luke 16:16 (NKJV)

"Then spake Jesus to the multitude, and to his disciples, Saying,
- The **scribes** and the **Pharisees** sit in **Moses' seat:**
- All therefore whatsoever they bid you observe, that **observe** and **do**;

but do not ye after their works: for **they say, and do not**. For they bind heavy burdens and grievous to be borne, and lay them on men's shoulders; but they themselves will not move them with one of their fingers." **Matthew 23:1-4 KJV**

Today (and after 70A.D.), There are no longer any Scribes and Pharisees who sit on the seat of Moses to obey. This commandment was given before the cross; It cannot and is not to be kept today. [163] [164] [165]

Also, The disciples "did not do (obey) as they (*Scribes, Pharisees, and Priests*) said," while the pharisees were still around and in Moses' seat.

Saying, Did not we straitly command you that **ye should not teach in this name?** and,
- behold, ye have filled Jerusalem **with your doctrine**,
- and **intend to bring this man's blood upon us**.

Then Peter and the other apostles answered and said, **We ought to obey God rather than men. Acts 5:28-29 KJV**

---

[163] https://bible.org/seriespage/7-scribes (June 5, 2019)
[164] Antiquities of the Jews, Book 13, Chapter 10
[165] https://en.wikipedia.org/wiki/Pharisees (June 5, 2019)

Did The Apostles Keep The Law?

"And to him they agreed: and when they had called the apostles unto them, **they beat them** and **charged them not to speak in the name of Jesus**, and let them go. 41 They therefore departed from the presence of the council,
- rejoicing that they **were counted worthy to suffer dishonor for the Name**. 42
- And every day,
    - in **the temple**
    - and **at home**,
- they ceased **not**
    - **to teach** and
    - **to preach**

Jesus as the Christ." **Acts 5:40-42 (ASV)**

Notice, that nothing is said about the apostles preaching and teaching "**The Law**" or "**The Law** plus **Jesus Christ**" as the so-called **Hebrew Israelites** would have us to believe.

In fact, it was the now "*believing in Christ*" Pharisees who tried to promote "**The Mosiac Law** plus **Jesus Christ**" in order for a person to be saved. (**Acts 15:1-4 KJV**)

"But there rose up certain of **the sect of the Pharisees which believed**, saying,
- That it was needful **to circumcise them**,
- and **to command them to keep the law of Moses**." **Acts 15:5 (KJV)**

The apostles and elders (Jews) came to gather to consider the matter and that there should be no difference between the **Jews and Gentiles** when it came to purifying their hearts by faith. (**15:6-9**)

"Now therefore why tempt ye God, **to put a yoke upon the neck of the disciples**, which neither **our fathers nor we were able to bear**? 11 But we believe that through the grace of the Lord Jesus Christ **we shall be saved, even as they**." **Acts 15:10-11 (KJV)**

James after his deliberation says

Did The Apostles Keep The Law?

"Wherefore my judgment is, that **we trouble not them that from among the Gentiles turn to God**; 20 but that we write unto them,
- that they abstain from the pollutions of idols,
- and from fornication,
- and from what is strangled, and from blood." **Acts 15:19-20 (ASV)**

Then the apostles (**Jews**) and elders (**Jews**) wrote letters to their brothers in Christ who are Gentiles:
"Forasmuch as we have heard that certain who went out from us
- have **troubled you** with words,
- **subverting your souls**;
- to whom **we gave no commandment**;

25 it seemed good unto us, having come **to one accord**, to choose out men and send them unto you with our beloved Barnabas and Paul, 26 men that have hazarded their lives for the name of our Lord Jesus Christ. 27 We have sent therefore Judas and Silas, who themselves also shall tell you the same things by word of mouth. 28 **For it seemed good to the Holy Spirit, and to us, to lay upon you no greater burden than these necessary things**: 29
- that ye abstain from things sacrificed to idols,
- and from blood, and from things strangled,
- and from fornication;

from which if ye keep yourselves, **it shall be well with you**. Fare ye well." **Acts 15:24-29 (ASV)**

Aren't these passages included in the KJV 1611 Bible with the Apocrypha which the so-called **Hebrew Israelites** love to swear (literarily) over? Or do they even care? Or is it that they are blinded by their traditional "precept" method of understanding the Bible as passed down to them from Abba Bivens who is dead and rotting in a grave.

DID JESUS KEEP THE MOSIAC LAW?

ISUPK BHI camp in a YouTube video titled, " Christ said Keep The Law - ISUPK"[166]

IUIC BHI camp in a YouTube video titled, "15 Minutes With The Captains: Did Christ Keep The Law?"[167] [168]

The **BHI** adherent starts out by reading **Matthew 9:20 (KJV)** to pull out "and touched **the hem of his garmen**t:"

- He goes to the Zondervan Compact Dictionary to look up "**Hem of a Garment**" It is defined as "fringes or tassels on the border of the Jewish outer garment."
- He then reads **Mark 6:56** to pull out "might touch if it were but **the border of his garment**:

BHI asked, why would Jesus have borders on His Garments? Reading the Numbers passage (he *asks and answers himself*) is Jesus an Israelite from the Tribe of Judah:

> "Speak unto the **children of Israel**, and **bid them that they make them fringes in the borders of their garments** throughout their generations, and that **they put upon the fringe of the borders a ribband of blue**:" Numbers 15:38 (KJV)

What are the Christians talking about that the Law was done away with when Jesus came on the scene? **BHI** then reads:

Mark 14:12,13-18 and **Luke 22:1** to point out that **the feast of the unleavened bread** and **the Passover** are the same things. And that Jesus and His disciples kept them. Meaning Jesus Christ kept the feast of the unleavened bread.

BHI has **Leviticus 23:5** read to point out that he is reading from the Law about the Passover, and we are to keep the Passover on the fourteenth day of the first month, and you also read it in the New Testament by Our Lord and Savior Jesus Christ doing the exact same thing.

---

[166] https://www.youtube.com/watch?v=zS7eBoa5Y4A (June 5, 2019)
[167] https://www.youtube.com/watch?v=fLy7hvoESQo (June 5, 2019)
[168] https://www.youtube.com/watch?v=rwJ1mYHFN24 (June 5, 2019)

Did Jesus Keep The Mosiac Law?

The so-called **Hebrew Israelite** reads John 7:1 and says the Jews sought to kill Jesus because He spoke openly of the Law and put them to shame. Verse 7:2 he says the Jew's feast of Tabernacle, which was a Law of God was at hand.

Eisegeting the text (vv. 7:10-16), the **BHI** adherent goes through great pain to point out that although Jesus life was in great danger, and He could have been killed at any moment, yet **He still made a way to keep the feast** meaning that **He still "kept the Law" no matter what the circumstance could be**. He drops to v.37 and says He didn't just keep one day of the feast of the Tabernacle, but He kept all of the days of it.

He ignores what Jesus said in v7:37 "....**If any man thirst, let him come unto me, and drink**." And jumps to Leviticus 23:34. His focus is **Law keeping of the feast of tabernacles**. He says we see that Christ kept all seven days.

Perhaps the so-called **Hebrew Israelite** don't understand that we (Christians) understand that Christ was born under the Law, under Jewish Culture, and came to a Jewish people (first). If anything, the so-called Hebrew Israelite is proving our assertion (based on Scripture) that Christ fulfilled the Law in all points.

BHI reads:
>**Deuteronomy 32:4 (KJV)** "**He is the Rock**, his work is perfect: for all his ways are judgment: **a God of truth** and **without iniquity**, just and right is he."

The **BHI** believer points out that the verse says "**the Rock**" here (Deut 32:4) **is without sin**. But strangely, he does not comment on the fact that it also says, He is "a **God of Truth**."

Then **BHI** reads:
>**1 Corinthians 10:4 (KJV)** And did all drink the same spiritual drink: for they drank of that spiritual Rock that followed them: and **that Rock was Christ**.

The **BHI** adherent says this shows "**the Rock**" in (1 Cor. 10:4) kept the commandments and the Law. But **BHI** says nothing about Him being a "**God of Truth**," as stated in Deut. 32:4.

Did Jesus Keep The Mosiac Law?

Finally, **BHI** closes on **John 5:30** where Jesus said He came to do the will of the Father, and **BHI** says according to Psalm 40:8 is to keep His commandments.

Rebuttal:
I believe that posing the question of whether *Jesus kept the Mosiac Law or Not*, demands a negating question: Was the **Mosiac Law** made for Jesus? The Bible answers that with an absolute **No**!

The Law was not made for Jesus! It was made for all men: all who are born with the nature of sin.

> **"knowing this: that the law is not made for a righteous person**, but for the lawless and insubordinate, for the ungodly and for sinners, for the unholy and profane, for murderers of fathers and murderers of mothers, for manslayers,..." **1 Timothy 1:9 (NKJV)**

Was Jesus born under the Law? The Bible answers that with an absolute **Yes,** and tells us why!

> "But when the fullness of the time had come, God sent forth His Son, born of a woman, **born under the law**, 5 **to redeem those who were under the law**, that we might receive the adoption as sons." **Galatians 4:4-5 (NKJV)**

Jesus did not become the righteousness of the law; He was the righteousness of the Law.

Breaking the Mosiac Law would have been a sin, and Scripture repeatedly affirms that Jesus was sinless (**2 Corinthians 5:21, 1 Peter 2:22, Hebrews 4:15**). Apostle James says:

> "For whoever shall keep the whole law, and **yet stumble in one point, he is guilty of all**. "James 2:10 (NKJV)"

The question for the so-called **Hebrew Israelites** is this; "at point of the law did Jesus stumble?" If the answer is **none**, then He **fulfilled** the Law (Matthew 5:17). If you name one, then you have claimed that He is a sinner.

Did Jesus Keep The Mosiac Law?

Jesus didn't actually break an Old Testament command. He violated the interpretations religious leaders had developed around the biblical commands of keeping the Sabbath day holy (**Luke 23:2**).

BHI says that Jesus instructed the Jews to keep the Mosaic Law (**Matthew 19:16-22**). But a close examination of this demonstrates the opposed.

> 'So He said to him, "Why do you call Me good? No one is good but One, that is, God. But if you want to enter into life, **keep the commandments**."' Matthew 19:17 (NKJV)

While it can be said that the ten commandments were added among the Law, the reverse is not true.

Jesus gives the young man **at least four commandments** that was never given in **the Mosiac Law** nor listed among the **Ten Commandments**:

'Jesus said to him, "If you want to be perfect,
- **go,**
- **sell what you** have and
- **give to the poor**, and you will have treasure in heaven;
- and **come**,
- **follow Me**."'

Matthew 19:21 (NKJV)

Jesus never instructed people not to keep the Law, but He makes it clear that if you think you are going to enter the Kingdom of God **by keeping the Law** that a camel has a better chance than you (**Matthew 19:24-28**). Jesus taught the young man that if he wanted to be **perfect**, follow Him who the Law taught you about, "**ME**" (**John 15:5**). The solution is to follow Him whom God sent to redeem them born under the law.[169]

> "**for the law made nothing perfect**; on the other hand, there is the bringing in of a better hope, through which we draw near to God." **Hebrews 7:19 (NKJV)**

---

[169] https://factsandtrends.net/2018/07/13/did-jesus-break-the-law/ (June 5, 2019)

Did Jesus Keep The Mosiac Law?

"For what the law could not do in that **it was weak** through the flesh, God did by sending His own Son in the likeness of sinful flesh, on account of sin: He condemned sin in the flesh, 4 **that the righteous requirement of the law might be fulfilled in us who do not walk** according to the flesh but according to the Spirit." **Romans 8:3-4 (NKJV)**

The Law Had NO Dominion Over Jesus! Jesus did not Come to be a law keeper; By His very nature, He did that which was contained in the Law! His Holiness met the requirements of **The Law**!

"For I came down from heaven, not to do mine own will, **but the will of him that sent me**. 39
- And **this is the Father's will** which hath sent me, **that of all which he hath given me I should lose nothing**, but should raise it up again at the last day. 40
- And **this is the will of him that sent me**, that every one which seeth the Son, and believeth on him, may have everlasting life: and I will raise him up at the last day." **John 6:38-40 (KJV)**

"Yet I say to you that in this place there is **One greater than the temple**. 7 But if you had known what this means, I desire mercy and not sacrifice,' you would not have condemned the guiltless. 8 **For the Son of Man is Lord even of the Sabbath." Matthew 12:6-8 (NKJV)**

"12:8. Jesus completed this conversation with an authoritative claim: For the Son of Man is Lord of the Sabbath. This is the reason he had the right to determine what was appropriate and inappropriate on the Sabbath, as well as the right to offer covenant rest in 11:28–30. As author of the law, he had authority to clarify its correct application. Jesus used the title "Son of Man" for himself to claim the prophetic authority that accompanied this messianic title." [170]

"12:8 Then the Savior added, "For the Son of Man is Lord even of the Sabbath." It was He who had instituted the law in

---

[170] Weber, S. K. (2000). Matthew (Vol. 1, pp. 171–172). Nashville, TN: Broadman & Holman Publishers.

the first place, and therefore He was the One most qualified to interpret its true meaning."[171]

Jesus:
Change - New Covenant
Change In Priesthood
Change In The Law

"Now if perfection had been attainable through the Levitical priesthood **(for under it the people received the law)**, what further need would there have been for another priest to arise after the order of Melchizedek, rather than one named after the order of Aaron?" Hebrews 7:11 (ESV)

"For when
- there is **a change** in **the priesthood**,
- there is necessarily **a change** in **the law** as well.

13 For the one of whom these things are spoken belonged **to another tribe**, from which no one has ever served at the altar. **For it is evident that our Lord was descended from Judah**, and in connection with that tribe Moses said nothing about priests. **Hebrews 7:12-14 (ESV)**

"This becomes **even more evident** when another priest arises in the likeness of Melchizedek, 16 who has become a priest,
- not on the basis of **a legal requirement** concerning bodily descent,
- but by **the power of an indestructible life**.

17 For it is witnessed of him," **Hebrews 7:15 (ESV)**

"'**You are a priest forever**, after the order of Melchizedek." 18 For on the one hand, a former commandment is set aside because of its weakness and uselessness 19 (**for the law made nothing perfect**); but on the other hand, a better hope is introduced, through which we draw near to God."' **Hebrews 7:17-18 (ESV)**

---

[171] MacDonald, W. (1995). Believer's Bible Commentary: Old and New Testaments. (A. Farstad, Ed.) (p. 1247). Nashville: Thomas Nelson.

Jesus did, in fact, stress the importance of keeping the law but throughout his teachings and the emphasis of His differences with the Pharisees (self-defined keepers of the law) He also stressed that the purely legalistic keeping of the law could not replace the need to do good. But it was NOT the keeping of the law that would redeem them born under the Law, It was simply the schoolmaster that taught the need of a Savior. The Law and Grace (Jesus) could not both reign together. Jesus was on His way to the cross to take His rightful reign. One was being ushered in (Grace and Truth(Jesus)), and the other was being ushered out (Law):

"Tell me, you who desire to be under the law, do you not hear the law? 22 For it is written that Abraham had **two sons**: the one by **a bondwoman**, the other by **a freewoman**. 23 But

- he who was of the bondwoman was born according to the flesh,
- and he of the freewoman through promise,

24 **which things are symbolic**.

For these are the two covenants: the one from Mount Sinai which gives birth to bondage, which is Hagar— 25 for this Hagar is Mount Sinai in Arabia, and corresponds to Jerusalem which now is, and is in bondage with her children— 26 but the Jerusalem above is free, which is the mother of us all. 27 For it is written:...." **Galatians 4:21-27 (NKJV)**

"Now we, brethren, as Isaac was, are children of promise. 29 **But, as he who was born according to the flesh then persecuted him who was born according to the Spirit**, even so it is now. 30 Nevertheless what does the Scripture say? **"Cast out the bondwoman and her son**,
- for the son of the bondwoman shall not be heir with the son of the freewoman." 31
- So then, brethren, we are not children of the bondwoman **but of the free**." **Galatians 4:28-31 (NKJV)**

Did Jesus Keep The Mosiac Law?

Did Jesus Keep The Mosiac Law?

PROBLEM SEVEN

HEBREW ISRAELITES BLAME THE WOMEN FOR THE WOES OF THE FAMILY

ISUPK BHI camp YouTube video titled, "**The Christian Church Is Full of Dumb, Loud Mouth Black Women**."[172]

IUSPK on a corner Eisegeting Genesis chapter 3 says the woman knew she had commandments that her man, Adam, had taught her not to follow the customs of the other nations, and the teachings of other racists of people getting into their philosophies like Christianity, the philosophy of the white man. But the **BHI** adherent says the Serpent goes to your house and try to get that madness in your house. He says when she saw the tree was good for food, and she found out that she could rule and become a leader. She was entrapped because it was pleasant to her eyes. He says "*the knowledge*" in the church telling the women that they are wise. But she cannot teach the Bible; she can't teach anybody about God.

BHI adherent says **God got strict commandments in the Bible that forbids a woman from teaching the Bible. Reading Job 39:17, He says God has deprived her of wisdom.**

> **Rebuttal**: He has no clue this passage is talking about an Ostrich when reading in the context of the surrounding verses. The ostrich is a wonderful animal, a very large bird, but it never flies. Some have called it a winged camel. God here gives an account of it and observes.

BHI adherent proclaims that God did not give the Black, Hispanic, and Native American women any wisdom. God has **with-holden it** from them. He didn't get her the wisdom to understand these Scriptures.

God did not give the woman the wisdom to raise her household by herself and to raise her sons and daughters by herself. This is why brothers and sisters are becoming homosexuals because she doesn't have wisdom to control the

---

[172] https://www.youtube.com/watch?v=84BNf0e9PkE (May 20, 2019)

house. This is why we have two million black men in prison because the woman doesn't have wisdom to raise a family. Yelling, (*as he has the passage read again*) he says God has purposely taken and withheld wisdom and understanding of the Bible from Black, Hispanic, and Native American women.

BHI says our communities are being destroyed, our families are being destroyed because the Christian church and the white man has taught our black leaders to tell the Black, Hispanic, and Native American women that she can be a leader and that she knows God; Telling her woman thou art loosed, and she can do bad by herself. Now we have two million brothers in prison! Your woman is not suppose to be in any church learning from another man. Why are all these married Christian women in the church? Women, why are you going to another man that you are not sleeping with [married] to learn about God?

He says brothers do not let your Black, Hispanic, and Native American women go into the Christian church. Make sure she does not go to church. He has read **1 Corinthian 14:34-35**), where it says, "…women are to keep silent in the church."

You are supposed to have **your mouth shut** in the churches; he says they are not suppose to be teaching, reading the Bible, and desiring to be ministers and evangelists wanting to spread the gospel across the earth. When the woman doesn't follow her man, the children becomes bloods and crips (gangs); commit murders and two million of them end-up in prison. He says this is what happens when women are in charge.

1 Timothy 2:11-15. He says God charged the woman and punished her for it.

GMS in a Youtube video titled, "***The destruction of our race is because of the black women***"[173] They spew the same rhetoric about women.

It is enough to make one wonder what did their grandmothers, mothers, aunts, and sisters do to these men of color to make them hate women of color and even their own lives. On a

---

[173] https://www.youtube.com/watch?v=5_iQH_rSKNU **(May 23, 2019)**

street corner in public, the GMS adherent yells as he rants, nobody is paying any attention to her fat nappy headed black **A*&$**. He says we don't give a **S*&^%** about her. He points to a poster with Africa on it and says we don't subscribe to this. He says this is why you **N*&^%$** are getting shot in the streets. He says thanks to **the BLACK WOMAN**.

Hebrew Israelites Distorted View of Women

GMS BHI in a YouTube video titled, "**GMS Hebrew Israelites Say White Woman Look Better Than African American Woman**."[174]

GMS says white women are the devil, but **it is ok to have sex with them because they are spoils of war**. The GMS adherent says technically when the white man conquered he had the right to have his way with our women. She is just a piece of poontang, and there is no wrong in that according to the Scriptures. You have a right to her because that woman is spoil. So when we are talking about popping the white woman in technicality, we got it in the Scriptures. **He said, African women don't look good in books, but some of these white women be looking good**. In the future, if you get with some white **B*&%%^^**, and you just want to get your S*&^% off, that is where your mind should be because that is what she is a piece of meat. He says you are not supposed to be getting with a white woman, falling in love, marrying, and making a family with her; and all that. The white woman is the **G*%$ D%^&*(*** devil. The **GMS** reader reads:

> "**When you go out to war against your enemies**, and the Lord your God delivers them into your hand, and you take them captive, 11 **and you see among the captives a beautiful woman**, and desire **her and would take her for your wife**, 12 then you shall bring her home to your house, and she shall shave her head and trim her nails. 13 She shall put off the clothes of her captivity, remain in your house, and mourn her father and her mother a full month; **after that you may go in**

---
[174] https://www.youtube.com/watch?v=9t57wExdT-0 (May 23, 2019)

> to her and be her husband, and she shall be your wife." Deuteronomy 21:10-13 (NKJV)

The **GMS** Adherent says this does not mean your wife "wife", it means **concubine**, which means **your meat**. No other man is suppose to touch her. You have your fun with her and then just get rid of her. But you should not do this with Black, Hispanic, or native American women.

Rebuttal: God allowing something does not mean that God approved **(Matthew 19:8)**. The word **concubine**[175] is never used in relation to a Christian in The New Testament. Christians should be reminded that, just because God allowed a sin for a time, does not mean that God was pleased with it.

"Now concerning the things of which you wrote to me: It is good for a man not to touch a woman. 2 Nevertheless, because of sexual immorality, let each man have his own wife, and let each woman have her own husband" 1 Corinthians 7:1-2 (NKJV).

Former IUIC Member: Youtube inside view from a woman that used to be a member of IUIC **BHI** camp. Titled, *"#IUIC MEN HATE BLACK WOMEN - BIBLE USED TO ABUSE Black WOMEN - Black Hebrew Israelite"*:

"A short lesson on what IUIC thinks about Black women and how they influence their followers and those who watch their videos that Black women are the scum of the earth." By Gina Blue.

THE NATION OF ISRAEL IS NOT THE TRUE (ROOT OR VINE)!

ISRAEL IS NOT THE ROOT!

> "And if **some of the branches were broken off**,
> - and **you, being a wild olive tree**,
>   - ❖ were **grafted in among them**,
>   - ❖ and **with them**
>   - became **a partaker of the root**

---

[175] https://www.gotquestions.org/concubine-concubines.html (May 23, 2019)

The Nation Of Israel Is Not The True (Root or Vine)!

- and **fatness of the olive tree**," **Romans 11:17 (NKJV)**

"**do not boast against the branches**. But if you do boast, remember that
- you do not support **the root**,
- **but the root supports you**. Romans 11:18 (NKJV)

"You will say then, "**Branches were broken** off that **I might be grafted in**." Romans 11:19 (NKJV)

"You [*Gentiles*] will say then, "**Branches** [*Israel*] **were broken** off that I [*Gentiles*] might be **grafted in**."
20 Well said. Because of **unbelief they** [*Israel*] were **broken off**, and you [*Gentiles*] stand by faith. Do not be haughty, but fear." **Romans 11:19 (NKJV)**

"For if God did not spare the **natural branches** [*Israel*] , He may not spare you [*Gentiles*] either." **Romans 11:21 (NKJV)**

"And **they** [*Israel*] also, if **they** [*Israel*] do not continue in unbelief, will be grafted in, for God is able to graft **them** [*Israel*] in again." **Romans 11:23 (NKJV)**

CHRIST IS THE TRUE ROOT AND VINE:

"**I am the true vine**, and My Father is the vinedresser. 2 **Every branch in Me** that does not bear fruit He takes away, and every branch that bears fruit He prunes, that it may bear more fruit." **John 15:1 (NKJV)**

"Abide in Me, and I in you. **As the branch cannot bear fruit of itself**, **unless it abides in the vine**, neither can you, unless you abide in Me." **John 15:4 (NKJV)**

Christ is the root of that tree, and it is from His rich nature that all the freshness and fatness, all the quickening and energy, all the love and grace of the Hebrew Scriptures and heritage of promises are gained.

Revelation 5:5 (KJV) And one of the elders saith unto me, Weep not: behold, the Lion of the tribe of Juda, **the Root of**

David, hath prevailed to open the book, and to loose the seven seals thereof.

Revelation 22:16 (KJV) I Jesus have sent mine angel to testify unto you these things in the churches. **I am the root and the offspring of David and the bright and morning star.**

SO-CALLED HEBREW ISRAELITES IGNORANCE OF THE TRINITY CONCEPT

IUIC BHI YouTube video titled, **"The Israelites: Trinity Debunked and Love applied"** [176]

GMS BHI YouTube video titled, **"The Trinity is false."** [177]

In summary of the GMS adherent elaboration, he goes to **1 John 5:7**:

> "For there **are three that bear witness in heaven**: the Father, the Word, and the Holy Spirit; and **these three are one.**" 1 John 5:7 (NKJV)

GMS says this does not mean that they are all rolled up together (one God), but it means that they are **on one accord**. He then reads:

> "that they all may be one, as You, Father, are in Me, and I in You; **that they also may be one in Us**, that the world may believe that You sent Me. 22 And the glory which You gave Me I have given them, that **they may be one** just **as We are one**:" John 17:21-22 (NKJV)

GMS asked so does that mean that the elect is rolled up together (one God)? He says it means that they are on the same accord and in agreement with each other.

Sicarii BHI YouTube video titled, **Catholic "Apologist VS. Hebrew Israelites (Trinity Debunked)"** [178]

Sicarii adherent (out on the street) asked a man that was a Catholic if he was a trinitarian, to which the man replied he was. He then asked the man, so you believe that Jesus Christ is equal to the Father? **Sicarii** tells the man to be a **Trinity**

---

[176] https://www.youtube.com/watch?v=g--PqsplviE (June 2, 2019)
[177] https://www.youtube.com/watch?v=jsJKYheBsYM (June 2, 2019)
[178] https://www.youtube.com/watch?v=aZDx62pZPYY (June 2, 2019)

you have to be co-equal, and you have to be co-eternal. He says he is not talking about the hierarchy of position, but equal in power. **Sicarii** goes on to say to be God; you have to know all things. **Sicarii** then asks, did Jesus Christ know all things? He then asks was Jesus Christ Omniscient while He was on earth? **Sicarii** says the hypostatic union of Christ (two natures) sounds schizophrenic. He has **James 1:17** read saying he is not allowing the Catholic to get away from the fact that during the incarnation that Jesus was not omniscient.

> "Every good gift and every perfect gift is from above, and comes down from **the Father of lights, with whom there is no variation or shadow of turning.**" **James 1:17 (NKJV)**

Sicarii then asked what does variance mean? And replies it means that God does change. He asked if God took on Human nature does that mean He changed? He asked if you add humanity to your nature did your Nature Change? **Sicarii** is purposely carrying the man on a merry-go-round trip of which there will never be an answer that the subscriber to Hebrew Israelism will accept.

Rebuttal:
Jesus has two complete natures—one fully human and one fully divine. What the doctrine of the **hypostatic union** teaches is that these two natures are united in one person in the God-man. Jesus is not two persons. He is one person. **The hypostatic union is the joining of the divine and the human in the one person of Jesus**.

'Scripture, while making it "perfectly evident that only one person is intended,"[1] makes some statements that seem to apply specifically to **one nature** or **the other**. For instance,
- **Romans 1:3-4** says Jesus "was descended from David according to the flesh and was declared to be the Son of God in power according to the Spirit of holiness." Similarly,
- Philippians 2:6-8 says He "was in the form of God" and also was "found in human form." Someone might be tempted to ask, "Which is it? Was Jesus in the form of God or in human form? Was He descended from David

or the Son of God?" But the doctrine of His two natures in one person allows us to respond, "It's both.'" [179]

According to Wayne Grudem, "
- On the one hand, with respect to his **human nature**, he had limited knowledge (**Mark 13: 32; Luke 2: 52**).
- On the other hand, Jesus clearly knew all things (**John 2: 25; 16: 30; 21: 17**).

Now, this is only understandable if Jesus learned things and had limited knowledge with respect to his human nature but was always omniscient with respect to his divine nature, and therefore he was able any time to "call to mind" whatever information would be needed for his ministry.

In this way we can understand Jesus' statement concerning the time of his return: "But of that day or that hour no one knows, not even the angels in heaven, nor the Son, but only the Father" (Mark 13: 32). **This ignorance of the time of his return was true of Jesus' human nature and human consciousness only**, for in his divine nature he was certainly omniscient and certainly knew the time when he would return to the earth." [180]

Strangely, **GMS** has no problem with Jesus referring to His Father ("**My Father**")" as "**My God**" (**John 20:17**), . But GMS rejects what **the Father calls His Son "O GOD"** (**Hebrews 1:8**).

> "Jesus said to her, "Do not cling to Me, for I have not yet ascended to **My Father**; but go to My brethren and say to them, I am ascending to My Father and your Father, and to **My God** and your God.' " **John 20:17 (NKJV)**

> "**But to the Son He says**: "Your throne, **O God, is forever and ever**; A scepter of righteousness is the scepter of Your kingdom." **Hebrews 1:8 (NKJV)**

---

[179] https://biblemesh.com/blog/was-jesus-omniscient-during-his-earthly-life/#_edn2 (June 2, 2019)
[180] Grudem, Wayne A.. Systematic Theology: An Introduction to Biblical Doctrine (Cómo Entender) (p. 561). Zondervan. Kindle Edition.

THE CHART FOR TRINITY THOUGHT:

	FATHER	SON	HOLY SPIRIT
Called God	Phil. 1:2	John 1:1, 14, Col. 2:9	Acts 5:3-4
Creator	Isaiah 64:8	John 1:3, Col. 1:15-17	Job 33:4, 26:13
Resurrects	1 Thess. 1:10	John 2:19, 10:17	Rom. 8:11
Indwells	2 Cor. 6:16	Col. 1:27	John 14:17
Everywhere	1 Kings 8:27	Matt. 28:20	Psalm 139:7-10
All-knowing	1 John 3:20	John 16:30, 21:17	1 Cor. 2:10-11
Sanctifies	1 Thess. 5:23	Heb. 2:11	1 Pet. 1:2
Life-giver	Gen. 2:7, John 5:21	John 1:3, 5:21	2 Cor. 3:6, 8
Fellowship	1 John 1:3	1 Cor. 1:9	2 Cor. 13:14, Phil. 2:1
Eternal	Psalm 90:2	Micah 5:1-2	Rom. 8:11, Heb. 9:14
A Will	Luke 22:42	Luke 22:42	1 Cor. 12:11
Speaks	Matt. 3:17, Luke 9:25	Luke 5:20, 7:48	Acts 8:29, 11:12, 13:2
Love	John 3:16	Eph. 5:25	Rom. 15:30
Searches the heart	Jer. 17:10	Rev. 2:23	1 Cor. 2:10
We belong to	John 17:9	John 17:6	. . .
Savior	1 Tim. 1:1, 2:3, 4:10	2 Tim. 1:10, Titus 1:4, 3:6	. . .
We serve	Matt. 4:10	Col. 3:24	. . .
Believe in	John 14:1	John 14:1	. . .
Gives joy	. . .	John 15:11	John 14:7
Judges	John 8:50	John 5:22, 30	. . .

SCRIPTURE EVIDENCE FOR TRINITY DOCTRINE:

A. **There is only One God (Deuteronomy 6:4).**
For There are three that bear witness record in heaven, the Father, the Word (Son (**John 1:1, 14**)), and the Holy Ghost: and these three are one. (**1 John 5:7**)

B. **Three Persons Are Called God**
1. **The Father is God**
   (**Romans 1:7; Galatians 1:1; Matthew 6:9**).
2. **The Son is God**
   (**Isaiah 9:6; Psalms 110:1; Hebrews 1:8; Zech. 12:10; John 8:58, Mark 2:5-7; John 5:23; Colossians 2:9; Titus 2:13**)
3. **The Holy Spirit is God**
   a. He has the names of God (God: **1 Corinthians 3:16;** Lord: **2 Corinthians 3:17**)
   b. He has the attributes of God (**eternal: Hebrews 9:14; Omnipresence: Psalms 139:7; Omniscience: 1 Corinthian 2:11; Holiness: Ephesians 4:30**)
   c. He performs the acts of God (**creating: Genesis 1:2; Psalms 104:30;** redeeming: **Ephesians 4:30;** doing miracles: **Hebrews 2:4;** giving supernatural gifts: **1 Corinthians 12:4-11**)
   d. He is associated with God in benedictions (**2 Corinthians 13:14**)
   e. He is associated with God in prayers (**Jude 1:20**).
   f. He has all the glory of God (**2 Corinthians 3:18**).
   g. He can be lied to (**Acts 5:3-4**)
   h. He can be grieved (**Ephesians 4:30**)
   i. He speaks (**Acts 13:2; 21:11**)
   j. He comforts (**John 14:26**)
   k. He bears witness (**Romans 8:16**)
   l. He hears (**John 16:13**)
   m. He makes intercession for us (**Romans 8:26**)

C. **All Three are Distinct Persons**

Person = one with **a mind**, **will**, and **feeling** (He can think, choose, and feel).
  1. **The Father is a Person**
     a. He has a mind (**Matthew 6:32**).
     b. He can choose (**Matthew 6:9-10**).
     c. He can feel (**Genesis 6:6**).
  2. **The Son is a Person**
     a. He has a mind (**John 2:25**).
     b. He can choose (**John 10:18**).
     c. He can feel (**John 11:35**).
  3. **The Holy Spirit is a Person**
     a. He has a mind (**John 14:26**).
     b. He can choose (**1 Corinthians 12:11**).
     c. He can feel (**Ephesians 4:30**).
D. Hence, there are three distinct Persons in one God = The Trinity.

TRINITY ACTING IN UNITY[181]

1. **In Creation:**
   a. **The Father**: God the Father spoke (**Genesis 1:3**).
   b. **The Son** was the Word, (**John 1:1**); all things made through Him, (**John 1:3**).
   c. **The Holy Spirit**: God the Holy Spirit moved (**Genesis 1:2. Job 26:12-13**).
2. **In the Incarnation**:
   a. **Father** gave His only Son (**John 3:16**).
   b. **Son** born into the world (**Luke 2:11**).
   c. **Holy Spirit** caused conception (**Luke 1:35**).
3. **In Redemption:**
   a. **The Father** accepted the sacrifice of Calvary (**Hebrews 9:14**).
   b. **The Son** offered Himself as the sacrifice (**Hebrews 9:14**).
   c. **The Holy Spirit:** Jesus offered Himself through the Holy Spirit (**Hebrews 9:14**).
4. **In Salvation**:
   a. **The Father** receives the prodigal (**Luke 15:22**).
   b. **The Son** seeks the lost sheep (**Luke 15:4; Luke 19:10**).

---

[181] Ultimate Cross Reference Treasury by Jerome Smith (2016): E-Sword Electronic Software

c. **The Holy Spirit** seals the new convert (**Ephesians 1:13**).
5. **In Communion:**
   a. **The Father** invites us to come to Him for fellowship (**Ephesians 2:18**).
   b. **The Son** is the reconciliation, (**2 Corinthians 5:19**).
   c. **The Holy Spirit** effects union and communion (**Ephesians 2:18**).
6. **In Prayer:**
   a. **The Father** receives our requests (**John 16:23**).
   b. **The Son** is the One in whose Name we pray, (**John 16:23**).
   c. **The Holy Spirit** directs us in our requests (**Romans 8:26**).
7. **In Glory:**
   a. **The Father** ultimately receives the millennial kingdom (**1Corinthains 15:24**).
   b. **The Son** changes our body to be like His (**Philippians 3:21**).
   c. **The Holy Spirit** gives the invitation (**Revelation 22:17**).
8. **In Regeneration:**
   a. **The Father** records the new name in glory (**Luke 10:20**).
   b. **The Son** cleanses sin in His blood (**Ephesians 1:7**).
   c. **The Holy Spirit** performs the miracle of the new birth (**John 3:3-8**).
9. **In the Resurrection of Christ:**
   a. **The Father**: God raised up Jesus (**Acts 2:32**).
   b. **The Son**: Jesus said He raised **Himself from the dead**, (**John 2:19; John 10:18**).
   c. The **Holy Spirit** raised Jesus from the dead, (**Romans 8:11; 1 Peter 3:18**).

PLURALITY SCRIPTURES:

1. **Isaiah 44:6 (the Lord the King of Israel** and **his Redeemer** the Lord of hosts; I am the first and I am the last, and **besides me there is no God**).
2. **Isaiah 6:8** Also I heard the **voice of the Lord**, saying, Whom shall I send, and **who will go for us**? Then said I, Here am I; send me.
3. **Psalm 45:6 Thy throne, O God**, is for ever and ever: the sceptre of thy kingdom is a right sceptre. **Psalm 45:7** Thou lovest righteousness, and hatest wickedness: **therefore God, thy God**, hath anointed thee with the oil of gladness **above thy fellows**.
4. **Matthew 28:19** Go ye therefore, and teach all nations, baptizing them **in the name of the Father, and of the Son, and of the Holy Ghost**:
5. **Matthew 3:16** And **Jesus,** when he was baptized, went up straightway out of the water: and, lo, the heavens were opened unto him, and he saw **the Spirit of God descending like a dove**, and lighting upon him: 17And lo **a voice from heaven, saying, This is my beloved Son**, in whom I am well pleased.
6. **2 Corinthians 13:14** The grace of **the Lord Jesus Christ,** and **the love of God,** and **the communion of the Holy Ghos**t, be with you all. Amen.
7. **Genesis 1:26** And God said, **Let us** make man in our image, after **our likeness**: and let them have dominion over the fish of the sea, and over the fowl of the air, and over the cattle, and over all the earth, and over every creeping thing that creepeth upon the earth.
8. **Genesis 3:22** And the LORD God said, Behold, the man is become as **one of us**, to know good and evil: and now, lest he put forth his hand, and take also of the tree of life, and eat, and live for ever:
9. **Genesis 11:7** Go to, **let us** go down, and there confound their language, that they may not understand one another's speech. 8 So the LORD scattered them abroad from thence upon the face of all the earth: and they left off to build the city.

10. **John 14:23** Jesus answered and said unto him, If a man love me, he will keep my words: and my Father will love him, and **we will come** unto him, and make **our abode with him.**
11. **1 Corinthians 12:** 4 Now there are diversities of gifts, but the same Spirit. ⁵And there are differences of administrations, but the same Lord.⁶And there are diversities of operations**, but it is the same God which worketh all in all**.
12. **Isaiah 42:8** I am the LORD: that is my name: and **my glory will I not give to another**, neither my praise to graven images.
13. **Isaiah 48:16** Come ye near unto me, hear ye this; I have not spoken in secret from the beginning; from the time that it was, **there am I**: and now **the Lord GOD**, and **his Spirit**, hath sent me.
14. **John 15:26** But when **the Comforter** is come, whom **I will** send unto you from **the Father**, even the Spirit of truth, which proceedeth from the Father, he shall testify of me:
15. **John 14:16** And **I will** pray **the Father**, and he shall give you **another Comforter**, that he may abide with you for ever;

PROBLEM EIGHT

THE SABBATH AND SUNDAY

IUIC BHI YouTube videos Sabbath vs. Sunday: [182]
- Titled, "**The Israelites: Is Sunday The Day of Worship?**" [183]
- Titled, "**The Israelites: Sunday Church Worship**" [184]
- Titled, "**The Israelites: Truth Be Told DC: Sunday Sabbath Deception.**" [185]

ISUPK BHI YouTube videos Sabbath vs. Sunday:
- Titled, "**The Sabbath is The 7th Day After Working 6, but Christians say Its Sunday – ISUPK Kentucky.**"

GOCC BHI YouTube videos Sabbath vs. Sunday:
- Titled, "**Christians Lies About The Day of The Sabbath. (1 of 6)**" [186]

DID CONSTANTINE CHANGE THE SABBATH TO SUNDAY?

Answer: **No!** In the year 321 A.D., **Constantine decreed**, "On the venerable day of the Sun
- let the magistrates and people residing in cities rest,
- and let all workshops be closed." [187]

Constantine Did Not change the Sabbath; he merely made Sunday the official day of rest for the Roman Empire.

There Is No Evidence that his motivation was born out of hatred for the Jews but out of a desire to adopt what the Christians had practiced for nearly two and a half centuries.

SCRIPTURE DETERMINED THE LORD'S DAY NOT CONSTANTINE

---

[182] https://www.youtube.com/playlist?list=PL-djiOgtDTUWYl9pj60IRkm0-qA5Cvtya
[183] https://www.youtube.com/watch?v=_A2LZe3_3U8 (June 2, 2019)
[184] https://www.youtube.com/watch?v=-IrHyeopAZk (June 2, 2019)
[185] https://www.youtube.com/watch?v=-w75HnQaNAc (June 2, 2019)
[186] https://www.youtube.com/watch?v=CjL8PkCC940&list=PLjBS9YYwPucNRVrPi6UDk5L8WwOub4ePO (June 2, 2019)
[187] (Codex Justinianus lib. 3, tit. 12, 3; trans. in Philip Schaff, History of the Christian Church, Vol. 3, p. 380, note 1).

Did Constantine Change the Sabbath to Sunday?

It is well documented that the early church adopted Sunday as their day of worship.

> "**The first day of the week** *cometh Mary Magdalene early, when it was yet dark, unto the sepulchre, and seeth the stone taken away from the sepulchre.*" **John 20:1 (KJV)**

> "*Then the same day at evening,* **being the first day of the week**, *when the doors were shut where the disciples were assembled for fear of the Jews, came Jesus and stood in the midst, and saith unto them, Peace be unto you.*" **John 20:19 (KJV)**

> "*And upon* **the first day of the week**, *when the disciples came together to break bread, Paul preached unto them, ready to depart on the morrow; and continued his speech until midnight.*" **Acts 20:7 (KJV)**

> "**On the first day of the week** *let each one of you lay something aside, storing up as he may prosper, that there be no collections when I come.*" **1 Corinthians 16:2 (NKJV)**

> "*having wiped out the handwriting of requirements that was against us, which was contrary to us. And He has taken it out of the way, having nailed it to the cross. 15 Having disarmed principalities and powers, He made a public spectacle of them, triumphing over them in it. 16* **So let no one judge you in food or in drink, or regarding a festival or a new moon or sabbaths**, *17 which are a shadow of things to come, but the substance is of Christ.*" **Colossians 2:14 (NKJV)**

> "**One person esteems one day above another; another esteems every day alike. Let each be fully convinced in his own mind.** *6* **He who observes the day, observes it to the Lord**; *and he who does not observe the day, to the Lord he does not observe it. He who eats, eats to the Lord, for he gives God thanks; and he who does not eat, to the Lord he does not eat, and gives God thanks.*" **Romans 14:5 (NKJV)**

BEFORE CONSTANTINE – THE CHURCH - SABBATH OR SUNDAY

The Quartodeciman controversy arose because Christians in the churches of Jerusalem and Asia Minor celebrated Passover on the 14th of the first month (Aviv), while the churches in and around Rome changed to the practice of celebrating Easter on the following Sunday calling it "the day of the resurrection of our Saviour" (The Lord's Day). The difference was turned into an ecclesiastical controversy when synods of bishops which held to Apostolic tradition condemned the practice.

> Synods and assemblies of bishops were held on this account, and all, with one consent, through mutual correspondence drew up an ecclesiastical decree, that the mystery of the resurrection of the Lord should be celebrated on no other but the Lord's day, and that we should observe the close of the paschal fast on this day only. [188]

The earliest reference we have to the Lord's day, besides the comment made in the Book of Revelation (1:10), is in the letter to the Magnesians written by **Ignatius of Antioch in A.D. 110:**

> If those who have been brought up in the ancient order of things [i.e., converted Jews] have come to the possession of new hope, **no longer observing the Sabbath but living in observance of the Lord's day**, on which also our life has sprung up again by him and his death …

The Lord's day is the day on which "our life has sprung up again by him." In other words, **it is the day of Jesus' resurrection, the first day of the week.**

> Saint Justin Martyr (110-165):
> "And on the day called **Sunday,** all who live in cities or in the country gather together in one place, and **the memoirs of the apostles or the writings of the prophets are read** …" [further description of the Sunday meeting is given here]. **(First Apology 67)** [189]

---
[188] Eusebius. History of the Church (p. 250). Acheron Press. Kindle Edition.
[189] http://www.logoslibrary.org/justin/apology1/67.html

AFTER THE CROSS, CHRISTIANS – FOLLOWERS OF JESUS CHRIST

"having abolished in His flesh the enmity, that is, the law of commandments contained in ordinances,
- ➤ so as to **create** in **Himself**
  - **one** new man
  - from **the two,**

thus making peace," **Ephesians 2:15 (NKJV)**

PROBLEM NINE

WHO ARE THE GENTILES?

SO-CALLED HEBREW ISRAELITES BELIEF ABOUT THE GENTILES

According to many so-called **Hebrew Israelites, the word gentile**[190] is not used in reference to non-Israelite nations in the Bible. They contend, it refers to non-believing Israelites or Israelites that had been disbursed among other nations.

- **Hebrew Israelites** teach that when Jesus gives the great commission to his apostles in **Matthew 28:19 "Go ye therefore, and teach all nations……….."** (KJV), He was sending them out to where the Jews had been scattered among the nations, using **James 1:1** "………… **to the twelve tribes which are scattered abroad**, ….." (KJV).
- While they do acknowledge that gentile means a non-believer, they say it also means an Israelite who has been carried away into the philosophy of the world:
  John 7:35, "**Then said the Jews among themselves**, Whither will he go, that we shall not find him? **will he go unto the dispersed among the Gentiles**, and teach the Gentiles? (KJV)
- They teach that Israelites had become gentiles by serving others gods of Christianity, Islam, etc. and because of that God had scattered them, Quoting from **Deuteronomy 28:64** "And **the Lord shall scatter thee among all people, from the one end of the earth even unto the other; and there thou shalt serve other gods, which neither thou nor thy fathers have known**, even wood and stone." (KJV)
- They even teach that Cornelius was an Israelite, contrary to the text (**Acts 10: 1- 7**).
- They contend that these gentiles were Israelites who were exposed to the philosophy of the Greeks: **Ephesian 2:11** Wherefore remember, **that ye being in**

---

[190] https://www.bibletools.org/index.cfm?cx=006538976850733148404%3Aotqd4eea0gk&cof=FORID%3A9&ie=UTF-8&fuseaction=search.results&q=Gentile&sa=Search

Who Are The GENTILES?

time past Gentiles in the flesh, who are called **Uncircumcision** by that which is called the Circumcision in the flesh made by hands. (KJV)

- So-called **Hebrew Israelites** believe that Jesus Christ is coming back to save only Israelites quoting:
  - **Romans 9: 4 Who are Israelites**; to whom **pertaineth the adoption**, and **the glory**, and **the covenants**, and **the giving of the law**, and **the service of God**, and **the promises**; (KJV)
  - **Hebrews 8: 8** For finding fault with them, he saith, Behold, the days come, saith the Lord, when I will make a new covenant with **the house of Israel** and with **the house of Judah**: (KJV)
- They don't believe that all nations shall be saved in Christ.
- **BHI** quote the Apocrypha **2 Maccabee 6:6** "Neither was it lawful for a man to keep sabbath days or ancient fasts, or **to profess himself at all to be a Jew**."
  - They teach that **Israelites were not allowed to be called Jews** and **allowed themselves to be transformed** into the Greek world and called themselves Greek. So this is why the Israelites in Jerusalem was looking down on the Greek Israelites (Gentiles).
- They say the law was not done away with, **but it was the punishment (works) that was done away with**. In other words, we don't stone you. **Romans 3: 31** "Do we then make void the law through faith? God forbid: yea, we establish the law. (KJV)
- **BHI** explains the **resurrection** in **Romans 6: 3-5** as getting rid of your old self (man) and becoming a new creature. The old man eating pork (dietary laws) and committing adultery, etc.
- They refer to the **works as works of the law**, meaning **the punishment of the law**.

Who Are The GENTILES?

DEFINING YOUR TERMS[191]

GENTILE: **Old Testament** the Concept is expressed most frequently by Heb. **gôy, gôyim** (so KJV; also "**heathen**, nations"; RSV "nations"; cf. Vulg. Lat. gentes).

GENTILE: **New Testament** is Gk. **éthnos**, which is the LXX equivalent for both Heb. gôy,gôyim and ʿammim "nations, peoples"; it generally is translated "Gentiles" with reference to non-Jews (e.g., Luke 21:24;

Jesus Said: "And they will fall by the edge of the sword and be **led away captive into all nations**. And **Jerusalem will be trampled by Gentiles** until the times of the **Gentiles** are fulfilled." **Luke 21:24 (NKJV)**

- Stranger = H1616 (gēr) a sojourner, alien, foreigner,
- Stranger = H2114 (zār)
- Stranger = G3581 (ξένος, η, ov) xenos, a guest, stranger, Alien, foreigner or host.
- Alien= H1616 (gēr)
- Foreigner = H5237 (nokrî) Alien, Foreign, stranger, foreigners, gentile
- Foreigner = H8453 (toshab) sojourner, stranger, a temporary dweller
- Foreigner = G3941 (πάροικος, ov) paroikos, non-relative, foreign, alien, subst: a foreigner, sojourner.
- **Gentile = H1471 (gôy, gôyim), Nation, People**
- Gentile = G1482 (ἐθνικός, ή, όν), (ethnikos) pagan, heathen, gentile; subst: a Gentile, non-Jew.
- **Gentile = G1483 (ἐθνικῶς), (ethnikós) As a Gentile, to live as a non-Israelite (see Gal 2:14)**
- Gentile = G1484 (ἔθνος, ους, τό), (ethnos) a race, people, nation; the nations, heathen world, Gentiles.
- **Gentile = G1672 (Ἕλλην, ηνος, ὁ), a hellene, a Greek.**

GENTILE: (גוים, goyim; ἔθνος, ethnos). A word of Latin origin meaning, "belonging to a people." **The Hebrew and Greek words translated as Gentiles mean "people" or "nations."**

Who Are The GENTILES?

Bible translations selectively use Gentiles to designate non-Jews.

GENTILE: A biblical term "**nations**" usually applied to non-Jews. The meaning of the corresponding Latin word, "**gentiles**," used in the *Vulgate to translate the Heb. and Greek, has changed during the centuries. In post-Augustan Latin, it meant 'fellow-countrymen' and in still later Latin more generally '**foreigners**.'

HEATHEN[192]: Heb. plural goyum).
- At first, the word **goyim** denoted generally all the nations of the world (Gen. 18:18; comp. Gal. 3:8).
- The **Jews** afterward became a people distinguished in a marked manner from the other **goyim.**

"since Abraham shall surely become a great and **mighty nation**, and **all the nations of the earth shall be blessed in him**?" **Genesis 18:18 (NKJV)**

"And the Scripture, foreseeing that God would justify the Gentiles by faith, preached the gospel to Abraham beforehand, saying, "**In you all the nations shall be blessed**." 9 So then those who are of faith are blessed with believing Abraham." **Galatians 3:8-9 (NKJV)**

SOJOURNER [193] (Heb. gēr). A technical term (from gûr "sojourn") **designating persons living in a place other than their own home or home country**. The gēr (RSV, KJV often "stranger"; RSV also "alien") **was not a native member of the community in which he resided** (in most cases as a permanent resident)

They had certain rights as a resident, hence the alternate translation "resident alien." The sojourner's "community" could be a household of which that person became a dependent (usually a servant) during difficult times (e.g., Gen. 32:4; Exod.

---

[192]
https://www.bibletools.org/index.cfm?cx=006538976850733148404%3Aotqd4eea0gk&cof=FORID%3A9&ie=UTF-8&fuseaction=search.results&q=Gentile&sa=Search

[193]
https://www.bibletools.org/index.cfm?cx=006538976850733148404%3Aotqd4eea0gk&cof=FORID%3A9&ie=UTF-8&fuseaction=search.results&q=Gentile&sa=Search

Who Are The GENTILES?

20:10 (Stranger); 1 Kgs. 17:20; cf. Job 19:15; RSV "guests"; KJV "they that dwell"),
or a town, region, or nation in which the sojourner
had taken up residence (e.g., Gen. 19:9; Exod. 2:22;
Judges 19:16; Ruth 1:1; 2 Sam. 4:3; 2 Kgs. 8:1–2; 2 Chr. 15:9).

FOREIGNER[194] (Heb. nēḵār, zār; Gk. allogenḗs, bárbaros).* **A non-Israelite who comes into temporary contact with the Hebrews** as merchant, traveler, or military invader; thus distinguished from the **SOJOURNER or resident alien**. The term also indicates the gods of foreign nations (e.g., Josh. 24:20; Jer. 5:19; 8:19).

JEW = H3054 (יָהַד) (verb) yahad: to become a Jew. Denominative from a form corresponding to Yhuwd; to Judaize, i.e., Become Jewish -- become Jews.

> "The Jews had light and gladness, joy and honor. 17 And in every province and city, wherever the king's command and decree came, the Jews had joy and gladness, a feast and a holiday. Then many of the people of the land became Jews, because fear of the Jews fell upon them."
> **Esther 8:16-17 (NKJV)**

GOCC Hebrew Israelite camp; There is much dispute concerning the identity of the Gentiles in the New Testament. Though there are references pertaining to natural gentiles (non- Israelites). the majority of gentiles mentioned in the NT are in reference to Israelite foreigners.[195]

Great Millstone (GMS) Hebrew Israelite camp posted a YouTube video titled "The Gentiles Explained (The Elders Of GMS)"[196]

According to **GMS BHI** camp, there is a lot of ignorance based on the word, **Gentile**, and people don't understand what the word Gentile means, and how to correctly apply that word in Scripture.

---

[194] https://www.bibletools.org/index.cfm?cx=006538976850733148404%3Aotgd4eea0gk&cof=FORID%3A9&ie=UTF-8&fuseaction=search.results&q=Gentile&sa=Search
[195] https://gatheringofchrist.org/faqs-1/ (May 19, 2019)
[196] https://www.youtube.com/watch?v=Feq2JRtRz0k (May 9, 2019)

Who Are The GENTILES?

BHI reader is asked to read:

> "That at that time ye were without Christ, being aliens from the commonwealth of Israel, and strangers from the covenants of promise, having no hope, and without God in the world: "**Ephesians 2:12 (KJV)**

GMS BHI camp articulates that Paul was talking to the Israelites living in Ephesus Greece who called themselves Ephesians. So, because they were not calling themselves Israelites, but were calling themselves Ephesians they didn't have the truth of (**Yahshuah**) the Messiah. Because they were worshipping the customs of the Greeks. This goes back to Alexander the Great, who conquered our people. The Israelites were forced to worship their customs.

GMS BHI camp declares Paul was sent to Ephesus to bring them back to their true nationality, which was Israelites. Bring them back into the fold, which is happening right now. It is happening again, and therefore we are out there on the streets. Bringing back those twelve groups you see, beginning with the so-called Negroes, Mexicans, Porta Ricans, Haitians. Bringing them back to their nationality; to who they really are which are Israelites. The promise is only with Israelites. And the covenants are the agreements that God made with the nation of Israel to follow His Laws, Statutes, and Commandments. This Covenant means agreement. If you are calling yourself by any other **Nationality** than who you are, then you have no hope. Because He is **NOT** coming to save any Porta Ricans, Mexicans, African Americans, or Negroes. He is coming to save Israelites. It begins with You knowing your Nationality. It was the same thing back during the time of Paul and that is why we are reading the Scripture. Just like during the time of the Greeks: Alexander a Greek, the White man, captured our people and put different names on them.

> "Now therefore ye are **no more strangers** and **foreigners**, but fellow citizens with the saints, and of the household of God; **Ephesians 2:19 (KJV)**

GMS Redefines Biblical Usage of Gentile

So-Called **Hebrew Israelites** say another word for Strangers and Foreigners is Gentile. But the other Nations are actually heathens that are strange away from us. The label that was on you of "**stranger**" was put away from you; now you are back in the fold of Hebrew Israelites. The Most-High considers all the other Nations to be strangers and foreigners to Him. Yes, He created all people, but He didn't create all people to serve him. The things that cleaned up Israel were the Laws, statutes, and the commandments. These the Most-High only gave to Israel; He didn't give them to any other Nations (Psalms 78:5). (Psalms 138:14, 50:5, 148:14) the Saints are the Israelites.

"Now concerning spiritual gifts, brethren, I would not have you ignorant. 2 Ye know that ye were Gentiles, carried away unto these dumb idols, even as ye were led." **1 Corinthians 12:1-2 (KJV)**

GMS says people don't understand the difference between Natural Gentile and the unnatural Gentile.

ISUPK Redefines Biblical Usage of Gentile

This **BHI** camp says in a YouTube video titled, "**The Gentiles In The New Testament Are Hebrews Not Heathens**." [197]

ISUPK says Christians teach that the Gentiles are not Israel and are so quick to try and love everybody and save the white man. They say Christians hate themselves but value everyone else. They say when the Bible speaks of **Gentiles**, it is speaking about **Blacks, Hispanics, and Native Americans**.

ISUPK says in a YouTube video titled, "**Who Are The Gentiles That Can Be Saved?**" [198]

They say that Christ died to save the world (**everybody**) is not in the Bible.

---

[197] https://www.youtube.com/watch?v=wKSgmsH-Uco (May 18, 2019)
[198] https://www.youtube.com/watch?v=74mpTS3a46c (May 18, 2019)

Who Are The GENTILES?

ISUPK says in a YouTube video titled, "**The Gentiles – Paul Went to Israelites Only.**"[199]

IUSPK says they are going to prove in Scripture that the word Gentiles is not referring to other nations. The Most-High is only dealing with the Twelve Tribes, and the Most-High is Separatist.

They teach the word Gentile and Samaritans in Matthew 10:5-6 means:

- Here they use Gentile to mean other nations.
- And they say the Levites came back from captivity and they started teaching the Samaritans. So here, the word **Samaritans** is referring to the descendants of those Levites and does not refer to other nations.
- But go to the brothers that are scattered abroad (v.6).

"*These twelve Jesus sent out and commanded them, saying*: "**Do not go into the way of the Gentiles**, and **do not enter a city of the Samaritans**. 6 *But go rather to the lost sheep of the house of Israel.*" **Matthew 10:5-6 (NKJV)**

ISUPK reads **Matthew 15:24** and says this is what Christ told the woman; and this is also who he sent His disciples. **BHI** adherents say they must be sure to point this out.

"*But He answered and said,* "**I was not sent except to the lost sheep of the house of Israel.**" **Matthew 15:24 (NKJV)**

The **ISUPK** adherent reads **John 4:7-9,22** and says that this Samaritan woman knew that the Jews did not have to deal with other nations (v. 9). He says Christ points out the Samaritans don't know what they Worship, but the Jews do and that He makes a difference between them and the Jews (v.22). The **BHI** adherent says you can't take one Scripture and say all nations can come.

"*A woman of Samaria came to draw water. Jesus said to her,* "*Give Me a drink.*" **John 4:7 (NKJV)**

---
[199] https://www.youtube.com/watch?v=FvubkP3GXT4 (May 18, 2019)

Who Are The GENTILES?

> "Then the woman of Samaria said to Him, "How is it that You, being **a Jew**, ask a drink from me, **a Samaritan** woman?" For **Jews** have no dealings with **Samaritans**." **John 4:9 (NKJV)**
>
> "You worship what you do not know; we know what we worship, for salvation is of the Jews." **John 4:22 (NKJV)**

The **ISUPK** adherent says The Most-High wants you to **LOVE** your brethren (Blacks, Hispanics, Native Americans) but **HATE** Esau (so-called White man).

Rebuttal:
1675. Ἑλληνιστής Hellēnistés hel-lay-nis-tace' Definition: **a Hellenist or Greek-speaking Jew** KJV Translation(s): Grecian.
- Origin: from a derivative of 1672; Ἕλλην Héllēn hel'-lane Definition: **a Hellen (Grecian) or inhabitant of Hellas; by extension a Greek-speaking person, especially a non-Jew** KJV Translation(s): Gentile, Greek.
    - Origin: from 1671;Ἑλλάς Hellás hel-las' Definition: **Hellas (or Greece), a country of Europe** KJV Translation(s): Greece. Origin: of uncertain affinity;[200]

It was in Athens that Paul manifested evidence of his Hellenistic culture by familiarly quoting a verse taken from an invocation to Zeus, written by a minor Cilician poet, Aratus (312-245 B.C.).[201]

The Grecians mentioned in Acts 6:1 **were Jews who had lived abroad and spoke Greek**. At this time, there **were no Gentiles in the Church.**

HEL' LENIST (hel' en-ist). A term employed of a person who spoke Greek **but was not racially of the Greek nation**. The expression is especially used of Jews who adopted the Greek. language and, to some extent, Greek customs and culture (**Acts 6: 1; 9: 29**).

---

[200] Strong, James. Dictionary Strong's of the Bible
[201] Unger, Merrill F.. The New Unger's Bible Dictionary (p. 123). Moody Publishers. Kindle Edition.

Who Are The GENTILES?

- **The Hellenists are the Christian converts among the Jews who had returned to Judea after having lived abroad in the Greek world.** Despite being Jewish, the Hellenists had adopted Greek cultural elements and spoke Greek.
    - "**The Hebrews**" in this verse are **the Christian converts among the Jews who were born and raised in Israel**.
- The Hellenists influence can be seen early in the church's history (**Acts 6:1; 9:29**; variant reading in **11:20**). In **Acts 6:1** there was a dispute in the early Christian community at Jerusalem between the Hebrews and the Hellenists (KJV "Grecians") because the widows of the Hel. group were being neglected in the daily allocation from the common pool of the property.

CERTAIN GENTILES ARE PROMINENT CHARACTERS IN THE BIBLE:

- Ruth, a Moabite, was devoted to Naomi (Ruth 1:4).
- Job was from the land of Uz (Job 1:1).
- Cyrus, a non-Jewish king, was called the Messiah (Isa 44:28–45).
- The Genealogy of Jesus in Matthew included at least three Gentile women:
    - Tamar (Matt 1:3),
    - Rahab (Matt 1:5),
    - Ruth (Matt 1:5);
    - it could possibly include a fourth: Uriah's wife, Bathsheba—if Uriah was actually a Hittite.

The problem is to identify these Hellenists. In observing the context, one notices from **Acts 2:5-11** that **the Jews from several different lands throughout the Near and Middle East had gathered in Jerusalem for the observance of Pentecost**. These foreign-born Jews were able to understand the disciples' message **in their own language** and no doubt one of the languages was Greek. Hence, in Acts 6:1 it refers to Jews who spoke Greek as opposed to the Jews who spoke Aramaic.

HELLENISTS DOES NOT REFER TO GREEKS

Some think that the Hellenists refer to Greeks (i.e., non-Jews), but this is not likely because
1) the context of Acts 1-5 is **the spread of the church among Jews in Judea**;
2) **the Gentiles being admitted into the church marked a new phase** which begins in Acts 10; 11;
3) the later conflict of the church regarding the admission of **the Gentiles without circumcision** (Acts 15) would have been pointless **if the Gentiles were admitted in the church at its inception**; and
4) the reference to Hellenists in Acts 9:29 makes no sense if it means "**Greeks**," for Paul **was not disputing with Gentiles in Jerusalem**.

Regarding the reading in Acts 11:20, the word Ἕλληνας has a slight edge over the variant, and clearly, the context indicates Greeks, for it was the **Greek-speaking Jews** in 11:19 who preached to the **Greeks or Gentiles** in 11:20.

The believing Jews are here divided into two groups.
- The first were those who had **remained in Judea, near Jerusalem, who used the Hebrew language**, and who were appropriately called "Hebrews."
- The second group consisted of **those who were scattered among the Gentiles, who spoke the Greek language, and who used the Greek translation of the Old Testament, called the Septuagint**. These were called "Hellenists," from a word meaning "Greek" or "Greek-speaking." To "Hellenize" is to adopt Greek culture and ideas.

After Acts 6, the Hellenists appear again in Acts 9:29, when Paul "talked and debated with the Hellenistic Jews, but they tried to kill him" in Jerusalem. The KJV translates the word for the group as "Grecians." Among the Grecian Jews, just as among the Hebraic Jews, there were those who rejected

Who Are The GENTILES?

Jesus as the Christ and resisted the preaching of the gospel, even to the point of trying to kill the Christian missionaries.[202]

DOES THE BIBLE TEACH OR ENDORSE RACISM?

Does Race Matter According to the Bible?

According to the **GOCC's Hebrew Israelite** camp's website [203] : "As much as people like to disregard the importance of race, **the Bible makes it clear that race matters**. The Bible dedicates chapter upon chapter strictly for the genealogies of peoples. One of the important purposes of identifying race is the understanding of Bible prophecy. There is no way you can break down prophecy if you don't first identify the peoples in which the prophecies are referring to. We must also put an end to this emotional rampage that makes one believe that identifying someone's race, according to the Bible, is racist. If we can accept the labels that man gave us as badges of honor, then we surely should not have any problems with the labels that the Most-High gave us.

No one had a problem with Biblical race when they believed that we were the seed of Ham and that the Khazarian converts were the real Jews. It only seems to be a problem when we (African Americans, Jamaicans, Haitians, West Indians, Indigenous peoples of North, Central, and South America, etc.) begin to identify ourselves as the real Jews and Israelites, **that the world now wants to label Biblical genealogy to racism**."

Rebuttal to GOCC: According to the Bible, there is only one race, Human:

> "And **He has made from one blood every nation of men** *to dwell on all the face of the earth, and has determined their preappointed times and the boundaries of their dwellings,*" **Acts 17:26 (NKJV)**

There is **Only** one race born in sin, Human (**Romans 3:23**). There is **Only** one race that the Blood of Jesus atones for, Human (mankind ~ the believers) (**John 3:16; 1 John 2:2**).

---

[202] https://www.biblegateway.com/resources/encyclopedia-of-the-bible/Hellenism-Hellenists
[203] https://gatheringofchrist.org/faqs-1/ May 19, 2019

Who Are The GENTILES?

According to the **GOCC's Hebrew Israelite** camp's website:[204]

They ask and state, "how was Race Classified in Ancient Biblical Times?

> In ancient Biblical times, your race or national origin was identified by **the seed of your father** (Num. 1:3-4;20). **In other words, if your father was an Israelite, then you were an Israelite** (regardless of your mother's nationality). The same goes for any other nation."

They state, "If This is True, Can A Person Truly Be Mixed? Common sense would tell you that the answer is no. Nature itself teaches us that the seed determines the "genus." For instance, apple seeds produce apple trees. Lemon seeds produce lemon trees. Though the seed is planted in the earth, there is no such thing as a half earth or half apple tree. Though the earth nourishes the seed and allows it to grow, it still does **NOT** determine the genus of the seed. The same goes for people."

Rebuttal to GOCC: Who determined Adam's race, or Eve's race (**Genesis 1:26-27**)? What about Jesus, who had NO earthly (biological) father **(Luke 1: 34-35)**? And What about Titus, who was a Greek **(Galatian 2:3)**, and Timothy, whose father was Greek (**Acts 16:2-3**); and then there is Jacob and Esau; both of Isaac's seed (**Genesis 25:23**).

PROSELYTES GENTILES

Proselytes were Gentiles (Acts 2:9-11; Acts 8:26-38) **who had completely accepted Judaism**. Once they were circumcised and immersed in a mikvah (ritual bath), they were bound to all the doctrines and precepts of the Jewish religion and were considered full members of the Jewish people. Their religion was Judaism, but not their ethnicity.[205]

The Jewish leaders then tried to exterminate Jerusalem Christians. "... **and they were all scattered throughout the regions of Judea and Samaria**..." **(Acts 8:1)**

---
[204] https://gatheringofchrist.org/faqs-1/ May 19, 2019
[205] https://melkite.org/faith/brethren-who-are-of-the-gentile

Who Are The GENTILES?

The disciples traveled even further in preaching that Jesus was the Messiah. In Acts 11:19, **we read that they went "as far as Phoenicia, Cyprus, and Antioch"** where the Lord Himself had never gone. These regions were not Jewish areas, but they each had Jewish communities, made up chiefly of merchants and dating back hundreds of years before Christ.[206]

'PROSELYTES' THE INCORPORATION OF GENTILES INTO THE JEWISH COMMUNITY

Two Key Factors
1. Devotion to God
2. Circumcision for Males

"*You shall have* **the same law**
- for **the stranger**

and
- for **one from your own country**;

for I am the Lord your God." **Leviticus 24:22 (NKJV)**

"**And when a stranger dwell with you and wants to keep the Passover to the Lord**, *let all his males be circumcised, and then let him come near and keep it; and*
- **he shall be as a native of the land**.

For no uncircumcised person shall eat it." **Exodus 12:48 (NKJV)**

"**One law shall be for the native-born**
and **for the stranger**
who dwells among you." **Exodus 12:49 (NKJV)**

"And **if a stranger shall sojourn among you**, *and will keep the passover unto the Lord; according to the ordinance of the passover, and according to the manner thereof, so shall he do:* **ye shall have one ordinance, both for the stranger, and for him that was born in the land.**" **Numbers 9:14 (KJV)**

"**One ordinance** shall be both
- for you of the congregation,

---

[206] https://melkite.org/faith/brethren-who-are-of-the-gentiles

Can Gentiles Be Saved?

and also
- for the stranger that sojourneth with you,

an ordinance for ever in your generations: **as ye are, so shall the stranger be before the Lord.**" **Numbers 15:15 (KJV)**

"**One law** and **one manner** shall be for
- **you**,

and for the
- **stranger**

that sojourneth with you." **Numbers 15:16 (KJV)**

"**One and the same law** applies to everyone who sins unintentionally, whether
- **a native-born Israelite** or
- **a foreigner**

residing among you. **Numbers 15:29 (NIV)**

"But anyone who sins defiantly, whether
- **native-born** or
- **foreigner**,

blasphemes the Lord and must be cut off from the people of Israel." **Numbers 15:30 (NIV)**

CAN GENTILES BE SAVED?

GENTILES (NON-JEWS) INTO THE BODY OF CHRIST

"*Then Peter opened his mouth and said: "In truth I perceive that* **God shows no partiality**. 35 But in **every nation whoever fears Him and works righteousness is accepted by Him.**" **Acts 10:34-35 (NKJV)**

"*For there* **IS NO** *respect of persons with God.*" **Romans 2:11 (KJV)**

SICARII Hebrew Israelite camp has a YouTube video posted entitled, "**Can Gentiles Be Saved Israelite Street Debate.**"[207]

Sicarii BHI camp members on the street use selective Scriptures to pull what they call precepts out of the verses (here a little, there a little) to prove that these verses are

---

[207] https://www.youtube.com/watch?v=ILY3l3vjM5E May 9, 2019

reconciled by Ezekiel that Salvation is only for one group of people, Israelites.

> *"These twelve Jesus sent forth, and commanded them, saying, **Go not into the way of the Gentiles**, and into any city of the Samaritans enter ye not: 6 **But go rather to the lost sheep of the house of Israel**."* **Matthew 10:5-6 (KJV)**

"But he answered and said, **I am not sent but unto the lost sheep of the house of Israel**." **Matthew 15:24 (KJV)**
"And **other sheep I have**, which are not of this fold: them also I must bring, and they shall hear my voice, and there shall be one fold, and one shepherd." **John 10:16 (KJV)**

> *"And that he might **reconcile both unto God in one body** by the cross, having slain the enmity thereby: 17 And came and preached peace to you which **were afar off, and to them that were nigh**. 18 For through him, **we both have access by one Spirit unto the Father**."* **Ephesians 2:16-18 (KJV)**

The **Sicarii** tell the people that are gathered around them, let's see who was prophesied to come back into one:

> "21 And say unto them, Thus saith the Lord God; Behold, I will take the children of Israel from among the heathen, whither they be gone, and will gather them on every side, and bring them into their own land: 22 And I will make them one nation."

They say if this is talking about everybody outside of the children of Israel, then you are insinuating that twelve tribes of Israel were already together at the time of Christ.

> "in the land upon the mountains of Israel; and one king shall be king to them all:"

They point out: one king, one shepherd, one-fold, one nation.

> "and they shall be no more two nations, neither shall they be divided into two kingdoms any more at all:" **Ezekiel 37:21-22 (KJV)**

Can Gentiles Be Saved?

Sicarii say it was prophesied that the nation of Israel was going to be brought back into one Spirit, one body, one-fold, one nation.

They teach that Isaiah chapter 42 is calling Israel Gentiles in verse 6.

They explain that Israel is called Gentiles because they are blind (v. 7), and deaf (v.19), but they are also called my servant (Isaiah 44:1). The same people are robbed and spoiled, and for a prey (v. 22). It was Jacob (Israel) given for a spoil Israel to Robbers.

Sicarii contend that they showed Israel was the only people that were blind, deaf, and spoiled, but early the Scripture called them Gentiles (v.6).

> "He sheweth his word unto **Jacob**, his statutes and **his judgments unto Israel. 20 He hath not dealt so with any nation**: and as for his judgments, they have not known them. Praise ye the Lord." **Psalms 147:19-20 (KJV)**

Rebuttal: The Bible, when reading it in context, informs the readers that in **Acts Chapter 15**: Yes, there were some among the believing Jews who attempted to enforce **The Mosaic Law** on followers of Jesus Christ (Both Jews and Gentiles).

> "*But some of the sect of the Pharisees who believed rose up, saying,* "**It is necessary to circumcise them, and to command them to keep the law of Moses.**" Acts 15:5 (NKJV)

Contrary to the teaching of Hebrew Israelism, the Bible teaches that salvation was open to mankind, which includes the Gentiles. All who call on the name of the Lord and who turn to Him.

> "*So that* **the rest of mankind** *may seek the Lord,* **Even all the Gentiles** *who are called by My name, Says the Lord who does all these things.*" **Acts 15:17 (NKJV)**

> "Therefore I judge that we should not trouble those from among **the Gentiles who are turning to God**," **Acts 15:19 (NKJV)**

And no, the **Gentiles** and believing **Jews DO NOT Have to KEEP THE LAW**!

> "*Since we have heard that* **some who went out from us have troubled you** with words, *unsettling your souls, saying, "You must be circumcised and **keep the law**"*—to whom we gave no such commandment—" **Acts 15:24 (NKJV)**

Although Our Lord Jesus Christ went to areas **where non-Jews were numerous**, His call was first and foremost to the Jews. When He was passing through the region of **Tyre and Sidon,** a Canaanite woman begged Him to heal her daughter. "But He answered and said, 'I was not sent except to the lost sheep of the house of Israel'" (**Matthew 15:24**). The Acts of the Apostles tells us how, after Pentecost, the disciples of Christ took the Gospel **beyond the house of Israel as well.**

IN THE BEGINNING THERE WERE GENTILES

Five Importance Questions In Genesis Chapters 1 – 10 to ask the **So-called Hebrew Israelites**:
1. Where Are The **Jews**? NON-EXISTENCE.
2. Where Are The **Israelites**? NON-EXISTENCE.
3. Where Are The **Laws**? NON-EXISTENCE.
4. What **Nation** Did God Separate To Himself? NONE.
5. Who Did God Establish A **Covenant** With? NO-ONE.

"*And God said to Noah, "This is the sign* of **the covenant which I have established between Me and all flesh that is on the earth.**" **Genesis 9:17 (NKJV)**

"*I set My rainbow in the cloud, and it shall be for the sign of* **the covenant between Me and the earth.**"
- Noah
- Every Living Creature
- Earth
- All Flesh
- Creation" **Genesis 9:13 (NKJV)**

Before there were Jews, Israelites, and Laws; we see a form of Monotheistic worship to **One God:**

> "Then Noah **built an altar to the Lord**, *and took of every clean animal and of every clean bird, and* **offered burnt offerings on the alta**r. *21 And the Lord smelled a soothing aroma....*" **Genesis 8:20 (NKJV)** *(see Genesis 4:4)*

Before there were Jews, Israelites, and Laws; we see that God is aware of **the Heart of Man:**

> **Before Flood:** "*...the Lord saw that* **the wickedness of man** *was great in the earth, and that* **every intent of the thoughts of his heart was only evil continually.....**" **Genesis 6:5 (NKJV)**

> **After Flood:** "*....the imagination of man's heart is evil from his youth....*" **Genesis 8:21 (NKJV)**

Before there were Jews, Israelites, and Laws; we see that God gave C**OMMANDMENTS**:

> "*Every moving thing that lives shall be food for you. I have given you all things, even as the green herbs.* **4 But you shall not eat flesh with its life, that is, its blood.**" **Genesis 9:3-4 (NKJV)**

> "*Whoever sheds man's blood, By man his blood shall be shed; For in the image of God He made man.*" **Genesis 9:6 (NKJV)**

- > "Now the whole earth had **one language** and **one speech.**" **Genesis 11:1 (NKJV)**

> "These three were the sons of Noah**, and from these the whole earth was Populated."** **Genesis 9:19 (NKJV)**

> "**These are the families** *of the sons of Noah, after their generations***, in their nations:** *and by these were* **the nations divided in the earth after the flood. Genesis 10:32 (KJV)**

> "*Of these were the isles of* **the nations divided in their lands, every one after his tongue, after their families, in their nations.**" Genesis 10:5 (ASV)

THE GENTILE WHO WAS CALLED OUT:

> "*And Joshua said to all the people, "Thus says the Lord God of Israel:* **Your fathers, including Terah,** *the father of* **Abraham** *and the father of* **Nahor,** *dwelt on the other side of the River in old times*; **and they served other gods." Joshua 24:2 (NKJV)**

> "Now the Lord had said to Abram: **"*Get out of your country*,** *From your family And from your father's house,* **To a land that I will show you. Genesis 12:1 (NKJV)**

THE GENTILE WHO WAS ANOINTED AND THE SERVANT OF GOD

> "*Thus says the Lord* **to His anointed**, **To Cyrus, whose right hand I have held**— *To subdue nations before him And loose the armor of kings, To open before him the double doors, So that the gates will not be shut*: **Isaiah 45:1 (NKJV) (vs. 1-6)**

> "**Who says of Cyrus, 'He is My shepherd, And he shall perform all My pleasure,** *Saying to Jerusalem, "You shall be built," And to the temple, "Your foundation shall be laid." '"* **Isaiah 44:28 (NKJV) 28**

Cyrus is a king mentioned more than 30 times in the Bible and is identified as Cyrus the Great (also Cyrus II or Cyrus the Elder) who reigned over Persia between 539—530 BC. This pagan king is important in Jewish history because it was under his rule that Jews were first allowed to return to Israel after 70 years of captivity. [208] [209]

---

[208] https://www.gotquestions.org/Cyrus-Bible.html May 19, 2019
[209] https://www.britannica.com/biography/Cyrus-the-Great May 19, 2019

HEAVEN AND HELL

SO-CALLED HEBREW ISRAELITES BELIEF ABOUT HEAVEN AND HELL

BHI does not believe in heaven or hell in the Christian sense. **For them, heaven is rulership**.[210] They believe that right now we're in the Caucasian's heaven. Some call the Caucasians the devil.
1. **Hell is a metaphor** and is not a literal place where people suffer.
2. **There is no heaven and hell**. There is no place where people burn. **We are in the Caucasian heaven now**.

RESURRECTION:

BHI (some) explain the resurrection in **Romans 6: 3-5** as getting rid of your old self (man) and becoming a new creature.

The old man eating pork (dietary laws) and committing adultery, etc.

> "Or do you not know that as **many of us as were baptized into Christ Jesus** were baptized into His death? 4 Therefore **we were buried with Him** through baptism into death, that just as Christ was raised from the dead by the glory of the Father, **even so we also should walk in newness of life.** 5 For if we have been united together in the likeness of His death, certainly we also shall be **in the likeness of His resurrection**, 6 knowing this, that **our old man was crucified with Him, that the body of sin might be done away with, that we should no longer be slaves of sin.**" Romans 6:3-6 (NKJV)

- HEAVEN & HELL ARE CONDITIONS ON EARTH – BOSTON[211]
- HEAVEN and HELL are CONDITIONS on THE EARTH[212]

- [CHRISTIANITY LIED : HEAVEN AND HELL ARE CONDITIONS ON EARTH - NO COWARDS][213]
- [HEAVEN & HELL IS NOT A PLACE BUT A CONDITION ON EARTH - ISUPK MINNEAPOLIS][214]
- [REVEALING THE MYSTERIES OF HEAVEN AND HELL, LIFE AND DEATH LECTURE 07/01/2017 - ISUPK BMORE][215]
- [OUR OPPRESSORS WILL NOT HAVE SALVATION IN THE KINGDOM OF HEAVEN - #ISUPK][216]

The Gospel of John is a very tough book on the issue of salvation.

> "For God sent not his Son into the world to condemn the world; but that the world through him might be saved. ^{18} He that believeth on him is not condemned: but **he that believeth not is condemned already** because he hath not believed in the name of the only begotten Son of God. ^{19} **And this is the condemnation, that lightcomes into the world, and men loved darkness rather than light because their deeds were evil.**" (John 3:17-19)

John makes it clear that anyone who does not accept Jesus Christ is already condemned. If people die in a state of unbelief, never accepting Jesus Christ as their Lord and personal Savior, they die in their sins.

> "I said therefore unto you, that ye shall die in your sins: for **if ye believe not that I am he, ye shall die in your sins**." (John 8:24)

Sadly, for them, physical death is not the end, and they don't go to heaven, but rather end up in hell.
Notice what Jesus tells us,
> "Marvel not at this: for the hour is coming, in the which **all that are in the graves shall hear his voice**, ^{29} **And shall come forth**;
> - they that have done good, unto the resurrection of life; and

---

[213] https://www.youtube.com/watch?v=XAF_L5fdfmM (May 14, 2019)
[214] https://www.youtube.com/watch?v=gYqtl7-Ja08 (May 14, 2019)
[215] https://www.youtube.com/watch?v=_e8kRXBWiOQ May 14, 2019
[216] https://www.youtube.com/watch?v=nxE_OwGLkFs May 14, 2019

> - ***they that have done evil, unto the resurrection of damnation.*** " (**John 5:28-29**)

The resurrection of damnation means the person who died in their sins will rise from the dead in a damnation body, and in that body, they will be cast into hell. Jesus provides more details:

> "*And if thy hand offend thee, cut it off: it is better for thee to enter into life maimed, than having two hands*
> - ***to go into hell, into the fire that never shall be quenched:*** *[44]* ***Where their worm dieth not, and the fire is not quenched.*** *[45] And if thy foot offend thee, cut it off: it is better for thee to enter halt into life, than having two feet*
> - ***to be cast into hell, into the fire that never shall be quenched:*** *[46]* ***Where their worm dieth not, and the fire is not quenched.*** *[47] And if thine eye offend thee, pluck it out: it is better for thee to enter into the kingdom of God with one eye, than having two eyes*
> - ***to be cast into hell fire:*** *[48]* ***Where their worm dieth not, and the fire is not quenched.***" (**Mark 9:43-48**)

> "*And shall cast them into a furnace of fire:* ***there shall be wailing and gnashing of teeth.***" (**Matthew 13:42**)

> "*And* ***the smoke of their torment ascendeth up for ever and ever:*** *and* ***they have no rest day nor night****, who worship the beast and his image, and whosoever receiveth the mark of his name.*" (**Revelation 14:11**)

The Scripture is clear that hell is where the person goes who does not accept Jesus Christ as their personal Savior. It is very important to know about hell. What it basically means is that one is separated from God throughout all eternity.

Now you might say, "Oh, you just trying to make me afraid by frightening me." You are correct. **YES, I AM!**
In fact, the Bible recommends the fear tactic:

> "*Keep yourselves in the love of God, looking for the mercy of our Lord Jesus Christ unto eternal life.* [22] *And of some have compassion, making a difference:* [23]

- ***And others save with fear,***
- ***pulling them out of the fire;***
- ***hating even the garment spotted by the flesh.***

²⁴ Now unto him that is able to keep you from falling, and to present you faultless before the presence of his glory with exceeding joy," (**Jude 21-24**)

Anybody with any sense should be afraid. Someone telling you that if you don't turn around, you are going to fall off the cliff, and you refuse to take heed? Healthy fear is good for you. Only people running around afraid of something that is not going to occur need psychiatric care. But in this case, hell is real, and if you don't want to go there, make sure that you are right with God. Simply, while the blood is running warm in your veins:

- *"That if thou shalt confess **with thy mouth the Lord Jesus**, and **shalt believe in thine heart that God hath raised him from the dead**, thou shalt be saved."* (**Romans 10:9**)

- *"Then Peter said unto them, **Repent**, and **be baptized every one of you in the name of Jesus Christ for the remission of sins**, and ye shall receive the gift of the Holy Ghost."* (**Acts 2:38**)

Yes, there are those who will say a loving God would not send anyone to hell to be tormented forever and ever for all eternity.

They are right! You send yourself to hell when you choose to reject Him. At the end of the day, what God is simply saying to you is, "Have it your way." You condemn yourself. It is not like God is going to send you to a place where you don't want to go. No person who goes to hell could survive a second in heaven, because he or she doesn't want to be there. In heaven it will only be worshipping God and His holiness. Heaven is not the place for him or her. The person actually goes to the place of their own life's choosing, hell.

In fact, hell was not even made for man. God did not make hell as a place for a man to go.

> *"Then shall he say also unto them on the left hand, Depart from me, ye cursed, into everlasting fire, **prepared for the devil and his angels**:"* (**Matthew 25:41**)

So why would a person desire to go somewhere that was not made and designed for them? Hell was not designed for mankind. So it is simply a matter of choice.

> *"And this is the condemnation, that light is come into the world, **and men loved darkness rather than light**, because their deeds were evil. [20] For **every one that doeth evil hateth the light**, neither cometh to the light, lest his deeds should be reproved."* (**John 3:19-20**)

Everything in the universe belongs to God. God says at the end of the day I'm taking all that is mine, and since you want no part of me, there you go.

Some groups, such as the Jehovah Witnesses teach that there is no hell. They say that the dead (*non-Jehovah Witnesses*) are just annihilated. Ask them or any other recruiting group this question: "If you are wrong about hell, will you go to hell in my place?"

Physical Death: when you die, your body is buried, and your soul continues either in hell (unbeliever) or with the Lord in heaven.

> "And it came to pass,
> - that the beggar died, **and was carried by the angels into Abraham's bosom**:
> - the rich man also died, and was buried; [23] **And in hell he lift up his eyes, being in torments**, and seeth Abraham afar off, and Lazarus in his bosom." (**Luke 16:22-23**)

> *"We are confident, I say, and willing rather **to be absent from the body, and to be present with the Lord**."*(**2 Corinthians 5:8**)

And if people are living their life now in a state of unbelief while they are in the land of the living, even so, they are spiritually dead right now.

Spiritual Death: People who do not believe in Jesus Christ are dead right now spiritually. But the good news is that they can be recovered by accepting Jesus Christ as their personal savior, before dying physically. If they don't and they die in this state they go into the second death.

> "And you hath he quickened, who **were dead in trespasses and sins**;" **(Ephesians 2:1)**
> "*But she that liveth in pleasure **is dead while she liveth**.*" **(1 Timothy 5:6)**

The Bible informs us that:

Second Death: Physical death and Hades/Sheol were cast into the second death. Here people are in an Irretrievable place: Hell, and they are separated from God for all eternity in a damnation body. This is everlasting death and punishment away from God.

> "*Then shall he say also unto them on the left hand, Depart from me, **ye cursed**, **into everlasting fire**, prepared for the devil and his angels*:" **(Matthew 25:41)**
> "*And **these shall go away into everlasting punishment**: but the righteous into life eternal.*" **(Matthew 25:46)**

> "*And **death and hell** were cast into **the lake of fire. This is the second death.**" **(Revelation 20:14)**

The cult called **Christian Science** teaches **there is no death**[217], and they don't believe in the Biblical hell. **Death is not real. Heaven and hell are states of mind**. The way to reach heaven is by attaining harmony (oneness with God).[218] They teach that "*Sin makes its own hell, and goodness its own heaven (S&H 196:18-19). The sinner makes his own hell by doing evil and the saint his own heaven by doing right (S&H 266:20-21).*[219] *The evil beliefs which originate in mortals are hell. Man is the idea of Spirit; he reflects the beatific presence, illuming the universe with light. Man is deathless,*

---

[217] https://sentinel.christianscience.com/issues/1909/9/12-1/there-is-no-death (April 26, 2017)
[218] Publishing, Rose. Christianity, Cults & Religions (Kindle Locations 231-233). Rose Publishing, Inc.. Kindle Edition.
[219] https://sentinel.christianscience.com/issues/1909/9/12-1/there-is-no-death (April 26, 2017)

spiritual. He is above sin or frailty. He does not cross the barriers of time into the vast forever of Life, but he coexists with God and the universe. (SH 266-26)." **There is no devil**, S&H 469:13-17. "Matter, **sin**, and sickness are not real, but only illusions," S&H 335:7-15; 447:27-28. [220]

Ellen G. White, founder of the cult Seventh-Day Adventism, "How repugnant to every emotion of love and mercy, and even to our sense of justice, is the doctrine that **the wicked dead are tormented with fire and brimstone in an eternally burning hell**; that for the sins of a brief earthly life they are to suffer torture as long as God shall live. Yet this doctrine has been widely taught and is still embodied in many of the creeds of Christendom." [221]

ESAU SHALL BE LEAD INTO CAPTIVITY IN THE KINGDOM

The Israelites: Esau Is Not Getting Away With Slavery!!!
https://www.youtube.com/watch?v=P4P_Cn8APYM

Esau will be a complete slave in the kingdom of heaven
https://www.youtube.com/watch?v=JZnoOFT1av4

Esau is going to be slaves in the kingdom
https://www.youtube.com/watch?v=SQDdW3qFWXQ

The Judgment for Esau (whiteman) is death and slavery in the Kingdom of Heaven pt1
https://www.youtube.com/watch?v=Zjjgn6b3ClM

GOD WILL PUNISH ALL INVOLVED IN THE TRANS-ATLANTIC SLAVE TRADE - #ISUPK
https://www.youtube.com/watch?v=1dv2rXweJho

Rebuttal: Esau

Genesis 27:40 (NKJV) By your sword you shall live,
- (A) And **you shall serve your brother**; And it shall come to pass, when you become restless,
- (B) That **you shall break his yoke from your neck**."

---

[220] https://carm.org/what-does-christian-science-teach (April 26, 2017)
[221] http://text.egwwritings.org/publication.php?pubtype=Book&bookCode=GC&lang=en&pagenumber=535 (April 26, 2017)

Heaven and Hell

(A) **2 Samuel 8:13 (NKJV)** And David made himself a name when he returned from killing eighteen thousand Syrians in the Valley of Salt. 14 He also put garrisons in Edom; throughout all Edom he put garrisons, **and all the Edomites became David's servants**. And the Lord preserved David wherever he went.

(B) **2 Kings 8:20 (NKJV)** In his days **Edom revolted against Judah's authority, and made a king over themselves**.

By hating The Edomite you broke the Law:

"You shall not abhor an Edomite, for he is your brother. You shall not abhor an Egyptian, because you were an alien in his land. 8 The children of the third generation born to them may enter the assembly of the Lord." **Deuteronomy 23:7-8 (NKJV)**

'If you really fulfill the royal law according to the Scripture, "You shall love your neighbor as yourself," you do well; 9 but if you show partiality, you commit sin, and are convicted by the law as transgressors. 10 For whoever shall keep the whole law, and **yet stumble in one point, he is guilty of all**.' **James 2:8-10 (NKJV)**

"So when her days were fulfilled for her to give birth, indeed there were twins in her womb. 25 And the first came **out red. He was like a hairy garment all over**; so they called his name Esau. 26 Afterward his brother came out, and his hand took hold of Esau's heel; so his name was called Jacob. Isaac was sixty years old when she bore them." **Genesis 25:24-26 (NKJV)**
"And when the Philistine looked about and saw David, he disdained him; for he was only a youth, **ruddy and good-looking. 1 Samuel 17:42 (NKJV)** 42
"My beloved is **white and ruddy**[222], Chief among ten thousand. *Shulamite girl:* **Song of Songs 5:10 (NKJV)** I am dark, but lovely, O daughters of Jerusalem, Like the tents of Kedar, Like the curtains of Solomon.6 Do not look upon me, because I am dark, Because the sun has tanned me." **Song of Songs 1:5-6 (NKJV)**

---

[222] Youngblood, R. F., Bruce, F. F., & Harrison, R. K., Thomas Nelson Publishers (Eds.). (1995). In Nelson's new illustrated Bible dictionary. Nashville, TN: Thomas Nelson, Inc.

PROBLEM TEN
SO, KING JAME WAS BLACK?

According to the OFFICIAL **GOCC Hebrew Israelite WEBSITE!!!!** [223]

The King James Bible 1611 **should be the BIBLE we all read from**... and I know when you all hear the TRUE facts about King James, you will all agree... Now the KING JAMES 1611 has the 14 Books called the Apocrypha in it... No other BIBLE does...... Now that alone is a HUGE clue what not many people know about.... [224]

"King James was **a BLACK king** [225] who was **a HEBREW ISRAELITE from the TRIBE of JUDAH** who sat on three thrones at the same time... he was the 6th king of Scotland, and he became the 1st king of England in 1603.... it was at his ascension to the throne of England that he became known as King James the 1st...

He is LIED on because he was a staunch opponent against the establishment known as THE ROMAN CATHOLIC CHURCH.... making quotes such as

- ."ROME IS THE SEAT OF THE ANTICHRIST"
- "THE POPE IS ANTICHRIST"
- "THE SCRIPTURE FORBIDDETH US TO WORSHIP THE IMAGE OF ANYTHING THAT GOD CREATED..."

"Now King James knew his zealousness for TRUTH would cause his name to eventually be slandered and vilified by one of his biggest foes, the roman catholic church..."

So what King James did was call for a decree for the translation of the old and new testament out of the ORIGINAL HEBREW and GREEK tongues... this translation is known today as the KING JAMES VERSION 1611 WITH THE APOCRYPHA...(The Apocrypha had already been removed during the Roman Vulgate translation in 364AD by the Catholic church.. KJ knew this and put the 14 books back in)"

---

[223] http://www.gatheringofchrist.org/
[224] http://goccuk321.blogspot.com/2013/12/king-james-black-king.html May 19, 2019
[225] https://www.youtube.com/watch?v=qeh9CsGVvpl May 19, 2019

- All this went on in a time period in history known as the DARK AGE...
- 800yrs where apparently NOTHING of historical value occurred... HOW CONVENIENT!!!
- During this time, **BLACK KINGS**..... "HEBREWS" sat on thrones all over Europe...
- King James was one of the last kings of this era to reign over Europe...
- King James was later beheaded by his enemies (him and his children); and England, Scotland, Ireland, and France took control off... These same people responsible are still in power today... shortly afterwards the Apocrypha was then again removed.... however if you get the kjv1611 today you can find it with the Apocrypha, or you can just get hold of it separately... [226]

IUIC Hebrew Israelite camp teaches that King James was black. [227] [228]

IUSPK BHI camp teaches that King James was Black and that Scotland was Jewish. [229] They teach that the Roman Catholic church tried to assassinate King James because they didn't want a black man sitting on the throne.

GMS BHI camp teaches that King James and other men in Europe were so-called Black Men. [230] These BHI adherents even teach that Constantine was a so-called Black man.

The **Hebrew Israelite** camps may wear different "Power Ranger" like outfits. They may argue amongst the various camps, which is the rightful and true representative of the Most-High. But at the end of the day, their foundational source is the same Erroneous ERROR. They distort Biblical History, Church History, Secular History, and anything else they can wrap their satanic claws around.

WHY IS THE APOCRYPHA NOT IN YOU CHRISTIANS BIBLE?

---

[226] http://goccuk321.blogspot.com/2013/12/king-james-black-king.html May 19, 2019
[227] https://www.youtube.com/watch?v=vQNWDWmWDVc May 19, 2019
[228] https://www.youtube.com/watch?v=aPdsWQf3Ppw (June 3, 2019)
[229] https://www.youtube.com/watch?v=F9zr39vrQFs May 19, 2019
[230] https://www.youtube.com/watch?v=XSVoasaaklY May 19, 2019

IUIC BHI camp says the so-called white man took the **Apocrypha out of the Bible.**[231] Out on the corners, they have doctored (Photoshopped) up images of old black and white images smudged to give the illusion that he appears to have an afro hairstyle. They teach that King James included the Apocrypha because the fourteen books belonged in the Bible.

THE APOCRYPHA DOES NOT CARRY THE WEIGHT OF THE BIBLE

"The Jewish canon, or the Hebrew Bible, was universally received, while the Apocrypha added to the Greek version of the Septuagint were only in a general way accounted as books suitable for church reading, and thus as a middle class between canonical and strictly apocryphal (pseudonymous) writings. And justly; for those books, while they have great historical value, and fill the gap between the Old Testament and the New, all originated after the cessation of prophecy, and they cannot, therefore, be regarded as inspired, nor are they ever cited by Christ or the apostles" (Philip Schaff, History of the Christian Church, book 3, chapter 9)[232]

God determined the books of The Canon (Bible):

"All Scripture is given by inspiration of God..." (GOD-BREATHED) **2 Timothy 3:**16

"Knowing this first, that no prophecy of Scripture is of any private interpretation, for prophecy never came by the will of man, but holy men of God spoke as they were moved by the Holy Spirit." **2 Peter 1:20-21**

"**Thus said the LORD**" or Similar occurs some 1500 times in the Old Testament.

The unique claims within the Bible itself bear witness to its unusual character. Some **thirty-eight hundred** times the Bible declares, "God said," or "Thus says the Lord."[233]

---

[231] https://www.youtube.com/watch?v=eAqAhiSxjuQ May 19, 2019
[232] http://www.bible.ca/catholic-apocrypha.htm
[233] Paul Enns. The Moody Handbook of Theology (Kindle Locations 1520-1521). Kindle Edition.]

So, KING JAME WAS BLACK?

On What Basis Were They Chosen? "**God's Fingerprints**"

- A. **Was it written by a prophet of God?** (2Pet. 1:20-21; Mt. 5:17-18; Lk. 24:27)
- B. **Was he confirmed by an act of God?** (Ex. 4:1-9; Jn. 3:2; Heb. 2:4; 2 Cor. 12:12)
- C. **Did it tell the truth about God?** (Deut. 13:1-3; 18:21-22; Acts 17:11; 1 Jn. 4:1-6)
- D. **Did it have the power of God?** (Isa. 55:11; Heb. 4:12; Rom. 1:16; 2 Tim. 3:17)
- E. **Was it received by the people of God?** (Deut. 31:26; 1 Thes. 2:13)

When Were They Chosen?
Initial acceptance –as they were written (1500-400 B.C.)
Eventual recognition by all (400 B.C. to present)

14 Apocryphal Books (3 Rejected by Rome)

1) The Wisdom of Solomon (C. 30 B.C.)
2) Ecclesiasticus (Sirach) (c. 132 B.C.)
3) Tobit (c. 200 B.C.)
4) Judith (c. 150 B.C.)
5) 1 Esdras (c. 150-100 B.C.) [3 Esdras in Catholic Bible]
6) 2 Esdras (c. **100 A.D.**) [4 Esdras in the Catholic Bible]
7) 1 Maccabees (c. 110 B.C.)
8) 2 Maccabees (c. 110-70 B.C.)
9) Baruch (c. 150-50 B.C.) ---Baruch 1-5
   (Letter of Jeremiah [c. 300-100 B.C.])--Baruch 6
*10) Addition to Esther (140-130 B.C.)
*11) Prayer of Azariah (2nd or 1st cent. B.C.)-Daniel 3:24-90
*12) Susanna (2nd or 1st cent. B.C.) --Daniel 13
*13) Bel and the Dragon (c. 100 B.C.) --Daniel 14
14) Prayer of Manasseh (2nd or 1st cent. B.C.)

The Council of Trent 1546: Roman Catholicism recognizes fifteen books as authoritative in addition to the sixty-six books of Scripture. These are known as the Apocrypha (meaning "**hidden**"). They are

- First and Second Esdras,
- Tobit,
- Judith,

- additions to Esther,
- Wisdom of Solomon,
- Ecclesiasticus,
- Baruch,
- Letter of Jeremiah,
- Song of the Three Children,
- Susanna,
- Bell and the Dragon,
- Prayer of Manasseh,
- and First and Second Maccabees.

The Council of Trent also decreed the Latin Vulgate as the standard Bible for reading and teaching. A further important decree of the council was that the Roman Church is to be the interpreter of Scripture.

The Roman Church declared it is the official interpreter of the faith; no one is to interpret Scriptures for himself in a way that is contrary to the Roman Catholic interpretation.[234]

The Apocrypha Rome **accepts includes eleven** books or twelve, depending on whether Baruch 1– 6) is split into two pieces, Baruch 1– 5 and The Letter of Jeremiah (Baruch 6).

The Deuterocanon includes all the fourteen (or fifteen) books in the Protestant Apocrypha except the Prayer of Manasseh and 1 and 2 Esdras (called 3 and 4 Esdras by Roman Catholics. Ezra and Nehemiah are called 1 and 2 Esdras by Catholics).

Although the Roman Catholic canon **has eleven more** pieces of literature than does the Protestant Bible, **only seven extra books, or a total forty-six, appear in the table of contents** (the Protestant and Jewish Old Testament have thirty-nine).[235]

The Apocrypha Is NOT Inspired Writings:

1. **NT never once quotes any Apocryphal books.**
    a) At best, it only alludes to an event in them (cf. Heb. 11:35).

---

[234] Paul Enns. The Moody Handbook of Theology. Kindle Edition
[235] [Geisler, Norman L.. Baker Encyclopedia of Christian Apologetics (Baker Reference Library) (p. 28). Baker Book Group - A. Kindle Edition.]

- b) It never cites them as inspired or as "Scripture."
- c) It quotes from pagan poets but not as inspired (Acts 17:28).

2. **Greek OT of the 4th cent. A.D. had them, but--**
   a) It is not known if the first Greek OT (250 B.C.) had them.
   b) No Hebrew Bible ever had them.
   c) Palestine, not Egypt, was the place of OT canonization.

3. **Some early Fathers cited them, but--**

a) Many early Fathers clearly rejected them (Athanasius, Cyril of Jerusalem, Origen, and Jerome).
b) Almost no early Father clearly accepted the Apocrypha.
c) Many alleged patristic citations are not from the Apocrypha.
d) Those books cited are not clearly cited as Scripture.

4. **Early Catacombs pictured scenes from them because those events happened, not because those books relating them were inspired.**

   The Bible also cites non-inspired writings (Act 17; 1 Cor. 15; Titus 1; Jude 9, 14).

5. **Some Greek Mss. of the 4th cent. A.D. had them, but Judaism never accepted them.**

   Palestine was the place of canonization. Alexandria (Egypt) was merely the place of translation (into Greek).

6. **Augustine accepted them in the 4th cent. A.D., however—**

   a) His contemporary St. Jerome (who translated the Bible into Latin) rejected all of them;
   b) Most earlier Fathers rejected them;
   c) Augustine's basis for accepting them was wrong;
   d) He recognized that the Jews (whose books they were) rejected them (City of God, 19.36-38).

7. **The Eastern Church was not Consistent about them:**

a) No record of early official acceptance of them.
b) Some late Synods of the 17th century. accepted them,
c) But the larger Catechism (1839) omits them.

8. **Many Protestant Bibles had them up to 19th cent., but—**

   a) Protestants **did not accept them as canonical**;
   b) They were often printed between the OT and NT but not as part of either inspired section.

9. **Some were found in Dead Sea Scrolls, but—**

   a) There is no indication they were considered inspired;
   b) No commentaries were found on them as there were on the inspired books.
   c) None had the special parchment and script used only of inspired books.

10. **Some church councils accepted them, but—**

    a) They were local councils, not universal ones.
    b) They were late councils, not early ones (Councils of Rome, Hippo, and Carthage were all late 4th cent. A.D.—some 600 years after most of the Apocrypha was written).
    c) They were not officially accepted by Rome until the counter-Reformation Council of Trent in A.D. 1546.

11. **Roman Catholic Church canonized them in A.D. 1546 (at The Council of Trent), but this was—**[236]

    a) The wrong group (Christians not Jews);
    b) At the wrong time (c. 1700 years later!);
    c) On the wrong basis: On the authority of the church Not on the authority of God (through a prophet of God).
    d) For the wrong reason: to defend its dogma against Protestants

An Authority on the OT Canon Said:

---

[236] Council of Trent, Session IV (April 8, 1546), as quoted in Henry Denzinger, The Sources of Catholic Dogma, trans. Roy J. Deferrari (Fitzwilliam, NH: Loreto, 1954), 245.

"When one examines the passages in the early Fathers who are supposed to establish the canonicity of the Apocrypha, one finds that
- some of them are taken from the alternative **Greek text of Ezra** (1 Esdras)
  - or from additions
  - or appendices to Daniel, Jeremiah or some other canonical book, which...are not really relevant;
- others of them **are not quotations from the Apocrypha** at all;
- and those who are, **many don't give any indication that the book is regarded as Scripture.**" [237]

The **Roman Catholic Church** Canonized the Books of the Apocrypha (A.D. 1546) at The Council of Trent to defend its doctrine against the Protestant Church.

They approved 2 Maccabees, which was in favor of praying for the dead. Giving money as an offering for the sins of the dead: (**2 Maccabees 12:44-46**):

12: 44 For **if he were not expecting** that those who had fallen would rise again, **it would have been superfluous and foolish to pray for the dead.**

12: 45 But if he was looking to the splendid reward that is laid up for those who fall asleep in godliness, it was a holy and pious thought. **Therefore he made atonement for the dead, so that they might be delivered from their sin.**

But they rejected: 2[4] 7:88,104, 105 Esdras which was against it praying for the dead.

THE APOCRYPHA DOES NOT CLAIM TO BE INSPIRED BY GOD [238] [239]

1. The Apocrypha **does not claim to be inspired by God**.
2. Apocrypha **was not written by prophets of God** (400 years of Silence):

---

[237] (Roger Beckwith, The Old Testament Canon in the New Testament Church..., 387)
[238] https://apologeticjunkie.blogspot.com/2012/05/is-apocrypha-scripture.html May 20, 2019
[239] https://carm.org/catholic/errors-apocrypha May 20, 2019

> **1 Maccabees 4:45** "And they thought it best to tear it down so that it would not be a lasting shame to them that the Gentiles had defiled it. So they tore down the altar, 46 and stored the stones in a convenient place on the temple hill **until a prophet should come to tell what to do with them**." (NRSV)
>
> **1 Maccabees 9:27,** "So was there a great affliction in Israel, the like whereof was not since the time that **a Prophet was not seen amongst them**."
>
> **1 Maccabees 14: 41** "The Jews and their priests have resolved that Simon should be their leader and high priest forever **until a trustworthy prophet should arise**, "(NRSV)

3. The Apocrypha was **not confirmed by supernatural acts of God:**

    Hebrews 2: 3 "how can we escape if we neglect so great a salvation? It was declared at first through the Lord, and it was attested to us by those who heard him, 4 while God added his testimony by signs and wonders and various miracles, and by gifts of the Holy Spirit, distributed according to his will. "

4. The Apocrypha **does not always tell the truth** of God:

    - On praying for the dead (2 Mac. 12:43-46);
    - On working for salvation:

    Tobit 12:9 "**For almsgiving saves from death and purges away every sin**. Those who give alms will enjoy a full life,"

    Tobit 4: 10 "**For almsgiving delivers from death and keeps you from going into the Darkness**. 11 Indeed, almsgiving, for all who practice **it, is an excellent offering in the presence of the Most-High**.

5. The Apocrypha **was not accepted by the people of God (Judaism)**.

6. The Apocrypha **was not accepted by Jesus** the Son of God

> "Then beginning with Moses and all the prophets, he interpreted to them the things about himself **in all the scriptures.**" Luke 24:27 (NRSV)

> "Do not think that I have come to abolish **the law or the prophets**; I have come not to abolish but to fulfill. 18 For truly I tell you, until heaven and earth pass away, not one letter, not one stroke of a letter, will pass from the law until all is accomplished." **Matthew 5:17 (NRSV)**

> "Then he said to them, "These are my words that I spoke to you while I was still with you—**that everything written about me in the law of Moses, the prophets, and the psalms must be fulfilled.**" Luke 24:44 (NRSV - Strong's)

7. The Apocrypha **Condones the use of magic**:
Tobit 6:5-7, "Then the angel said to him: Take out the entrails of this fish, and lay up his heart, and his gall and his liver for thee: **for these are necessary for useful medicines.** 6 And when he had done so, he roasted the flesh thereof, and they took it with them in the way: the rest they salted as much as might serve them, till they came to Rages the city of the Medes. 7 Then Tobias asked the angel, and said to him: I beseech thee, brother Azarias, **tell me what remedies are these things good for**, which thou hast bid me keep of the fish? 8 And the angel, answering, said to him: If thou put a little piece of its heart upon coals, **the smoke thereof driveth away all kind of devils, either from man or from woman, so that they come no more to them.**"

8. The Apocrypha was **not accepted by the Apostles of God (who didn't quote it).**

9. **The Apocrypha was not accepted by the Early Church of God.**

10. The Apocrypha **was rejected by the great Catholic translator of the Word of God (Jerome).**

11. The Apocrypha **was not written during the period of the prophets of God (according to Jewish Teaching):**

    a) Jewish OT prophets ended by 400 B.C.
    b) Apocrypha was written 200 B.C. and following.

The Jewish Historian Josephus: "From Artaxerxes [4th cent. B.C.] until our time everything has been recorded but has not been deemed worthy of like credit with what preceded, **because the exact succession of the prophets ceased**" **(Contra Apion 1.8).** [240] [241]

The Jewish Talmud: "With the death of Haggai, Zechariah and Malachi the latter prophets, **the Holy Spirit ceased out of Israel**" **(Tosefta. Sotah 13:2).**

The Apocrypha Contains Offensive Materials to Women Contrary To The Inspired Writing of God:

1. **Ecclesiasticus 25:19 Any iniquity is small compared to a woman's iniquity**; may a sinner's lot befall her!
2. **Ecclesiasticus 25:24** From a woman sin had its beginning, **and because of her we all die**.
3. **Ecclesiasticus 22:3** It is a disgrace to be the father of an undisciplined son, **and the birth of a daughter is a loss.**

APOCRYPHA CONTAINS INACCURATE HISTORICAL FACTS:

The book of Judith incorrectly says that Nebuchadnezzar (Nabuchodonosor) **was the king of the Assyrians** when he was the king of the Babylonians.

- Judith 1:1 (NRSV - Strong's) "It was the twelfth year of the reign of **Nebuchadnezzar, who ruled over the Assyrians** in the great city of Nineveh."

---

[240] F.F. Bruce, The Canon of Scripture (Downers Grove, IL: InterVarsity, 1988), 46.
[241] Webster, The Old Testament Canon and the Apocrypha, 1

- Judith 1:7 (NRSV - Strong's) "Then **Nebuchadnezzar, king of the Assyrians**, sent messengers to all who lived in Persia and to all who lived…"
- Judith 1:11 (NRSV - Strong's) "But all who lived in the whole region disregarded the summons of **Nebuchadnezzar, king of the Assyrians**…"
- Judith 2:4 (NRSV - Strong's) "When he had completed his plan, **Nebuchadnezzar, king of the Assyrians**, called Holofernes, the chief general of his army…"

https://www.kingjamesbibleonline.org/1611_Judith-Chapter-1/#5

Nebuchadnezzar II was the most powerful and longest reigning **king of the Neo-Babylonian** (625-539 b.c.)." Achtemeier, Paul J., Harper's Bible Dictionary, San Francisco: Harper and Row, 1985.

Letter of Jeremiah 6:3 (NRSV – Baruch 6:2) 3 "Therefore when you have come to Babylon you will remain there for many years, for a long time, up to **seven generations**; after that I will bring you away from there in peace.."

Baruch 6:2 says the Jews would serve in Babylon for **seven generations**. Where As: **Jeremiah 25:11** says it was for **70 years.**

> "And this whole land shall be a desolation, and an astonishment; and these nations shall serve the king of Babylon seventy years." **Jeremiah 25:11 (KJV)**

NO! John 10:22 Can Not Be Used as proof that Jesus or an Apostle quoted the Apocrypha. [242]

> "And it was at Jerusalem the feast of the dedication, and it was winter. 23 And Jesus walked in the temple in Solomon's porch." **John 10:22-23 (KJV)**

John 10:22 The eight-day Feast of Dedication celebrates the rededication of the Jewish temple in December 164 B.C., after its desecration by the Seleucid ruler Antiochus Epiphanes IV in 167 (1 Macc. 1:59; 1 Macc. 4:52-59). [243]

---

[242] https://www.youtube.com/watch?v=mParOC-So4k May 20, 2019
[243] Freeman, James M.. The New Manners and Customs of The Bible (Kindle Locations 7401-7402). Kindle Edition.]

It is not a Quote, but an Observed Event dating back to the intertestamental period as read in History provided in 1 Macc. 1:59). **We never said that Apocrypha did not provide some Jewish history**, we said the Books are NOT Scripture (GOD BREATHED) based on the books themselves. Going into the Temple during that day is not a quotation from the Apocrypha.

CUSSING AND FOUL LANGUAGE

The leaders of the GreatMillStone call themselves **Apostles**.

Christian Apologists Vocab Malone, Shield Squad, and Brotha J expose the vile teachings of the Great Millstone in a YouTube video called "Great Millstone "Hebrew Israelites" - The Worst of the Worst (Part 1)" [244]

GMS Hebrew Israelites in three YouTube videos attempts to justify their filthy mouth and what flows out of it. Titled Pt3 Is Cussing Against the Bible? [245] [246] [247]

GMS BHI commenting on a previous conversation says, If he had known the Scriptures, he would have told his woman to shut the F*#$@* up.

The **GMS Hebrew Israelite** has his street corner **BHI** reader read:

> "But now you yourselves are to put off all these: anger, wrath, malice, blasphemy, **filthy language out of your mouth**. 9 Do not lie to one another, since you have put off the old man with his deeds," **Colossians 3:8-9 (NKJV)**

The **GMS BHI** adherent says Christians will say this is talking about cussing, so you can't cuss. But the text is talking about **lying to one another;** that is what **filthy communication** means. It is not talking about profanity. A cuss word is a word that society has deemed unfit to use, **not God**. God doesn't say don't use this word but use this word. The only thing that God says about what words not to use **is lies**.

---

[244] https://www.youtube.com/watch?v=CWI8RYXzT54 (May 22, 2019)
[245] https://www.youtube.com/watch?v=zLc096MMb1A (May 21, 2019)
[246] https://www.youtube.com/watch?v=ekQOeVB_-Dw (May 21, 2019)
[247] https://www.youtube.com/watch?v=LvCFIyD3Zls (May 21, 2019)

Cussing and Foul Language

Rebuttal: Colossians 3:8-9 is addressing the things that believers "**are to put off**"; these verses are not defining lying as a filthy conversation. But as we look at Ephesians 4:25 - 5:5 we actually see what should and should not be spoken out of a Christian's mouth (only what is good for the building up of someone in need, in order to give grace to those who hear (**Ephesians 4:29)**.

The filthy language would include all bitterness , anger, and wrath, insult, and slander. These must be "**put away**" from you, with **all wickedness** and evil speaking (**Ephesians 4:31**).

This is the complete list that was violated in Colossians 3:8
- anger g3709
- vengeance.
- rage g2372
- outburst of passion.
- malice g2549
- vicious disposition spite.
- slander
- g988 abusive or scurrilous language.
- filthy language
- g148 foul language.

. which the GMS adherent redefined as "**lying**."

GMS BHI adherent says to the Christian get the F$%*^& out of here man. Corrupt communication is not no D*%#$ cussing man. The **BHI** Reader reads:

> "**A wholesome tongue** is a tree of life: but perverseness therein is a breach in the spirit." **Proverbs 15:4 (KJV)**

GMS BHI adherent asks why is the wholesome tongue a tree of life? He says because the wholesome tongue is **the words** of the Most-High. Jeremiah said I'm a man of unclean lips and Jeremiah was a prophet. So how in the hell can a tongue be wholesome, only if the words of The Most-High are coming off of it? The **BHI** Reader reads:

> "To the law and to the testimony: **if they speak not according to this word**, it is because there is no light in them. "**Isaiah 8:20 (KJV)**

Cussing and Foul Language

The **GMS BHI** says, what you are supposed to speak is this word, and not what you think. It is not what you think is corrupt communication, but what the Bible says is corrupt communication.

People want to speak according to their heart, but the Most-High says lean not to your own understanding (**Proverbs 3:5; 28:26**). The understanding that you lean on are the words of the Most-High. If you trust in your own heart, you are a **D&^*$#** fool. If you tell me a curse word is a sin, you are a **D&^*$#** fool because the Scripture doesn't say that. If you are going to tell me that saying "**F*&%#$** or **S*&^%** is corrupt communication, you are **D*&%$#** fool, man. Because the Scripture doesn't say that.

Rebuttal: As to his quote of **Isaiah 8:20** "to the law and to the testimony if they speak not according to these words, it is because there is no light in them ... "
It means that they are void of the spirit of GOD. In **Matthew 5:22** but whoever is angry with his brother without a cause shall be in danger of the judgement . and **whoever says to his brother, raca** shall be in danger of the council. But **whoever says, "fool"** shall be in danger of hell fire.

The **GMS** adherent tells another member to go on Wikipedia and look up curse words (profanity)[248]:

I am not sure what **BHI** looked up because it was not this Wikipedia page, and it seemed that they read whatever they were reading the same way as they do the Bible (here a little, and there a little).

https://en.wikipedia.org/wiki/Profanity: Profanity is socially offensive language,[Definition of Profanity", Merriam-Webster Online Dictionary, retrieved on 2014-08-31.] which may also be called curse words or swearing (British English), cuss words (American English and Canada), swear words, bad words, crude language, coarse language, oaths, **blasphemous language**, vulgar language, lewd language, choice words, or expletives.

---

[248] https://en.wikipedia.org/wiki/Profanity (May 22, 2019)

Cussing and Foul Language

Used in this sense, profanity is a language that is generally considered by certain parts of a culture to be strongly impolite, rude, or offensive. It can show a debasement of someone or something or be considered as an expression of strong feeling towards something.

In its older, more literal sense, "profanity" **refers to a lack of respect for things that are held to be sacred, which implies anything inspiring deserving of reverence**, as well as **behavior showing similar disrespect or causing religious offense**.["Definition of profanity". Longman Dictionary of Contemporary English – online. Retrieved 11 September 2014.]

> "But though **I be rude in speech**, yet not in knowledge; but we have been throughly made manifest among you in all things." **2 Corinthians 11:6 (KJV)**

GMS BHI focusing on the word "rude" says isn't that true for us, right? Though we are rude in speech, we are not rude in knowledge, and we have thoroughly manifested Jesus. Meaning we broke the Scripture down. Even though we were rude in speech, we were not rude in knowledge.

The **GMS BHI** Reader reads:

"The heart is deceitful above all things, and desperately wicked: who can know it? **Jeremiah 17:9 (KJV)**

The GMS Hebrew Israelite with Bible in his hand says, your heart is **F*^%#$@$** wicked, man.

Rebuttal: Addressing his reading of **Philemon 1:6**
The verse is telling Philemon that his practice in CHRIST is being acknowledged by the good things that he is doing; And not that he was communicating wholesome words but that his actions were being seen.
Going to the book of Sirach, The GMS adherent attempts to change the topic: "to good" speech is "**the speaking or communication of GODS LAW.**"
This leads us to the book of **Proverbs 15:4** a wholesome tongue is a tree of life , which is actually saying

- **he whose tongue is wholesome brings life, the latter part of the verse says,**

- But perverseness in your tongue **breaks the spirit**.

Proverbs 15:1 a soft answer turns away wrath but a soft word stirs up anger so **GOD would never tell you to curse a person**. **Isaiah 5:20** says woe to those
- who **call good evil and evil good**
- who **put darkness for light and light for darkness**
- who put bitter for sweet and sweet for bitter.

Gms HollandZ[249] a **Hebrew Israelite adherent**, seeking to justify the use of such words, comments on his YouTube video as follows:

> "Now do I ADVOCATE cussing? NO. but IF it HAPPENS to come out? It comes out. but in no way should it be considered corrupt speech. Is it always pleasant to cuss? NO. there is a time and place for it. I speak as the common folk. a serial killer doesn't speak all vile and foul. he presents himself as the supreme gentlemen. so does a child F#%^&* in the churches... Yes, CUSSING Words Are in The Bible, Cussing and Cursing Are NOT the Same. plus, we are not advocating cussing, but sometimes it comes out."

BHI Camp Believes Rape Is Ok

GMS BHI members in a YouTube video titled "GMS cult exposed says they can rape 9 - 12year-old girls". [250] GMS says they would allow one of their brothers to rape one of their daughters. **Tahar**, the leader of GMS, says, "when the kingdom is established, they are going to get women when they are twelve years old. In the Kingdom of Heaven, when their period starts, that is when they start to become a woman. So, we are going to deal with them when their period starts. We are going to have sex with them and have babies with them. In the Kingdom, we are going to get them young. **Tahar** says lookup and google women that were pregnant under the age of twelve.

---

[249] https://www.youtube.com/watch?v=MbyKLPW1BDs (May 22, 2019)
[250] https://www.youtube.com/watch?v=_DeQtFZgJEU (May 22,2019)

Tahar says most women dream and fantasizes about being raped. In YouTube video titled "Polight Vs. **GMS Israelites** Is Rape Legal in God's Kingdom," [251] GMS says that you can rape. GMS says in this society it is not alright, and that the law doesn't allow what the Most-High has permitted. The Scriptures says it is alright. The GMS reader reads:

> "If a man find a damsel that is a virgin, which is not betrothed, **and lay hold on her, and lie with her**, and they be found; 29 Then the man that lay with her shall give unto the damsel's father fifty shekels of silver, and she shall be his wife; because he hath humbled her, he may not put her away all his days." **Deuteronomy 22:28-29 (KJV)**

GMS says in the kingdom you are going to beat woman off you with a stick. [252] This is the day that is fast approaching. The GMS reader reads:

> "**And in that day seven women shall take hold of one man**, saying, We will eat our own bread, and wear our own apparel: only let us be called by thy name, to take away our reproach." **Isaiah 4:1 (KJV)**

GMS even speaks hatefully of other **BHI** camps and says Women (black) will feel the bitterness of the Kingdom. [253] They say that when you look at these women, you have to look down upon them in a condescending manner.

ISUPK BHI camp also believes that **a man can have more than one women** using **Isaiah 4:1**. [254] Although they appear to frown on rape.

WHAT ARE HEBREW ISRAELITES SOURCES OF AUTHORITY?

---

[251] https://www.youtube.com/watch?v=vhM98Mx6tC4 (May 22, 2019)
[252] https://www.youtube.com/watch?v=gTU6h3bjXZA&t=9s (June 4, 2019)
[253] https://www.youtube.com/watch?v=3AJaNkZRXi4 (May 22, 2019)
[254] https://www.youtube.com/watch?v=cEgiekxPTXk (May 23, 2019)

What are Hebrew Israelites sources of AUTHORITY?

Source of Authority: It is difficult to determine where these Hebrew Israelites get their ultimate source of authority since they do not have any official writings.

Hebrew Israelites Use Bible (both the Old and New Testaments), preferably the King James Version 1600, as an authoritative source, but they just argue that there have been a number of mistranslations.

- Some hint that the canon of the Bible is not fixed.
- Most **Hebrew Israelites** believe that the Torah(Law) must be observed.
- Uses extra-biblical sources to support their ideas, such as the Apocrypha and Pseudepigrapha (meaning literally "false writings").
- Some **BHI**'s adhere to the Talmud (Jewish collection of teachings, laws, and interpretations based on Genesis through Deuteronomy) while others do not.
- The Talmud is not God's revelation.

They also attach scholarly acclaim to books such as:

- Arthur Koestler, "The Thirteenth Tribe: The Khazar Empire and Its Heritage," Random House, 1976.
- Rudolph R. Windsor, "**From Babylon to Timbuktu**: A History of the Ancient Black Races Including the Black Hebrews, " Windsor Golden Series, (1988).
- Shadrock, "The Forgotten Israelites: God's Chosen People," Fifth Ribb Pub., (1991).
- Shadrock, "The Truth, The Lie, and The Bible III," Fifth Ribb Pub., (1995).
- Shadrock, "The Word, The Israelites, and The Damned by Shaddrock," ISBN# 9694907-3-9, at: http://www.israelitenation.com/

What are Hebrew Israelites sources of AUTHORITY?

PROBLEM ELEVEN

WOULD YOU LIKE TO ACCEPT CHRIST, TODAY?

Would you like to enter the Kingdom of God? It is simply a matter of being born again from above.

Do you confess with your mouth that you are a sinner; and believe that Jesus Christ died for your sins (**Romans 10:9-10**); and that He rose on the third day never to die again? **If you do, may I encourage you to pray a simple prayer of repentance?**

Please understand that it is not this or any other prayer that saves you. It is only through trusting in Christ that can save you from your sins.
This prayer is simply a way to express to God your faith in Him and thank Him for providing for your salvation.

> *"God, I know that I have sinned against you and am deserving of punishment. But Jesus Christ took the punishment that I deserve so that through faith in Him, I could be forgiven. I place my trust in You for salvation. Thank You for Your wonderful grace and forgiveness— the gift of eternal life! Amen!"*

If you prayed that prayer, welcome to the Body of Christ! Now that you have given your life to Christ, in obedience to Him, you want to find a good Bible teaching church (***Hebrews 10:24-25***) and be baptized (**Acts 2:38; 8:35--37**).
If you like, I can help you with that. You can write, email, or call me. My information is in the back of the book.

Here are a few verses about your salvation; what God has done for you:

"And you hath **he quickened**, who were dead in trespasses and sins;" (**Ephesians 2:1**)

"Therefore if any man be in Christ, **he is a new creature**: old things are passed away; behold, all things are become new." (**2 Corinthians 5:17**)

Would you Like To Accept Christ, today?

"*We know that **we have passed from death unto life**, because we love the brethren. He that loveth not his brother abideth in death.*" (**1 John 3:14**)

"*²⁹ Take my yoke upon you, **and learn of me**; for I am meek and lowly in heart: and ye shall find rest unto your souls. ³⁰ For my yoke is easy, and my burden is light.*" (**Matthew 11:29-30**)

Did you make your decision to accept Jesus Christ based on what you read in this book?
We would love to hear from you!

Would you Like To Accept Christ, today?

QUESTIONS TO ADDRESS BEFORE DIALOGUING WITH SO-CALLED HEBREW ISRAELITES:

1. Do You Believe The "Whole Bible" Is the Word of God (OT and NT)?
    a. When Was the Bible Written And By Who?
    b. Are There "Missing Inspired Books" of The Bible Like the Apocrypha; And If **NOT**, Biblical And External Evidence?
    c. Was King James a Black Man and A Jew, And If **NOT**, What Is The Evidence?
    d. Is the Bible Coded So That You Can Only Understand It by Precepts? If **NOT**, Explain?
    e. What Does the Bible Teach About The Trinity; Is The term or Concept Biblical? Explain?
    f. What Does the Bible Teach About God?
2. What Does the Bible Teach About the Virgin Mary?
    a. What Was the Importance of The Virgin Birth and Is It the Immaculate conception?
    b. What Does the Bible Teach About Joseph and Was He Jesus' Biological Father?
    c. What Does the Bible Teach About Jesus' Conception?
    d. Does the Bible Identify Jesus' Color, And If So Where?
3. Does the Bible Teach Race Identity?
    a. Does Race (Color of One's Skin) Play A part In Salvation? And If **NOT**, Biblical Evidence?
    b. Does the Bible Teach That You Must Speak Hebrew and/or Greek to Be Saved; And If **NOT**, Biblical Evidence?
4. What Does the Bible Teach About Who Will Be Saved?
    a. Does the Bible Teach That Only Israel (Jews) Will Be Saved?
    b. Does the Bible Identify That the Jews As Black?
5. What Does the Bible Teach About Christians (Biblically)?
    a. Did the Emperor Constantine Start Christianity; And If **NOT**, Biblical And External Evidence?

      b. Did the Emperor Constantine Change the Sabbath to Sunday; And If **NOT**, Biblical And External Evidence?
6. What Does the Bible Teach About the Biblical Church?
7. What Does the Bible Teach About The Purpose of The Law?
      a. Does the Bible Teach That Believers in Christ Are Under the Mosaic Law (613)?
      b. Can You Demonstrate Biblically What Law "Believers in Christ" Are Under?
      c. Can You Prove Biblically That Christians Do Keep the Commandments of God?
8. Are the Writings (Epistles) of Apostle Paul Scripture and Does He Write as By the Authority Given Him by Jesus Christ, And If So, What Is The Evidence?
9. Is the Transatlantic Slave Trade The Fulfilment of Deuteronomy Chapter 28, And If **NOT**, Biblical And External Evidence?
10. Does The Bible Teach and Demonstrate That Jesus Is God; Biblical Evidence?
11. What Does The Bible Teach About The Lake Of Fire; Biblical Evidence?

APPENDIX

GLOSSARY

AD, BC, BCE, and CE:
AD is Anno Domini or Year of our Lord referring to the year of Christ's birth.
BC is Before Christ.
CE is a recent term. It refers to Common Era and is used in place of A.D. the dates are the same, i.e., 2009 AD is 2009 CE.
BCE means Before Common Era. For example, 400 BC is 400 BCE.

Apocryphal Books: Deuterocanonical books 14 Books in the O.T. not deemed as inspired scriptures by Protestants, but later accepted as scripture by the Roman Catholics - Council of Trent 1546AD. They were written in the inter-testamental period (silent years).

Apologetics may be simply defined as the defense of the Christian faith.

Apostasy is the falling away from the Christian faith. It is a revolt against the truth of God's Word by a believer. It can also describe a group or church organization that has "fallen away" from the truths of Christianity as revealed in the Bible.

Apotheosis: Man becoming a god.
(from Greek ἀποθέωσις from ἀποθεοῦν, *apotheoun* "to deify"; in Latin *deificatio* "making divine"; also called **divinization** and **deification**) is the glorification of a subject to divine level. The term has meanings in theology, where it refers to a belief, and in art, where it refers to a genre. In theology, *apotheosis* refers to the idea that an individual has been raised to godlike stature. In art, the term refers to the treatment of any subject (a figure, group, locale, motif, convention or melody) in a, particularly grand or exalted manner.

Biblical Authority: The Bible alone is the Authority in the Christian life.

Glossary

Biblical Inspiration: It means that the Holy Spirit controlled and guided the authors of the biblical books. They wrote exactly what God wanted said. **(2 Peter 1:21, 1 Timothy 3:16)** God Breathed.

Biblical hermeneutics is the study of the principles and methods of interpreting the text of the Bible.

Biblical Inerrancy: The Bible is without error. The Bible is verbally inspired; it is infallible; it is inerrant in the manuscripts as they were originally written.
1. It is a technical phrase for the accuracy of the Biblical message.
2. It affirms that what the Bible teaches on any subject it addresses is true.
3. Properly understood, the message of the Bible gives correct information (**Hebrew 2:1-4**).

Inerrancy means without error, non-errant. In Christianity, inerrancy states that the Bible in its original documents is without error regarding facts, names, dates, and any other revealed information. Inerrancy does not extend to the copies of the Biblical manuscripts. [255]

Biblical infallibility is the belief that what the Bible says regarding matters of faith and Christian practice is wholly useful and true. It is the "belief that the Bible is completely trustworthy as a guide to salvation and the life of faith and will not fail to accomplish its purpose. Some equate 'inerrancy' and 'infallibility'; others do not."

Biblical Inspiration: What is meant by Biblical Inspiration? It means that the Holy Spirit controlled and guided the authors of the biblical books. They wrote exactly what God wanted said. **(2 Peter 1:21, 1 Timothy 3:16)**. The Bible Incapable of mistake.

BLASPHEMY—In the sense of speaking evil of God this word is found in Ps. 74:18; Isa. 52:5; Rom. 2:24; Rev.

---

[255] https://carm.org/dictionary-inerrancy (May 21, 2017)

13:1, 6; 16:9, 11, 21. It denotes also any kind of calumny, or evil-speaking, or abuse (1 Kings 21:10; Acts 13:45; 18:6, etc.). Our Lord was accused of blasphemy when he claimed to be the Son of God (Matt. 26:65; comp. Matt. 9:3; Mark 2:7). They who deny his Messiahship blaspheme Jesus (Luke 22:65; John 10:36).

Blasphemy against the Holy Ghost (Matt. 12:31, 32; Mark 3:28, 29; Luke 12:10) is regarded by some as a continued and obstinate rejection of the gospel, and hence is an unpardonable sin, simply because as long as a sinner remains in unbelief he voluntarily excludes himself from pardon. **Others regard the expression as designating the sin of attributing to the power of Satan those miracles which Christ performed**, or generally those works which are the result of the Spirit's agency.[256]

> **BLASPHEMY.** The sin of consciously using derogatory language about God. Secondly, it is the "reviling," "mocking," and "slandering" of another human being (cf. Rom. 3:8; 1 Cor. 4:13; 1 Pet. 4:4). In the New Testament the Jewish Sanhedrin considered that Christ deserved the death penalty on account of his confession at his trial (Gk.blasphēméō; Matt. 26:65–66 par. Mark 14:64, Gk.blasphēmía; cf. earlier accusations, e.g., Matt. 9:3; John 10:36).[257]

Canon: The word "canon," means "standard" or "rule." It is the list of authoritative and inspired Scriptures. Different religions have different canons.[258]

Canonization:
    a. Process of declaring a person to be a saint.
    b. The process by which the Scriptures were established by God and recognized in the Church; the process of determining the New Testament canon.

---

[256] Easton, M. G. (1893). In Easton's Bible dictionary. New York: Harper & Brothers.
[257] Myers, A. C. (1987). In The Eerdmans Bible dictionary (p. 162). Grand Rapids, MI: Eerdmans.
[258] https://carm.org/what-canon (May 21, 2017).

Glossary

Christology: The word "Christology" comes from two Greek words meaning "Christ / Messiah" and "word" - which combine to mean "the study of Christ." Christology is the study of the Person and work of Jesus Christ.[259] Some of the issues studied are His deity, His incarnation, His offices, His sacrifice, His resurrection, His teaching, His relation to God and man, and His return to earth.

Cognitive Dissonance: is the mental discomfort (psychological stress) experienced by a person who simultaneously holds two or more contradictory beliefs, ideas, or values. The occurrence of cognitive dissonance is the consequence of a person's performing an action that contradicts personal beliefs, ideas, and values; and also **occurs when confronted with new information that contradicts said beliefs, ideas, and values.**[260]

Ecclesiology is the study of the Christian church, its structure, order, practices, and hierarchy.

Eschatology is the study of the teachings in the Bible concerning the end times or of the period of time dealing with the return of Christ and the events that follow. Eschatological subjects include:
- the Resurrection,
- the Rapture,
- the Tribulation,
- the Millennium,
- the Binding of Satan,
- the Three witnesses,
- the Final Judgment,
- Armageddon,
- and The New Heavens and the New Earth.

In the New Testament, eschatological chapters include **Matt. 24, Mark 13, Luke 17, and 2 Thess. 2**.

In one form or another, most of the books of the Bible deal with end times subjects. But some that are more prominently eschatological are Daniel, Ezekiel, Isaiah,

---

[259] https://www.gotquestions.org/Christology.html (April 8, 2017)
[260] https://en.wikipedia.org/wiki/Cognitive_dissonance (May 28, 2017)

Glossary

Joel, Zechariah, Matthew, Mark, Luke, 2 Thessalonians, and of course Revelation.
(See Amillennialism and Premillennialism for more information on views on the millennium).

Eisegesis is when a person interprets and reads information into the text that is not there. [261]

Exegesis is when a person interprets a text based solely on what it says. That is, he extracts out of the text what is there as opposed to reading into it what is not there (Compare with Eisegesis). [262]

Gnostic Gospels: Found in Nagamadi Egypt in 1945. Written about the middle of the 3rd century – well after the so-called author died. These Gnostic gospels are often pointed to as supposed "lost books of the Bible."

Hamartiology is the study of the doctrine of sin. It encompasses topics, such as The Fall of Adam and Eve, degrees of sin, original sin, and human accountability for sin.

Hermeneutics is the Art and Science of Biblical interpretation. Theologically and Biblically speaking, it is the means by which a person examines the Bible to determine what it means. [263,264]

Historical Revisionism identifies the re-interpretation of the historical record, of the orthodox views about a historical event, of the evidence of the event, and of the motivations and decisions of the participant people. The revision of the historical record is to reflect the contemporary discoveries of fact, evidence, and interpretation, which produce a revised history.

Orthodoxy: a belief or a way of thinking that is accepted as true or correct. Orthodoxy is the belief in the standards of accepted and true doctrines taught in

---

[261] https://carm.org/dictionary-eisegesis (April 7, 2017)
[262] https://carm.org/dictionary-exegesis (April 7, 2017)
[263] https://carm.org/dictionary-hermeneutics (April 8, 2017)
[264] https://www.gotquestions.org/Biblical-hermeneutics.html (April 8, 2017)

Glossary

the Bible. That which is orthodox agrees with Biblical teaching and the interpretation of the Christian Church. False religions are not orthodox. They are heterodox.[265]

PHARISEES [făr´ə sēz] (Gk. Pharisaíoi).† One of the parties or movements within Judaism of the late Second Temple period (ca. 150 B.C.-A.D. 70). **The Pharisees were noted most for their exact observance of the Jewish religion**, their accurate exposition of the law, their handing down of extrabiblical customs and traditions, their moderate position with regard to the interplay of fate and free will, and their belief in the coming resurrection and in angels (Josephus BJ i.5.2 [110]; ii.8.14 [162–63]; Ant. xiii.10.6 [297]; xviii.1.3 [13–14]; Mark 7:3; Acts 23:6–9; Phil. 3:5; cf. Gal. 1:14). **The ancient sources variously describe the Pharisees as a political party, a philosophical school and scholarly class, or a sector voluntary association** (Heb. ḥaberôt devoted to ritual purity.[266]

Pneumatology: The study of the Holy Spirit, His person, works, relation to the Father and Son, relation to man, ministry in salvation and sanctification, conviction, and indwelling.

Polytheism: Polytheism believes that there are many finite gods in the world who actively influence the world. They are unlike theism in that there is no infinite God. They are unlike deism in that there is supernatural activity in the world. They are unlike finite godism in that there is no God beyond the universe. Some pantheists are also polytheists in that many gods are representative expressions of the god that is everything. Many people throughout the world are polytheistic, most notably modern Mormons. The ancient Greeks of the days of the New Testament were polytheists.

Postponement Theory (view): The term "prophetic postponement' refers to the delay of the messianic program of redemption for the nation of Israel. Between

---

[265] https://carm.org/dictionary-orthodoxy (April 7, 2017)
[266] Myers, A. C. (1987). In The Eerdmans Bible dictionary (p. 823). Grand Rapids, MI: Eerdmans.

Glossary

the first and second comings of Jesus Christ, national Israel is subject to a judicial hardening (see Matthew 13:13-15; Mark 4:11-12; Luke 8:10; John 12:40; Acts 28:26-27; Romans 11:8-10).

This prophetic postponement served to interrupt Israel's restoration as stipulated under the new covenant (Jeremiah 31:31-37).

This postponement is illustrated in the interruption between the first 69 weeks of Daniel and the seventieth week, which is the future seven-year tribulation period (Daniel 9:26- 27).

However, **at the end of the tribulation period, Israel will confess her sins and call out to her Messiah for deliverance at Armageddon.** (Matthew 23:37-39; Zechariah 12:10).

The Jewish remnant will be converted and restored. Israel will then experience the ultimate fulfillment of the land promises of the Abra- Hamic covenant and the throne promises of the Davidic covenant in Christ's 1000-year millennial kingdom, which follows the second coming of Christ (see Romans 9-11).

Delay of O.T. Promises until Christ Matthew 23:37-39. Zechariah 12:10. John 1:11.

Pseudepigrapha: falsely attributed works, texts whose claimed author is represented by a separate author or a work "whose real author attributed it to a figure of the past." The word *pseudepigrapha* (from the Greek: ψευδής, *pseudes*, "false" and ἐπιγραφή, *epigraphē*, "name" or "inscription" or "ascription"; thus when taken together it means "false superscription or title"; see the related *epigraphy*) is the plural of "pseudepigraphon" (sometimes Latinized as "pseudepigraphum").

Rapture: The word "**rapture**" does not appear in most English translations of the New Testament. Still, "rapture" is a thoroughly biblical term.

Glossary

In Latin translations of 1 Thessalonians 4:17, the term rendered "**caught up**" or "**taken up**" in English versions is the verb rapiemur, from the noun raptus. The word "rapture" simply comes from Paul's own words in the Latin Bible and means **"being caught up."**

Redemption means to free someone from bondage. It often involves the paying of a ransom, a price that makes redemption possible. The Israelites were redeemed from Egypt. We were redeemed from the power of sin and the curse of the Law (**Galatians 3:13**) through Jesus (**Romans 3:24, Colossians 1:14**). We were bought with a price (**1 Corinthians 6:20, 7:23**).[267]

Replacement Theology is the teaching that the Christian church has replaced Israel regarding God's purpose and promises.

Ruddy, rud'i (1 S 16 12; 17 42; Gen 26 25 RVm], [Cant 5 10]; vbs. ädham (Lam 4 7], and, "to blush" [Ad Est 16 5]): "Ruddy" is the form taken by the adj. "red" when used as a term of praise of the human skin, and this is its use in the Bible (the Heb and Gr words are all usual words for "red" or "to be red"). The dark-skinned Hebrews found great beauty in a clear complexion.[268]

Strong's Concordance
    admoni: red, ruddy
    Original Word: אַדְמֹנִי
    Part of Speech: Adjective
    Transliteration: admoni
    Phonetic Spelling: (ad-mo-nee')
    Short Definition: ruddy[269]

Rude (untrained, ignorant of rules), used in II Cor. 11:6 where Paul means "I am not a technically trained orator."[270]

---

[267] https://carm.org/dictionary-redemption (April 8, 2017)
[268] Zondervan Compact Bible Dictionary p. 510
[269] http://biblehub.com/hebrew/132.htm
[270] Zondervan Compact Bible Dictionary p. 510

HEBREW ISRAELITE - SUBJECT LINKS

- **History of the Israelite Schools - Disc 1 Excerpt** [271]
  https://www.youtube.com/watch?v=RL9QyhkjF4k&fbclid=IwAR1vvLYw7RM2nzxl72FfB5b-K54Q6WYt5M7bEFaPyqevsWUDMt0BaWjv8rw (May 11, 2019)
- **Are Black People Cursed? Are Blacks the Real Jews? Hebrew Israelites! (Full Show)**
  https://www.youtube.com/watch?time_continue=82&v=xg97LQQF354&fbclid=IwAR08XWNCwDJ_-duGAzhNo2QaeWTg_VNd1UYtAO_dKoyg4quO7Zh8T9c2mZl (May 11, 2019)
- **COMMANDING GEN.YAHANNA: THE TRUTH ABOUT AHRAYAH & THE ISUPK 12 TRIBES CHART, ABBA BIVENS &**
  https://www.youtube.com/watch?v=Xytz1eK-4K8
- **ABBA (AKA POP) BIVENS ADMITTED THE 12 TRIBE CHART WAS A HOOK, A LIE. UNDENIABLE PROOF**
  https://www.youtube.com/watch?v=NBg0SluYxXs&feature=youtu.be&fbclid=IwAR22rjBiFLIEaPhRVqMk9LqQdmLaOmZrNhkyNgrExVEJHCaDOjWaQgxST6Q (May 11, 2019)
- **The Destruction of Commandment Keepers, Inc. 1919-2007**
  http://www.blackjews.org/Essays/DestructionofCommandmentKeepers.html (May 22, 2019)
- **African Hebrew Israelites of Jerusalem**
  http://africanhebrewisraelitesofjerusalem.com/ (May 22, 2019)
- **Church of God and Saints of Christ**
  http://cogasoc.org/wordpress/ (May 22, 2019)
- **Israelite Church of God in Jesus Christ**
  http://www.icgjcmd.org/ (May 22, 2019)
- **Israel United In Christ**
  http://israelunite.org/ (May 22, 2019)
- **The Followers Of Yahweh Ben Yahweh**
  http://www.yahwehbenyahweh.com/ (May 22, 2019)
- **The GreatMillStone**
  http://greatmillstone.info/origsite/ (May 22, 2019)
- **The Israel School of U.P.K.**
  http://isupk.org/ (May 22, 2019)

The Gathering Of Christ Church (May 22, 2019)

---

[271] Anderson, Robert, Selling Something Nobody Needs, False Doctrine Cleaned Me Up! But God Saved me, pp173-195; TruthseekersRead Publishing (2016)

ABOUT THE AUTHORS

About Elder Robert Anderson

Elder Robert Anderson is a native of Detroit, Michigan, and has been married to his lovely wife Jo Ann for over 34 years.

Elder Anderson received his GED, a degree from Wayne County Community College (WC3) in Associate of Applied Science Computer and Data Processing, a degree from Detroit College of Business in Bachelor of Business Administration; and with honors in both degrees.

A salaried employee of AT&T, he learned about diversity through the opportunity to work with people from various cultures and ethnic groups. As he traveled the USA for AT&T, he learned there was more to the world than the streets of Detroit. After several promotions and 30 years of service, Robert chose to retire and pursue his goals as an entrepreneur, professional photographer, and videographer.

Elder Anderson dedicates his life to studying the sound doctrine of Scripture and apologetics with the hope of warning and teaching others how to come out of and/or avoid the cults and false doctrine. His first book is titled **"Selling Something Nobody Needs, False Doctrine Cleaned Me Up! But God Saved Me!**

Previously, as a Bible believing Christian he served as an Associate Pastor licensed under Pastor Emery Moss Jr. at Strictly Biblical Bible Teaching Ministries. Over the years as he has attended various classes and recorded them for his own studies, Elder Anderson was guided by the Holy Spirit to design a website www.bibletalkbbc.com where various class lectures (audios) and resource literature are available to those that have the desire to learn. He collaborated as co-author the book titled **"Essentials Simple But Biblical"** with his former Pastor and teacher, Pastor Emery Moss Jr.

Both books are available in bookstores and Amazon.com and the publisher's website: www.truthseekersread.com

About The Authors

Today, he serves on the elder's board under Bishop Quinton W. Wingate at Power Hope & Grace Bible Church

He and his wife, Jo Ann, witness together at Wendy's, McDonald's and anywhere else they can speak one-on-one and pass out tracts and cards pointing people to Jesus Christ.

You are invited to join **TruthSeekersRead** weekly "Facebook Live Stream" and "Tele-Conference" Bible Study on **Tuesdays from 7:00 p.m. – 9:00 p.m.**; Also **Thursdays and Fridays 6:00 p.m. – 8:00 p.m**. Send a FaceBook friend request to **TruthSeekersRead** and/or Call in Number (248) 607-0611 /Pin: 14251

For more information or to book Elder Robert Anderson for speaking engagements, or radio and television interviews, please contact:

Truth Seekers Read, LLC.
P.O. Box 23345, Detroit, MI 48223
Email requests to: truthseekersread@att.net
URL: http://www.truthseekersread.com
Phone: (313) 215-2576

YouTube: TruthSeekersRead
https://www.youtube.com/c/truthseekersread

Twitter: https://twitter.com/RLA_TSR

Send Friend Request to: "TruthSeekersRead"

Join our group: "The Bible Says What???"

About The Authors

About Minister Andrew E. Hooper

Andrew Eugene Hooper has served as a minister and apologist for the last five years. He currently is a member of Strictly Biblical Bible Teaching Ministries.

He has debated many Hebrew Israelite Camp leaders and individuals on Bible Doctrine. He teaches weekly on Facebook expounding on Hermeneutic approaches of Biblical study; Christian Living and exposing false doctrines of various cultic groups. He is a continuing student of the Bible and spends a considerable amount of time carrying the gospel of Jesus Christ to the streets weekly. The BUS-STOPS "is" his pulpit!

Previously served as an ironworker for local 25 for ten years building up metro Detroit and surrounding areas. Graduated from Mumford High School in 1992. I am currently dedicated to teaching the gospel, providing biblical counseling, and defending the faith.

OTHER BOOKS BY ELDER ROBERT ANDERSON

Selling Something Nobody Needs

ISBN: 978-0-9987221-0-8

Essentials Simple But Biblical

ISBN: 978-0-9987221-2-2

BOOK ORDER FORM

So-Called Black Hebrew Israelites

Name: _____

Address: _____

City: _____ State: _____ Zip: _____

Email: _____

Quantity	
Price (each)	$20.00
Subtotal	
(S&H)	$2.99
MI Tax 6%	
Total	

METHOD OF PAYMENT:

1. **Online Ordering:**
   http://www.truthseekersread.com
2. **Check or Money Order:** (Make payable to: **Truth Seekers Read**)

Mail your Payment with this form to:
Truth Seekers Read, LLC.
P.O. Box 23345, Detroit, MI 48223

Email: truthseekersread@att.net
URL: http://www.truthseekersread.com
Phone: (313) 215-2576

www.ingramcontent.com/pod-product-compliance
Lightning Source LLC
Chambersburg PA
CBHW070544010526
44118CB00012B/1221